Praise for *Fighting for Your Marriage*

"What distinguishes this fourth edition classic on marriage from other resources on marriage is the disclosure by the authors of the subtle but overlooked secret that 'how' couples deal with their differences is far more important than the issues themselves. Add emotional safety, intentional and timely engagement with the issues, and taking responsibility for one's role in conflict, and you have the perfect recipe for a thriving marriage. We recommend this book to *all* couples for research-based guidance they can trust, to all therapists who want to really help couples, and to everyone who would like to know how successful intimate relationships work."

—**Harville Hendrix, PhD and Helen LaKelly Hunt, PhD,** coauthors of the best-seller *Getting the Love You Want: A Guide for Couples* and cocreators of Imago Relationship therapy now practiced in more than 60 countries

"In my decades-long work with couples, I often hear, 'I wish marriages came with instructions.' The good news? They do! In this updated edition of *Fighting for Your Marriage*, you'll learn how to tackle the fundamental issues faced by all couples who are committed to keeping their relationships vibrant, as well as acquiring the necessary tools to deal with the unique challenges in our ever-changing culture. Best of all, this classic marriage-strengthening book is chock-full of pragmatic and easy-to-understand advice for creating joyful, satisfying, and long-lasting relationships."

—**Michele Weiner-Davis,** author of *Healing from Infidelity*; Michele@divorcebusting.com

"I work mostly with couples on the brink of divorce or, if not yet married, about to dissolve their relationship. Many have seen several couple therapists and found it unhelpful. Their number one complaint? 'The therapist didn't teach us any skills or tools for getting along better.' Based on decades of research, Markman,

Stanley, Rhoades, and Levine spell out succinctly and compellingly the attitudes and skills couples need to have a happy, successful relationship. As with previous editions and now thoroughly updated, it will be the core text I share with couples and teach to my graduate trainees in couple therapy."

—**Peter Fraenkel,** PhD, associate professor at The City College of New York, former faculty at the Ackerman Institute for the Family and New York University Medical Center, and author of *Last Chance Couple Therapy: Bringing Relationships Back from the Brink*

"This guide to modern couple relationships for the 2020s and beyond is written by the A-team of couple relationship education. Based on 40+ years of research and practice with couples, they offer practical advice and tips for having a great relationship. *Fighting for Your Marriage* is easy to read with lots of suggested activities to build a great relationship."

—**Kim Halford,** PhD, professor of clinical psychology, University of Queensland, Brisbane, Australia

Fighting *for* Your Marriage

FOURTH EDITION

Fighting *for* Your Marriage

Positive Steps for Preventing Divorce and Building a Lasting Love

FOURTH EDITION

Howard J. Markman

Scott M. Stanley

Galena K. Rhoades

Janice R. Levine

JB JOSSEY-BASS™

A Wiley Brand

Published by John Wiley & Sons, Inc., Hoboken, New Jersey.
Published simultaneously in Canada.

For general information on our other products and services or for technical support, please contact our Customer Care Department within the United States at (800) 762-2974, outside the United States at (317) 572-3993 or fax (317) 572-4002.

Wiley also publishes its books in a variety of electronic formats. Some content that appears in print may not be available in electronic formats. For more information about Wiley products, visit our web site at www.wiley.com.

Library of Congress Cataloging-in-Publication Data

Names: Markman, Howard, 1950- author. | Stanley, Scott, 1955- author. |
    Levine, 1954- author. | Rhoades, Galena, Janice R. (Janice Ruth),
    author.
Title: Fighting for your marriage : positive steps for preventing divorce
    and building a lasting love / Howard J. Markman, Scott M. Stanley,
    Galena K. Rhoades, Janice R. Levine.
Description: Fourth edition. | Hoboken, New Jersey : Jossey-Bass, [2024] |
    Includes index.
Identifiers: LCCN 2024025261 (print) | LCCN 2024025262 (ebook) | ISBN
    9781394220298 (paperback) | ISBN 9781394220304 (adobe pdf) | ISBN
    9781394220311 (epub)
Subjects: LCSH: Marriage. | Interpersonal relations. | Interpersonal
    communication.
Classification: LCC HQ734 .M349 2024 (print) | LCC HQ734 (ebook) | DDC
    306.81—dc23/eng/20240620
LC record available at https://lccn.loc.gov/2024025261
LC ebook record available at https://lccn.loc.gov/2024025262

Cover Design: Wiley
Cover Image: © Gexam/Adobe Stock

SKY10080736_080124

In memory of Mom and Dad: Your support, caring, and love continue to be an inspiration to me

To Mat and Leah: You two have been the centerpiece of my life, and I am so proud of you both

—HJM

To Nancy, for your love through all these years

To Kyle and Luke, for the joy you bring

—SMS

To my friend Betsy, who taught me the best of what I know about love

To my children, Langley and Emmett, whom I love with all my heart

—GKR

In loving memory of Brian, my greatest teacher

To Brennan and Sarah, my always inspiration and motivation

To Scott, for your abiding love and support, in all ways

—JRL

Contents

Acknowledgments

Many people have influenced us in the journey that underlies this work. We are grateful for the work of those specifically listed here as well as for the work of so many others.

Special and heartfelt thanks goes to our talented ghost writer, Adam Rosen. As a professional writer and careful editor, his input was indispensable. This fourth edition of *Fighting for Your Marriage* is immensely stronger because of his efforts.

We want to acknowledge one of our longest-time colleagues who not only collaborated with us on earlier editions of this book but who also was influential in our early efforts to disseminate the PREP approach to others—Susan Blumberg.

The PREP approach, on which this book is founded, is built from insights based on the research of scores of researchers who study relationships, marriage, and family. We specifically acknowledge the work of our amazing colleagues in building the knowledge basis for PREP, including Elizabeth Allen, Don Baucom, Steven Beach, Adrian Blow, Scott Braithwaite, Sarah Carter, Andy Christensen, Mari Clements, Brian Doss, Norm Epstein, Frank Fincham, Frank Floyd, Peter Fraenkel, John Gottman, Kurt Hahlweg, Kim Halford, Rick Heyman, Amy Holtzworth-Munroe, Neil Jacobson, Michael P. Johnson, Kayla Knopp, George Levinger, Kristin Lindahl, Ben Loew, Gayla Margolin, Clifford Notarius, Aleja Parsons, Gerry Patterson, Lane Ritchie, Caryl Rusbult, Shelby Scott, Amy Smith Slep, Doug Snyder, Ragnar Storaasli, Martha Wadsworth, Robert L. Weiss, and Sarah Whitton.

Having solid material that can help people in their relation-ships is one thing—getting it out to those who can use it is quite another. The team at PREP, Inc. has brought great drive, creativ-ity, and excellence to the task of disseminating the PREP approach to people around the world. They have been instrumental in developing and refining content and adaptations, training others to use the approach, and in disseminating PREP extensively. They are a creative, talented team who are leaders in the field of relationship education. As said previously, it is not possible to list everyone who has contributed to PREP's quality and influ-ence, but we give special mention to some of the past and present members of the team, including Jennifer Acker, Robert Allen, Todd Boyd, Maggie Corcoran, Miranda Egger, Jeff Erlacher, Sarah Healey, Natalie Jenkins, Lawrence Ramos, Kara Shade, and Nick Thayer.

We further acknowledge the work of numerous others who have coauthored books or worked on the dissemination of PREP with us: Abdallah Badahdah, Milt Bryan, Joel Crohn, Berger Hareide, Pamela Jordan, Savanna McCain, Daniel Trathen, Keith Whitfield, and Lee White.

Over the years, we've been excited to work with all the branches of our US armed forces. Bill Coffin, in particular, has been a true visionary in his efforts to support prevention efforts for building strong marriages in both military and civilian communities. He has been an especially potent force in helping bring evidence-based materials to couples throughout the US military services, beginning with the US Navy in the early 1990s. He saw a need and looked for ways to meet it.

Another person who deserves special notice is Chaplain Glen Bloomstrom of the US Army (retired). Glen has been a tireless leader in bringing PREP training to Army families through the work of the chaplain corps. In the Army, Navy, and Air Force, we've been privi-leged to get to know and work with hundreds of chaplains who go the extra mile in reaching and supporting the lives of service members.

In particular, we are very appreciative of the work of chaplains such as David Bynum, Pete Frederich, Paul Lepley, Dan Stallard, Ron Thomas, and Thomas Waynick in facilitating high-quality research on PREP in the US military. Across all the branches of service, we've also been privileged to work with those who work in many prevention and intervention roles on behalf of service members and their families, including those working in family advocacy, mental health, and substance use treatment and prevention roles.

These are just a few of the people in our armed forces who have put the military services on the cutting edge of efforts to prevent marital and relationship distress, and strengthen families. The military does not get nearly the credit it deserves for all these efforts, and we believe they are ahead of the curve in terms of prevention services to help couples and individuals reach their relationship goals.

We also thank Diane Sollee for her visionary efforts to put relationship education on the map through her creation of the Smart Marriages conferences, which ran from 1998 through 2013. We also acknowledge our friend Gary Smalley. Gary passed on some years ago, but not without giving to us and many others his support and encouragement to reach couples and families. Finally, we thank Mary Myrick and her team at Public Strategies in Oklahoma, whose insight, vision, and brilliance have helped numerous states and organizations implement family relationship strengthening efforts. She has significantly influenced our work.

As we've conducted research on this approach over the years, we have been assisted by bright and energetic research assistants and colleagues, including our graduate and undergraduate students at the University of Denver. The number of these people with whom we've been privileged to work has grown so very large that there are too many names to list here, but we deeply thank all these folks who have been so important in our work.

Most of the research reported in this book has been supported over the years by grants to several of us to the University of Denver, including funding from the National Institute of Mental Health, the National Institute of Child Health and Human Development, and the Administration for Children and Families. We are grateful for the support from these institutions; they have enabled us to develop the research basis for the program presented in this book (as well as much of the research behind the growing field of relationship education).

We are deeply grateful for the team at Wiley who has made it possible to bring this new edition of this classic work to you. We specifically thank Amy Fandrei, Navin Vijayakumar, and Sophie Thompson for all their advice, help, and support. Also, there could not be a new edition without there having been a first. We were fortunate to work on the very first edition of this book with our editor at Jossey-Bass/Wiley, Alan Rinzler. He was remarkably encouraging, wise, and deeply influential in the history of this book coming into being.

We acknowledge the role that clients and workshop participants have played over the years in enriching our sense of the challenges and mysteries of love. We also express our deep appreciation for the couples and families who have shared their lives with us in our various research projects. These couples have opened their hearts and their relationships to our interviewers and video cameras over time. They have shared their struggles and successes, and we hope that the knowledge presented in this book represents some small compensation to these couples, without whom the book could never have been written.

Although our knowledge of relationships has been deeply enriched by what we learned from all the couples and individuals along the way, the examples we share throughout this book are composites and thoroughly disguised. Nevertheless, the stories told by many couples over the years are often so strikingly common that the themes in our examples will speak to a variety of people. The examples will seem "real" to you as you read because they are all based on real human experience. We can all learn from each other.

Introduction

This is the fourth edition of *Fighting for Your Marriage*, a book first published in 1994, substantially revised in 2001, and then again in 2010. The first three editions were well received among couples and professionals alike, and all were bestsellers in the relationship and marriage fields. The first edition even had the illustrious honor of being mentioned on *Oprah*! This being the case, you may be wondering, "Why change something that already works?"

Well, a lot has happened in the last 14 or so years, to say the least. The dynamics of marriage, including who gets married (and divorced), have changed significantly, while national and global events have put additional stress on the institution of marriage. Widening political and social polarization, increased economic uncertainty, the opioid crisis, the COVID-19 pandemic, and the further entrenchment of technology into our everyday lives are just a few the major developments that have taken place over the past decade and a half.

What has not changed is that people benefit from having a happy, healthy relationship in terms of emotional, physical, and even financial well-being. Not surprisingly, children who grow up with parents in a happy, healthy relationship also do better in life.

Arguably the biggest news in the world of marriage is the fact that less than half of millennials, currently the largest generation in the United States, are married. When millennials do get married, it's at a later age. In 2022, the median age of marriage was 30.5 for men and 28.6 for women; in 2010, these figures were 28.2 and 26.1, respectively. We expect this trend for marrying later will continue, at least, through this decade.

At the same time, the divorce rate has been in steady decline, and we believe it likely will continue to decline for the foreseeable future. For example, between 2000 and 2020, the rate of divorce in the US has declined to 42 percent. Although many experts have said the probability of divorce for first-time marriages is approximately 40 percent, it is hard to know what the likelihood of divorce will be going forward for couples marrying for the first time today. We expect that divorce rates will continue to decline over the rest of this decade.

And then there are the growing income and education gaps when it comes to the likelihood of marrying. Americans in the top quintile of income are now significantly likelier to get married than those in lower ones. The same goes for Americans with a bachelor's degree versus those with only a high school education. This was not always the case. For comparison, the 1960s marriage rates in America were nearly the same across income and education levels.

There are also now more women enrolled in college, medical school, law school, and many other graduate-level fields than men. Not unrelatedly, 29 percent of women in heterosexual marriages now earn the same amount of money as their husbands, and 16 percent are the primary or sole breadwinners of their family. (In other words, just over half of men are their family's primary or sole breadwinner.)

Although this class divergence was clear in 2010, it has only accelerated since. Whether differing marriage rates are a cause or a consequence of inequality is a topic of much ongoing study and debate. Regardless, this reality must be taken into account when thinking about the role of marriage in peoples' lives today.

Another major change over time is the ascendance of living together without being married. This more ambiguous form of relationship encompasses a wide range of couples, from the highly committed to those for whom living together is much more like dating than a long-term commitment. Yet, at the same time, the vast majority of people still aspire to marry (though less than in the past). Regardless of their aspirations, however, the likelihood that people will marry has declined. For example, between 2011 and 2021 the marriage rate decreased 8.5 percent. It's not clear if trends toward fewer people marrying will continue in the coming decade.

These are not the only ways the makeup of who is married or not has changed in the United States. In 2015, the Supreme Court ruling *Obergefell v. Hodges* legalized same-sex marriage, extending the right to marry to hundreds of thousands of couples who had long been denied by the state. With the ruling, the United States became one of twenty-two countries (now thirty-two) to recognize same-sex marriage.

Looming over all of these changes has been the widespread adoption of smartphones, which have had a profound impact on dating (and, by extension, marriage). Although dating websites were already proliferating by the early 2010s, the presence of a constant and reliable internet connection in people's pockets all but ensured online dating would permanently shape how couples met. It's probably no surprise, then, that a 2019 study from Stanford University estimated that 39 percent of all heterosexual American couples met online in 2017, whether through dating sites or apps. Another study found that 77 percent of the online dating population in 2019 had been on at least one date with someone they met through a dating site or app; both figures are surely higher today. To offer some comparison, in the last edition, published in 2010, we noted (with no small sense of amazement) that the number of couples who met online was estimated to be 20 percent. The popularity of digital coupling represents an enormous and obviously unprecedented shift in human behavior.

What all of this boils down to is that marriages today require partners to be even more skilled in communication, conflict management, and negotiation than ever before. Because marriage is becoming somewhat rarer and partners choosier, partners (especially women, we feel it's important to note) are less likely to

What all of this boils down to is that marriages today require partners to be even more skilled in communication, conflict management, and negotiation than ever before.

automatically accept things. Many more issues are fair game for discussion. Assumptions are out.

Partners also have higher expectations for the positive sides of their relationships. They often expect their partner to be their best friend and soul mate. So when negative things happen, they have to realize that even best friends can have conflict, and that they must work through their issues in a way that doesn't threaten their relationship's success. The importance of productively managing conflict, especially today, cannot be overstated. We have even more evidence than in the past, increasingly drawn from more diverse samples of couples, that the negatives in relationships are more hurtful than the positives are beneficial. Accordingly, with this new edition we continue our focus on how to defeat negative patterns while also accentuating how to strengthen positive connections.

Just as in 2010, but to a far greater extent, there's a massive amount of information about relationships and marriage out there, especially online. If you go to any search engine and type in a question about relationships, you'll get back nearly infinite results. But how do you know what information you can trust?

That's where we come in. In this fourth edition of *Fighting for Your Marriage*, we have continued our commitment to science by refining our work based on research. We believe this gives our approach a strong foundation that you can trust. We wrote this book for everyone who is interested in learning research-based skills that will enable them to have and keep a satisfying current or future long-term relationship or marriage.

This book is for you if you want to do any of the following:

- Apply up-to-date, research-backed strategies to deepen your relationship.
- Prepare for marriage or a long-term relationship.

- Repair a relationship or marriage that is not going well.
- Bridge the emotional distance that has grown between you and your partner.
- Enhance your chances for relationship and marital success.
- Repair your or your partner's lack of desire for sensual and sexual connections.
- Fall back into love if you fear you've lost that loving feeling.
- Learn more about how to have a happy, healthy relationship, even if you are not in a relationship right now.

Many of the strategies in this book are based on our decades of research, much of it involving observing couples over time and noting how their communication strategies help or hinder them as they tackle common relationship problems. This process involved recording couples as they talked about their issues, and then having teams of coders assess the communication dynamics of these couples. This process has enabled us to describe key patterns when it comes to relationship success and failure—patterns that we will be passing on to you. As the famous New York Yankees catcher and philosopher Yogi Berra put it, "You can see a lot just by watching." Simply put, our research shows that what couples argue about is not as important as how they argue.

Simply put, our research shows that what couples argue about is not as important as how they argue.

The strategies in this book are based on the widely acclaimed Prevention and Relationship Education Program (PREP). Based on more than forty years of research, this book will show you how to talk more and fight less, protect your friendship, and keep the fun alive. You'll learn what it takes to have a more intimate, sensual relationship and how to clarify and act on priorities. Research has found that couples who are taught the strategies in this book can handle conflict more constructively, protect their happiness, and

Research has found that couples who are taught the strategies in this book can handle conflict more constructively, protect their happiness, and reduce the odds of breaking up.

reduce the odds of breaking up. No other approach in the field of relationship education has been studied and found successful by more researchers, and the program has reached hundreds of thousands of couples in the US and around the world. Accordingly, you might think of this book as your own relationship workshop.

Most people want a happy marriage that lasts a lifetime, but we know that many couples don't stay together. Although the likelihood of divorce has declined, many couples will divorce. Many couples who never marry will break up. As a result, children are still experiencing high rates of family instability. Whether married or not, too many couples who stay together are deeply unhappy. As a result, couples who want lasting love may have greater challenges now than ever before.

We are relationship optimists. We believe that a great deal of divorce, family instability, and marital and/or relationship unhappiness can be prevented. To that end, this book can help you achieve your goal of a fulfilling, lasting, happy, and healthy marriage or long-term partnership. It will teach you practical ways for building and sustaining a great relationship that can stand the test of time—even in the face of the obstacles life will inevitably put in your way.

The research-based skills, principles, and ideas in this book are relevant to all people and to all couples regardless of their age, race, ethnicity, sexual orientation, gender identity, income, or cultural background. No matter who you are, where you're from, or your life circumstances, this book will enable you (and your partner) to have and keep a lasting love. You deserve to be in a relationship that is happy and fulfilling.

One suggestion before we dive in. At the end of most chapters, we offer suggested activities to be completed. These brief activities are designed to reinforce the most important points of each chapter.

Some of the activities can be done with a partner and others are beneficial to do on your own. We want to note that, if you have a partner and they do not want to do an activity, that does not mean they do not care about you or the relationship.

You can consider this book a kind of travel guide for you and your relationship. But unlike most travel guides, which focus only on the best places to visit, ours spends as much time warning you about sites of danger (and how to safely navigate them). As you would read a travel guide, you can read this one cover to cover, or you can plan your own journey by reading the chapters that best meet your current needs and goals. Whatever your choice, we strongly suggest you begin with the first chapter, which highlights the three essential keys for a successful relationship.

Bon voyage!

PART 1

Understanding the Risks on the Road to Lasting Love

1

The Three Keys for a Great Relationship

Ask ten people what makes for a good marriage, and chances are you'll get back ten different answers. To lots of people, marriage is a slippery, subjective topic where internet based knowledge and folk wisdom are prized. Indeed, relationships are often talked about as if they're some sort of mystical or unknowable phenomenon, like dark matter or time travel. The result is a place where confusion and cliche too often reign.

The fundamentals of good relationships may *seem* hopelessly mysterious, but this couldn't be further from the truth. Decades of study have revealed ways in which happy couples make love last. Throughout this book, we present proven skills and strategies that you can use to make your relationship all it can be.

In this chapter we present the three research-based keys for relationship success. They are simple guidelines that will help you remember and act on the most important ideas from this book. By *simple* we mean easy to understand. Simple can be powerful, but simple does not mean easy to do—although, at times, small changes are all that are needed.

We want to challenge you to learn these keys and let them guide your action and thought so you can enhance your chances of enjoying a lifetime of love.

The three keys are as follows:

1. Make it safe to connect.
2. Decide, don't slide.
3. Do your part.

Simple enough, right? Not so fast. If they were, you probably wouldn't be reading this book. Let's explore each one.

KEY 1: MAKE IT SAFE TO CONNECT

What people want most in their relationship is to be accepted, understood, and loved—to feel safe to be themselves in their relationship. This happens when you feel assured that your partner has your back, that you are in this together.

Emotional safety is fundamental to a great relationship. Positive connections and intimacy thrive when things are safe—when you are confident that you can share your feelings and be at ease around each other. So many times, people tell us that feel like they have to walk on eggshells around their partner. That is surely not what you hope for in your relationship. When you have the skills to maintain connection and handle conflicts, you are better able to relax, to be yourself, and to open the doors to emotional and physical intimacy. We will show you how in the upcoming chapters.

Note that *safety* does not mean that conflict and emotional distress don't happen. On the contrary, being safe at home includes feeling safe to have difficult conversations. Making it safe for you and your partner to connect and stay close, especially when conflict arises (as it inevitably will), is the best thing you can do for your relationship.

Because conflicts are a common (and expected) part of relationships, many couples think that it's their differences and disagreements that cause the greatest problems in their marriage. This is a tempting explanation, but research makes it clear that by themselves they are rarely what drives people apart. To be sure, strong differences in backgrounds and viewpoints do make conflicts more likely. But over forty years of studies with an increasingly diverse population of couples tell us that success in relationships is less related to the nature of the differences between two partners than to *how they handle* the differences they have.

> *But over forty years of studies with an increasingly diverse population of couples tell us that success in relationships is less related to the nature of the differences between two partners than to how they handle the differences they have.*

Couples who handle their differences and conflicts poorly, with put-downs, escalation, and hostility are the most likely to struggle. However, even couples who disagree frequently can have a rock-solid relationship if their conflicts have established boundaries and remain respectful, even when heated.

Of course, emotional safety is not even possible when there is a lack of physical safety in a relationship. *If one or both partners do not feel free from the possibility of physical harm, nothing else is going to matter all that much.* If you do not feel physically safe in your relationship, please see "Getting More Help" at the end of the book. Also, see the box "Escalation and the Risk for Aggression" in Chapter Two.

When you make it safe to connect, you create the conditions for positive experiences to emerge. Conflicts are inevitable and need to be handled, but people do not marry for the joy of handling conflict together till death do they part. They want to be together for all the great things relationships offer: friendship, companionship, spiritual meaning, fun, passion, an opportunity to build a family, and shared values. (We will cover two important skills for helping you feel safe at home—taking a time out from destructive conflict and tools for talking without fighting—in Chapters Three and Six, respectively.)

KEY 2: DECIDE, DON'T SLIDE

There are many points in a relationship where it's important to make a decision. This can happen while facing down major life events and with lots of advance notice, or completely out of the blue and during routine conversations with your partner. Either way, whenever you find yourself in such a situation you have the choice to either let things happen as they will, or decide to move in a different direction. It may sound obvious, but the idea of deciding and not sliding is a powerful way to remember that a deliberate decision, big or small, can make a difference. (We describe more about the roots and implications of sliding versus deciding in Chapter Sixteen.)

Just letting things happen is fine in many situations. When you go on a trip, it can be fun to lay back and see what happens on a given day and not make any concrete plans. And when it comes to your relationship, you don't need to treat every moment as something requiring a hard analysis. For example, if you like your evening routine together, just letting things slide on a given night will likely work out just fine for both of you.

However, too many people apply this laissez-faire attitude to major transitions or life experiences. Rather than deciding in advance who they are as a couple, what their values are, and where they intend to go, they improvise as things come up, very often to their detriment. Why does that matter? Because major transitions and life experiences are opportunities to make a commitment to the path you most want to follow. Commitments are decisions, and such decisions anchor your sense of choosing and what you plan to follow through on. (We have much more to say about the topic of commitment in Chapter Sixteen.)

Big decisions take effort, energy, and teamwork. Consider the following questions, all of which touch on areas of major relationship stress, and then consider whether you'd be better served by discussing them carefully in advance or just dealing with them as they arise: Are you thinking about having children? Are there any major transitions coming up in your children's lives? What about how you manage money? Who does what around the home? How do you treat each other when you are upset?

Sometimes sliding is not merely allowing what will happen to happen. In effect, it means you are avoiding grappling with difficult issues and getting on the same page. We don't know how the two of you would answer the previous questions, but we do know that making a decision together demonstrates a greater commitment to follow through. So, where it matters, decide, don't slide. Discuss issues, make plans, and follow through.

This key of "decide, don't slide" applies as much to smaller moments in your relationship as big, obvious ones. As you will see starting in the next chapter, we have a lot to say and suggestions to offer about how a couple manages conflict. We make the important point that when an argument is flaring up and you are getting sideways with each other, there are many moments when one or both of you could step back and choose not to slide into a downward spiral. It's not inevitable! But interrupting that downhill slide requires a decision in the moment to take things in a different direction. Often, it only takes one of you to notice the decision point and decide to nudge the two of you in a better direction.

Similarly, decide, don't slide is a wonderful principle to guide you in making more positive moments happen. It is too easy in life to let moments pass where there could have been a kind word, a touch, an expression of appreciation—so many possibilities!—but without a moment of internal decision, the opportunity just slides away. On a day-to-day basis, a lot of "little" decisions to connect can add up to a lot of closeness over time.

Finally, the "decide, don't slide" principle applies just as well to this book. Don't *slide* into thinking that as a couple you must do everything we recommend. As you'll soon discover, we have a lot of suggestions; choose what you like and get after it, leaving the rest for the future. We are going to present so many different ideas, strategies, and skills that no couple is likely to want to do everything we recommend, at least not at first. Think of this book as a menu, not a twenty-course meal.

KEY 3: DO YOUR PART

When couples are struggling, it's tempting for each partner to blame the other for the problems at hand. In some relationships, it's true that one person is overwhelmingly more responsible for causing issues. More often, though, it takes two to tango (or wrangle—a new dance craze for unhappy couples). In the heat of a difficult moment, no one has more control over what *you* can do to help your relationship than, well, you. The reason is obvious.

You have more control over your behavior than anyone else in the world. You also have a lot less control over your partner's behavior. So if you want to make something better, do your own part.

Renowned couples therapist Shirley Glass once remarked that when it comes to relationship quality, it is more important to *be* the right person than to *find* the right person. We couldn't agree more. One way you can always be the right person in your relationship is to do the best thing for your relationship right now.

Ask Not

In 1961, John F. Kennedy famously uttered one of the greatest lines in the history of presidential speeches:

Ask not what your partner can do for you, but what you can do for your partner and your relationship.

Okay, that's not the exact quote. But it's in keeping with the spirit of the original. Both vividly illuminate the contrast between the strong human tendency to fixate first on what others should be doing, and what we can do to do our part. No matter your politics, JFK's line offers a powerful sentiment on human nature and how to make a difference.

One premise of this book, drawn from our decades of clinical practice, is that both partners in a relationship need to work on their own behavior to give themselves the best chance for lasting and committed love. This means, for example, that when conflict arises, or when you perceive your partner as acting unfairly, you try do the most constructive things *you* can do. Rather than thinking "Here we go again, they will never change" try reframing the situation to "I have the ability to change things in the direction I'd like it to go." This new perspective can feel very empowering—and is far more likely to set you up for relationship success.

Don't get us wrong: doing your part doesn't mean acting unilaterally or in isolation. Far too often, when people think their partner is being unfair or is behaving inappropriately, they feel relieved of the responsibility to be the best partner they can be. That's one of the easiest and most destructive things you can slide into. You need to hold up your end of the relationship *even when you think your partner isn't doing their share.* The major exception to this guideline is if there is ongoing victimization of one person by another. That calls for strong actions of a different sort than what we focus on here—professional help as from a domestic violence agency or therapist in leaving an unsafe relationship safely (See "Getting More Help").

To get the most out of the skills and strategies we describe in this book, you will need to decide to truly work as a team, and we cannot think of a better example of teamwork than two people each trying their best to do their part. This means that you agree to not fight destructively, to commit yourself to keeping fun and friendship in your relationship, and to make your relationship a safe emotional harbor.

Many people think they cannot bring their behavior under better control unless they first understand it. One final, essential idea to keep in mind: although it can be beneficial to have insight into why you and your partner repeat certain behaviors and patterns (for good or ill), you don't have to have it all figured out to take steps to make things better. So don't wait on insight when it's obvious that you could do something different right now that would be good for your relationship.

In the chapters to come we will give you some ideas for how you can do your part, make it safe to connect, and decide, not slide into a course of action. In fact, almost everything we cover embodies the spirit of these three keys. So try to keep them in the back of your mind as you read on.

Remember, when one of you changes your steps, the whole dance looks different!

Talking Points

1. The three keys can guide your actions in moments that matter in your relationship.

2. "Make it safe to connect" includes feeling safe to have difficult conversations.

3. "Decide, don't slide" captures the importance of being proactive and not letting things just happen.

4. "Do your part" is a powerful reminder that you have personal agency when it comes to making your relationship stronger.

Suggested Activity

Here are two specific ways you can try out doing your part:

1. Within the next twenty-four hours, do something small for your partner that you know they typically appreciate. Pick something totally under your control, and don't worry about whether or not your partner notices.

2. The next time your partner makes a comment that stings or is annoying, try letting it bounce off you. Instead of responding in a similar way, take the high road.

2

Destructive Patterns
Signs of Danger Ahead

When two people join their lives, there is always the possibility for friction. Sometimes our goals are not aligned, or we have different interests, values, or opinions on issues that feel important to us. Disagreements and conflict are inevitable—what matters is not that we have them, but how we handle them.

In this chapter we'll focus on four common ways couples mishandle conflict and damage their relationships. These four specific patterns—what we like to call Communication Danger Signs—are not the only ones that put couples at risk of unhappiness and divorce, but they are among the most important to address. Left unchecked, over time they will erode all the positives that drew partners together in the first place. Decades of work by many different researchers have confirmed the dark power of these Communication Danger Signs. Love may be a mystery, but the danger signs are not! You want to battle against these patterns, not one another—that's the essence of fighting *for* your marriage.

Here are the patterns:

1. Escalation

2. Invalidation

3. Negative interpretations

4. Withdrawal and avoidance

Once you understand these patterns, you can learn to recognize them and then use some simple tools to protect against them. Research shows that these patterns are fairly universal and apply to most relationships, which means the same goes for their solutions.

Before we dive into the Communication Danger Signs, we are going to do a quick exercise to get you thinking about the negative patterns you see in your own relationship. Years ago, in collaboration with Gary Smalley and his colleagues, we developed a Communication Danger Signs Quiz that we have subsequently used in scores of published studies. We now invite you to answer these same questions on a separate piece of paper (or in your mind). When you're finished, total up your score and then put your answers aside. If you are both reading this book, don't share them with your partner just yet. Try to wait until the end of the chapter, when we'll talk about what your scores might mean.

Here are the instructions: *please respond to each of the following statements about your relationship with your partner. We recommend that you answer these questions by yourself (not with your partner). Use the following 3-point scale to rate how often you and your mate or partner experience each situation described: 1 = almost never or never, 2 = once in a while, 3 = frequently.*

1. Little arguments escalate into ugly fights with accusations, criticisms, name-calling, or bringing up past hurts.

2. My partner criticizes or belittles my opinions, feelings, or desires.

3. My partner seems to view my words or actions more negatively than I mean them to be.

4. When we have a problem to solve, it is like we are on opposite teams.

5. I hold back from telling my partner what I really think and feel.

6. I feel lonely in this relationship.

7. When we argue, one of us withdraws—that is, doesn't want to talk about it anymore or leaves the scene.

Good work. Now let's get back to those danger signs.

COMMUNICATION DANGER
SIGNS = RED ALERT

Sometimes a crisis can lead to a stronger relationship. Maybe both partners make a pact to take on the challenge, working together to overcome it and developing a new level of support for each another. That's one way good things can come out of bad breaks in life. By contrast, the patterns of negative interaction we describe here have no upside; they are poison in your well.

How Many Positive Things Do You Need to Make Up for a Negative?

Have you ever wondered how many positives it might take to make up for one negative? If you hurl one insult at your partner and then you say something nice, are you back to being even? We don't think so, at least not usually. Cliff Notarius and coauthor Howard published a book in 1993 called *We Can Work It Out*, and in the book they attempted to answer this question. Based on their analyses of how couples talked, especially how they handled conflict, they concluded that it takes from five to twenty positive acts of kindness to wipe out the effect of one zinger. Put another way, one negative moment might wipe out the effect of five or more positives. Their colleague, John Gottman, has made this point in similar terms. One way to think about why negatives tend to carry more weight is simple. At any given moment, what is more threatening to your very existence: something dangerous coming your way or something good? We are wired to perceive threats to protect ourselves. The takeaway is that if one negative can wipe out a bunch of positives, we should be pretty motivated to prevent or interrupt those negatives. Acid burns!

This is why we emphasize Communication Danger Signs so early in the book. Couples who regularly exhibit these negative behaviors will find it hard to benefit from the positive things we recommend in the rest of the book. Limiting them sets the stage for protecting and/or restoring a great relationship.

ESCALATION: WHAT GOES AROUND COMES AROUND

Escalation occurs when partners respond back and forth negatively to each other, continually upping the ante so that their argument grows increasingly toxic. As this happens, negative comments spiral into increasing anger and frustration. It's not just the high emotional intensity that's the problem. Under these conditions, the tendency is to move from simple anger to hurtful comments to and about each other. We lose control of the conversation. What begins as a minor issue about the remote control or putting away the dishes may escalate to bigger relationship complaints or character attacks and, all too often for some couples, threats about the future of the relationship.

Jill, a thirty-four-year-old teacher, and Reese, thirty-two, who runs a catering business out of their home, had been married for six years. Like many couples, their fights started over small issues:

JILL: (sarcastically) You'd think you could put your dirty dishes in the dishwasher.

REESE: (equally sarcastically) Oh, like you never forget to put yours in.

JILL: As a matter of fact, I always load my dishes as soon as I'm done with them.

REESE: Oh, I forgot just how compulsive you are. You're right, of course!

JILL: I don't even know why I stay with you. You are so negative.

REESE: Maybe you shouldn't stay. No one's barring the door.

JILL: I'm not really sure why I do stay anymore.

One of the most damaging things about arguments that are escalating out of control is that people say things that threaten the very lifeblood of the relationship, things not easily taken back. As frustration mounts, people go from wanting to be heard by the other to wanting to hurt the other. At these times, people often hurl verbal (and sometimes even physical) weapons. You can see this pattern with Jill and Reese, where the stakes quickly rise to include threats of ending the relationship. Those reckless comments are often hard to take back, and they can do a lot to damage to the couple's sense of closeness and intimacy.

Recovery is possible, but it's better to prevent nasty, hurtful things from being said in the first place. Couples who are happy now and likely to stay that way are less prone to escalation. And if they do start to escalate, they are able to stop the negativity spiral before it erupts into a full-blown, nasty fight. Sometimes they do that with humor. Sometimes one partner decides (there's that word again—get used to it!) to soften. Sometimes they just both know it's time to back off. Too many couples, though, have trouble putting on the brakes even if they want to.

We are not recommending that you ignore negative or frustrating feelings when they inevitably arise. Rather, our advice is that you talk about the things that are bothering you in a safe, respectful way (as we discuss in later chapters).

One additional point: although partners can say the meanest things during arguments that escalate, such reckless remarks often don't reflect what each really thinks and feels about the other. You may believe or have been told that people reveal their "true feelings" in the midst of a fierce fight, but we don't believe this is usually the case. People express their true feelings when they feel safe talking to each other, not when they are angry.

People express their true feelings when they feel safe talking to each other, not when they are angry.

Escalation can deeply undermine emotional connection. Note how Reese mentioned Jill's compulsiveness, hitting her below the belt. At a more tender moment between them Jill once shared her concerns about being so driven, explaining that as a child she had learned to adapt this style to please her overly demanding father. Reese's escalating anger led her to wave this past hurt in Jill's face to win the argument. Reese may have "won" that round, but if he keeps it up he's all but guaranteed to lose his relationship.

Escalation and Chemistry

Why is escalation so hard to reign in? When we feel attacked or threatened, the stress hormone cortisol (and others) are released throughout our bodies. When that happens, our rational and empathic capacities take a back seat to our instinct to self-protect. Our bodies prepare to fight, flee, or freeze in self-defense. With each perceived attack, we fight back harder until we defeat the perceived threat. The goal is to conquer or win, not to listen or understand. It's nearly impossible to reach a mutually beneficial decision when either partner feels attacked and their body readies itself to fight back. It also takes a while to calm our bodies down. That's why when things start to get overheated, the best course of action is to pause and regroup, taking the matter up again later, when heads are cooler, as we discuss in the next chapter.

Scores of studies make it clear that conflict and the stress that can result from it not only affects the health of our relationships but also our physical well-being. So limiting and managing escalation may not just prolong your relationship, but your life, too.

When escalation leads to the use of intimate knowledge as a weapon, the likelihood of future tender moments—an essential element of a loving, long-lasting partnership—becomes jeopardized.

Who is going to share the deepest parts of themselves if the information may be used against them during a major blowup? Not you and not your partner. Wielding your partner's insecurities against them is the opposite of making it safe to connect. It's making it unsafe.

> *Who is going to share the deepest parts of themselves if the information may be used against them during a major blowup?*

You may be thinking, "We don't fight like cats and dogs—how does this apply to us?" Escalation is not always so overt. It can also be subtle. Voices don't have to be raised for you to get into the cycle of returning negative for negative. Yet research shows that even subtle patterns of escalation can lead to problems and even divorce later on. Consider the following conversation between Anthony and Alicia, a recently married couple in their twenties living together in an apartment.

ANTHONY: Did you pay the rent on time?
ALICIA: That was going to be your job.
ANTHONY: (*with an edge in his voice*) You were supposed to do it.
ALICIA: No, you were.
ANTHONY: (*sarcastically*) Did it get done?
ALICIA: No.
ANTHONY: (*muttering*) Great. Just like so many other things that don't get done.

Being newlyweds, Anthony and Alicia are happy to be married. But left unchecked, years of small arguments like this one will surely take a toll on their relationship, eroding the positive things that they now share. This process only gets worse over time, compounding as more and more damage is done.

For the future health of your relationship, then, it's essential to learn to counteract whatever tendency you have to escalate as a couple. If you don't escalate very much, great; your goal is to learn how to keep things that way. If you do escalate a fair amount, your goal is to recognize your behavior, stop the negative exchanges, and decide to talk about the issue at hand safely and at an appropriate time. (We will cover the all-important skill of calling Time Out in Chapter Three, and skills for how to talk without fighting in Chapter Six.)

INVALIDATION: PAINFUL PUT-DOWNS

Early in his career, coauthor Howard was working on a team including John Gottman and Cliff Notarius studying videotapes of couples talking about their top problem areas. They predicted that happy couples would differ from unhappy couples by how much they validate each other's viewpoints and feelings. They found,

---

Escalation and the Risk for Physical Aggression

One of the strongest risk factors for aggression in romantic relationships is high levels of escalation. When physical aggression occurs, it is often preceded by intense escalation. It's obviously extremely important for partners and any children in their home that this not be allowed to happen. Physical safety is a baseline requirement for any romantic relationship, end of story. Mastering the strategies we teach in this book can help couples reduce their risk for aggression. For some couples, what is taught in this book will be enough. Others may need outside help to learn to handle conflict more effectively. In some relationships, there is an even more serious problem than not handling conflict well, when one partner uses fear and aggression to control the other. In those cases, an individual at risk for serious harm should consider getting more help to be safe. See "Getting More Help" at the end of the book for resources if you as a couple or individual need more help.

instead, that these couples differed much more in how much they *invalidated* each other as they talked about their problem areas. This finding was part of the body of similar results that suggested that negatives might carry more weight than positives.

Invalidation occurs when one partner puts down the thoughts, feelings, or character of the other. Invalidation comes in many forms, including snide remarks and sarcasm, hurling harsh insults, or simply dismissing one partner's feelings. If you and your partner frequently speak with contempt or belittle one another, it is a serious risk to your relationship. Attacking the character of your partner cuts to the core, and it can do devastating relationship damage. Here are two arguments that illustrate what invalidation looks like.

REESE: (*very angrily*) You missed your doctor's appointment again! I even texted you to remind you. You are so irresponsible. I could see you dying and leaving me, just like your father.

JILL: (*bruised*) Thanks a lot. You know I'm nothing like my father.

REESE: He was useless, and so are you.

JILL: (*dripping with sarcasm*) I'm sorry. I forgot my good fortune to be married to such a paragon of responsibility. You can't even keep your own life organized. You're the messiest person I know, maybe except for your mother.

REESE: At least I'm not obsessed with stupid little things.

JILL: You are so arrogant.

Here's a more subtle example of invalidation.

MARIA: (*with a tear*) I'm so pissed off. Dan's evaluation of me was completely unfair.

ESTEVAN: I don't think he was all that critical, honestly. I'd be happy to have an evaluation as positive as that.

MARIA: (*turning away with a sigh*) You don't get it. It upset me.

ESTEVAN: Yeah, I see that, but I still think you're overreacting.

These examples are quite different in level of intensity, but both show what invalidation looks like. The first example is much more caustic, and hence damaging to the relationship, than the second. With Jill and Reese, you can *feel* the contempt seeping through. After finding its bearings, the argument has settled into an attack on each partner's character. That's the most invalidating language there is.

Although Maria and Estevan do not show the contempt displayed by Jill and Reese, Estevan is subtly putting down Maria for the way she's feeling. He may even think that he will cheer her up by saying, "It's not so bad." Nevertheless, this kind of communication is also invalidating. Maria feels more hurt now because he has said, in effect, that her feelings of sadness and frustration are inappropriate.

Any kind of invalidation sets up barriers in relationships. Invalidation hurts. It inevitably leads to covering up who you are and what you think because it's just too risky to do otherwise. Guarding our feelings and sharing less with each other slowly fractures the intimacy and safety of the relationship. Remember, your words have the power to build your partner up or tear them down. Use that power wisely.

NEGATIVE INTERPRETATIONS: DON'T BELIEVE EVERYTHING YOU SEE OR THINK

Negative interpretations occur when one partner believes that the motives of the other partner are more negative than they actually are. This can be a very harmful pattern. These interpretations are fueled by negative sentiment override, a concept first introduced and described by Robert Weiss in a foundational paper in 1980. He and his colleagues showed how people in distressed relationships regularly view their partner in a negative light, seeing more negatives than objective observers see.

Margot and David have been married twelve years, and they are generally happy together. Yet their discussions at times have been plagued by a specific negative interpretation. Every December, they have had trouble deciding whether to travel to her parents' house for the holidays or stay home. Margot believes that David dislikes her parents, but in fact, he likes them quite a bit. She has this mistaken belief because of a few incidents that happened early in their marriage that, for his part, David has long since forgotten. Here's how the conversation inevitably plays out every time the topic comes up:

MARGOT: We should start looking into plane tickets to go visit my parents for Christmas.

DAVID: (*thinking about their tight budget*) I was wondering if we can really afford it this year.

MARGOT: (*in anger*) My family is very important to me, even if you don't like them. I'm going to go.

As we said, David actually likes going to her parents' house, but he's concerned about what it will cost to get there. Still, what can he say or do to make a difference as long as her belief that he dislikes them is so strong? If a negative interpretation is strong enough, nothing the person on the receiving end of it can do will change things. When relationships become more distressed, partners tend to give each other less benefit of the doubt. This creates an environment of hopelessness and demoralization.

Negative interpretations are very hard to detect and counteract. We all have a strong tendency toward "confirmation bias," the tendency to look for evidence that confirms what we already think is true. That makes it hard to see something differently, especially if we've been viewing it a certain (negative) way for so long. We see what we expect to see, even though we should know better than to believe that what we "see" is always right.

Deciding to suspend judgment, even—especially!—when our instinct is to do the opposite, can go a long way in counteracting confirmation bias. When we have more grace and act charitably toward our partners, positive communication is far more likely to emerge.

WITHDRAWAL AND AVOIDANCE: PLAYING HIDE AND SEEK

Withdrawal and avoidance are different symptoms of a pattern in which one partner shows an unwillingness to get into or stay with important discussions. Withdrawal tends to happen when a conversation gets heated or when it is on a topic one partner feels uncomfortable talking about. Withdrawal can be as obvious as getting up and leaving the room or as subtle as changing the subject or just "turning off" or "shutting down" during an argument. The withdrawer often tends to get quiet during an argument or may agree quickly to some suggestion just to end the conversation, with no real intention of following through.

Avoidance reflects the same reluctance to get into certain discussions but describes how one partner attempts to prevent the difficult conversation from happening in the first place. A person prone to avoidance would prefer that the topic not come up, and if it does, may manifest the signs of withdrawal.

If one partner simply won't participate in hard conversations, there's little hope of cultivating the kind of safety and intimacy so essential to relationships that stand the test of time. A couple who frequently does the dance of one partner pursuing and the other withdrawing is at high risk for marital distress and divorce.

To see how these dynamics often play out, take Mike and Prithi, a couple who had been married ten years. Mike was the manager of a restaurant, and Prithi was a schoolteacher who was taking a few years off to be at home with their children while they were young. As is true for many couples, money was tight. Mike worked long hours to make ends meet. Prithi was torn between her desires to be home with the kids and to be back teaching, bringing in some income. Prithi deeply desired to talk with Mike about her conflicted feelings, but he never seemed interested in hearing what was on her mind about this subject. Prithi's frustration grew daily. She felt that Mike was avoiding talking with her about anything more important than the weather or what to eat for dinner. The following conversation, which took place one Saturday morning while the kids were out playing, was typical.

PRITHI: (sitting down by Mike and looking at him) I wish I could relax about money. When I see you worrying so much, it's just . . . I wonder if I'm doing the right thing, you know, being here at home.

MIKE: (not looking up from his phone) It'll all work out.

PRITHI: (She's thinking, "He doesn't want to hear it. I wish he'd put his damn phone down.") I don't know. Am I really doing the right thing taking time off? I think about it every day. Some days, I . . . you know, I'm not sure.

MIKE: (He tenses while thinking, "We always end up fighting when we talk about money. Why is she bringing this up now? I thought we'd settled this.") I really think you're doing the right thing. It's just harder to make the budget work, but we'll get back on track. I don't think we need to hash it out again.

PRITHI: (She's thinking, "Why can't he relax and open up more? I want to talk and know he is listening.") I can tell you really don't want to talk about it. It bugs me that you can't talk with me about this. You always either change the subject or get real quiet.

MIKE: (He takes a deep breath and lets out a loud sigh. He wants to say something to stop the escalation, but no good idea comes to mind. He says nothing. He feels tense.)

PRITHI: (feeling very frustrated, with anger growing) That's exactly what I mean. You just close me out, again and again, and I'm tired of it!

MIKE: (He's thinking, "I knew it. We always fight when we talk about money.") Why do you do this? I'm just sitting here relaxing. It's the only time I have all day to sit still, and you pick a fight. I hate this! (He throws his phone down, gets up from the table, and walks into the living room.)

Mike's withdrawal was very frustrating to Prithi. She wanted to talk through a significant concern: how the decision they had made for her to stay home with the children for a time was increasing his level of stress. Mike wasn't pulling back from talking because he didn't want to change, nor did his withdrawal have anything at all to do with flexing his power. His withdrawal was driven by his discomfort with having this kind of talk with Prithi. He'd come to believe that talking about issues like this usually led to fights between the two of them, and he did not want to fight with Prithi. He loves her. But his withdrawing was taking a toll on her confidence in their relationship. It avoided one problem for him while creating a different type of problem for their relationship.

There is an irony here, and we think it's a common one. Mike wanted to avoid a fight with her at all costs, yet his pulling back, if anything, guaranteed the fight. So, like most couples, when one of them withdraws, the other tends to up the ante and push harder. This can be motivated by frustration that something is not going to get resolved. On a deeper level, it can be motivated by panic that the partner is detaching from the relationship.

When you try to do something you think is good for your relationship, like bringing up a concern, and your partner does not seem to appreciate it or gets upset that you are bringing it up, it can leave you hanging out there and feeling alone. This could be why partners, especially women, lose confidence in their marriage when these negative patterns don't seem to get better. This might lead the woman to seek help and if her partner is not willing to participate, to eventually file for divorce.

Mike and Prithi were finding pursuit and withdrawal a painful dance. Imagine how much more destructive it could have become if each had started thinking the worst of the other. Prithi could have started to think that Mike's withdrawal meant he didn't love and care for her. That would be terribly serious if it were true. He might have started believing that Prithi just liked to stir up conflict to control him or nag him. These kinds of negative interpretations are devastating, and they are usually inaccurate. As we said previously, once negative interpretations get going, it's very hard to get things back on track. You can do it, but you have to work at it: by looking hard for evidence to the contrary, by asking questions to check out your assumptions, or by affording your partner the benefit of the doubt.

You think your partner doesn't care, and that's what's behind their withdrawal? Look for evidence that tells you they do care and give that equal weight. You think your partner gets some secret pleasure in hassling you? In our experience that's very unlikely. If you have concerns about something, find a soft way to raise them when you both can agree not to fight. Agree to pause if things get too fiery. Be kind. Ask questions and don't make assumptions or accusations. The loudest voice won't get the attention of someone who doesn't want to listen.

There are several popular assumptions as to why someone might pull away from talking with their partner. Let's take them one by one:

1. The withdrawer does not care about or love their partner.

2. The withdrawer simply does not want to change in some way and therefore refuses to talk about the subject.

3. The withdrawer is pulling a power move in which they are "showing" the pursuer that the pursuer does not have control.

4. The withdrawer fears arguing with the pursuer and is attempting to stop what looks like a fight coming.

We don't believe reason one is very common. We think most people do desire intimacy, though they may have different preferences for what form it will take. As for reason two, surely there are times when a person does not want to change something and avoids talking to their partner about the topic. That's likely pretty common. Reason three is obviously worse than one or two. There are times in some relationships when one shuts the other out, deliberately, as a kind of power move. That's also called being passive-aggressive, and it's very destructive. Whether one or both partners act this way, it undermines the relationship.

We believe that reason number four is more common than many people assume. And, on the plus side, it also offers a more positive interpretation for what's going on; not wanting to have a nasty fight isn't a bad impulse. Nonetheless, more often than not the pursuer interprets the behavior of the withdrawer as being driven by one of the three other reasons, ultimately concluding that the withdrawing partner just does not care about the topic at hand. This assumption is understandable, but, fortunately, doesn't seem to be well founded. In our many interviews with couples, we have learned that when withdrawers are given space to explain, more often than not they say they are not trying to avoid intimacy, but rather they are trying to avoid conflict.

What's interesting is that, in their own way, both the pursuer and the withdrawer feel threatened by the other's approach to conflict. The pursuer gets anxious and upset because they cannot get resolution to what they need to discuss, and the withdrawer feels threatened because they feel cornered or attacked. Both partners can get

---

Male-Female Relationship Trends

Decades of research make it clear that there are measurable and consistent differences in how men and women tend to communicate. When it comes to withdrawal, this research indicates that when talking with their (heterosexual) partner about difficult issues, women are usually the ones who want to open up and share their thoughts, whereas men are more likely to shut down and tune out, classic signs of withdrawal and avoidance. Although these trends can, of course, cross gender lines, the pursuer is left feeling like their partner doesn't care, and the one shutting down feels like their partner always wants to fight.

In our own practices, we find that women are much more likely to voice concerns about withdrawn, avoidant partners who will not open up and talk. When men act this way, women feel shut out and experience a double whammy: not only do they not get a chance to talk about something important to them but also their partners are now angry at them for bringing it up. The women feel that they are the only ones who care for the relationship and end up feeling lonely and unloved.

By contrast, men frequently complain that their wives get upset too often, griping about this or that and picking fights. Men generally feel hassled and criticized and want peace at any price. In essence, their biggest priority is to have harmony and calm in their marital relationships, even if the price is high. All too often we hear women say, "He won't talk to me and I often feel this is because he does not love me." And the men say, "I do love her, but the reason I often avoid talks is that I do not want to spend my life fighting with her."

In one way or another, we hear men saying they want to know how to stop having fights with their wives, and women wishing that their husbands would engage more directly to resolve their differences. Both wish for harmony but approach it differently, often alienating the other in the process.

stuck in fight-or-flight dynamics as things wind up. The pursuer fights and the withdrawer freezes or flees. Either are just going to result in damaging escalation.

There may be other individual differences that explain why a person withdraws as well, such as family background. Some families and cultures are very comfortable with, shall we say, *animated* conversations that involve high volumes and intensity. This may not feel at all threatening; indeed, it may feel like a normal (even loving) dinner table conversation. But to a person who grew up in a quieter household, the intensity of the conversation can feel intimidating.

What's sad is that most partners doing this pursuit-and-withdraw dance really want to make things better. We see this in our counseling practices: we ask couples to list their goals for therapy, and the people who put "to talk more" as their first goal often have "to fight less" as another major goal, and vice versa. But (as you no doubt know by now) just wanting these things to happen isn't enough. You need the tools we teach in upcoming chapters to recognize and counteract these dangerous patterns.

HOW'D YOU DO ON THE QUIZ?

Take out the sheet with your answers from the quiz earlier in the chapter. If you did not write down your answers, just reflect on how you answered those questions, or would now. Either way, total up the scores for your answers across the seven questions. Your score can range from 7 to 21.

The following ranges are based only on your individual total score—not your total as a couple. If one of you scores a lot higher than the other, we'd gently suggest that the higher score probably better reflects how your relationship is doing. That's not to say that the person with the higher score is "right," but rather that any higher score reflects significant concerns that both partners should take to heart.

Among the many surveys we've given out, the average score is a 10. Although you should not take a higher score to mean that your relationship is somehow destined to fail, it may mean that your relationship is in greater danger unless you and your partner make some changes.

7 to 11

If you scored in this range, your relationship is probably in good or even great shape *at this time*. We emphasize *at this time* because relationships don't stand still. In the next twelve months, you may have a stronger, happier relationship, or you could be headed in the other direction. To think about it another way: your score tells you that you are traveling along and have come to a green light. There is no need to stop, but it may be a great time to go in for a routine tune-up to ensure everything keeps working.

12 to 16

If you scored in this range, you are coming to a yellow light. You need to be cautious. Although you may be happy now in your relationship, your score reveals warning signs of patterns you don't want to allow to become worse. You'll want to take action to protect and improve what you have. Spending time to strengthen your relationship now could be the best thing you do for your future together.

17 to 21

If you scored in this range, think of yourselves as approaching a red light. Stop and think about where the two of you are headed. Your score indicates the presence of patterns that could put your relationship at significant risk. Your relationship is likely heading for trouble or is already there. Further, if you have children in the home, they are likely being negatively affected by your communication and conflict behavior. With a lot of effort, and by applying the tools in this book, couples can stop and start to learn ways to counter these patterns. Seeking a well trained couples therapist can also help. For others who have unrelenting destructive conflicts with no mutual, strong efforts to change (paired with aggression and refusal to seek outside help), it may be time to reconsider the viability of the relationship.

In this chapter, we've described common patterns of negative interactions that come out during conflicts. Common does not mean good, of course. It can be reassuring to realize everybody exhibits Communication Danger Signs from time to time, but it doesn't make them any less harmful. Because negative events are so potent, it is important to do your part when it comes to reducing these types of patterns. In Chapter Three we will show you how to do just that.

Talking Points

1. Even just a few negative interactions can cancel out the many positive ones in your relationship.

2. Most couples have some degree of difficulty with these patterns. You cannot wave a magic wand and have conflict disappear, but you can be more aware of the patterns you struggle with most.

3. It's easy for each partner in a relationship to think the other person started a negative interaction. In reality, it's usually a dance two people are doing together.

3

Changing the Dance
Counteracting Communication Danger Signs

All couples will experience some of these patterns as they deal with the inevitable conflicts inherent in their relationships. The presence of conflict isn't the problem. The problem occurs when couples refuse to address Communication Danger Signs—or use the wrong approach to do so, making things worse. In this chapter, we want to describe some of the specific ways you can minimize the recurrence of these patterns in your relationship.

CALLING TIME OUT: A MOST IMPORTANT SKILL

Research shows that the happiest couples tend to score lower in Communication Danger Signs. Perhaps more important, though, when negative patterns threaten to rear their ugly head, the couples are able to exit them relatively quickly. Some are able to deploy a little humor to cool things down or have a good sense of when to back off so things don't get too heated. For other couples, such abilities do not come naturally, and they easily roll right into the danger signs when a conflict is sparked. These couples will benefit the most from learning strategies that can help them step back from the brink.

39

Calling Time Out is a skill that can help counter any of the danger signs, but especially escalation. Once a conflict begins to escalate, all of the Communication Danger Signs can come into play within minutes (or even sooner). Calling Time Out is a powerful way to stop the negative cascade, especially if pumping the brakes doesn't come naturally to you or your partner. It may feel awkward or unnatural, but it's quick and easy.

By "Time Out," we do not mean the kind where a parent puts a child in the corner for five minutes. We mean the type of Time Out a sports team uses when they are losing their focus or need to reset their play. Just like them, *your* team needs to know how to call a Time Out to reset. Sometimes, just like in sports, negative momentum builds up and threatens to overtake you. Is your team going to let that happen? You don't have to allow it to—call a Time Out instead!

We strongly recommend you and your partner try out this approach. Beforehand, though, you should both agree on how to signal when one of you thinks it would be wise to take a Time Out. Otherwise one of you may not realize that the other is trying to do something to protect the relationship, and calling Time Out might feel like the partner is being controlling or trying to get out of the conversation for good (withdrawing). By agreeing on a signal, everyone will be on the same page.

It is often helpful to start by saying, "This is not going well," and then give your agreed-on Time Out signal. The signal could be the words "Time Out," as in, "Let's take a Time Out," or "Let's take a break," or a phrase like "How about we pump the brakes?" It could be some other term, a phrase, or even a hand gesture (a friendly one!) that you will both recognize as a sign the person is trying to do something good to protect the relationship.

It is often helpful to start by saying, "This is not going well," and then give your agreed-on Time Out signal.

You know what's *not* a good signal for taking a Time Out? One of you walking out of the room without saying anything. That's withdrawal, and, as you are well aware, it's a danger sign. It's also not useful to say, "You are getting angry, you need a Time Out." This will add fuel to the fires of relationship conflict. The whole point of using a skill like calling Time Out is that it shows you are acting in good faith, not to stonewall or bail but rather to protect your relationship. Of course, like many of the skills and principles we cover, Time Out can be used in other relationships as well.

Here are some pointers for using Time Out:

1. **Notice things are not going well for the home team.** At least one of you has to notice what is happening and that it's not good. That means being aware as early as you can of when your conversation is getting off track and beginning to engage in the Communication Danger Signs.

2. **Make the call.** One of you needs to give the signal, and in the most neutral way possible. Even though one of you will have to be the first to call Time Out, remember that it's something the two of you are doing together. That's the whole point. Otherwise, it can look as though one partner is just avoiding the other.

3. **Take a break.** That could be five minutes or a day. If you escalate fairly often, it's best to decide ahead of time the interval that works best for you so that you're not trying to figure it out in the heat of the moment. You could agree that the standard Time Out for the two of you is two hours, or perhaps twenty-four, or maybe thirty minutes. Try something out and then adjust it as needed.

4. **Calm yourself down.** It's easy when you're mad at each other to use your Time Out as a time to keep thinking about all the ways your partner was at fault. Don't do it! That's often an

exercise in negative interpretation, and it's not going to help. Instead, do something to relax your body and your mind. Think about something unrelated and neutral, and if you can't, push yourself to do your part for your relationship. While you're analyzing things, try to consider what the situation looks like from your partner's perspective.

5. **Get back in the game.** This has several possible meanings. Sometimes whatever caused the argument is not something you really need to talk more about. Suppose you got snippy with each other while driving to the grocery store, but you were both just hungry and had a bad moment. We don't suggest you get back into the game by replaying what happened and trying to figure it out. In fact, in this instance, the Time Out signal is simply for the purpose of taking a moment to reset. In fact, that could be your signal for this type of Time Out, such as "How about we take a moment to reset?" Other times, you will need to talk more about what caused an argument to escalate. In these cases, we highly recommend using the Speaker Listener Technique (Chapter Six) to communicate without fighting.

You don't have to keep driving down a road that has signs all over it declaring "Danger Ahead!" Get off that road until you're able to get on a better one together. Keep in mind, however, that your goal is to call a Time Out on negative patterns, not on each other. You are working together to stop the destructive process in the spirit of protecting your relationship.

We are often asked an important question about calling Time Out: "What do I do if we use Time Outs on important matters, but my partner will not come back to talking about these issues at another time?" We have come to believe that unless you are in a relationship that is physically dangerous, you are probably better off pursuing the issue assertively, but without hostility. Many of us in the field believe that it's usually better for the pursuer to bring the topic up again, even if it means more discomfort in the short run.

By not doing so, it could mean that important issues are going to be ignored.

Luke and Tara frequently had heated arguments that would escalate out of control quite easily. Before learning the Time Out technique, they would have shouting matches that often ended with threats about the future of the relationship, making dealing with issues unsafe. Both came from homes where open, intense conflict was relatively common, so changing their pattern wasn't easy. But the more they practiced calling Time Outs (in their case, "Lets Pause"), the better they became at exiting negativity spirals. Here's an example:

TARA: (*annoyed and showing it*) You forgot to get the trash out in time for the garbage company. The cans are already full.

LUKE: (*also annoyed, looking up from the paper*) It's no big deal. I'll just stuff it all down more.

TARA: Yeah, right. The trash will be overflowing in the garage by next week.

LUKE: (*irritated*) What do you want me to do now? I forgot, alright?

TARA: (*very angry now, voice raised*) You aren't getting the things done around here that you're supposed to.

LUKE: Let's pause, OK? This isn't getting us anywhere.

TARA: OK. When can we sit down and talk more about it?

LUKE: After the movie tonight?

TARA: OK. As soon as it's over.

Calling Time Out stopped an argument that was only going to damage Luke and Tara's relationship. Later, they sat down together and used the Speaker Listener Technique (Chapter Six) to talk without fighting. Then they used the problem-solving techniques we presented in Chapter Eight to come up with some solutions that they both agreed to try.

There is nothing magical going on here. Calling Time Out is simple but powerful. Sometimes people think this technique feels artificial or awkward. Maybe for some, but that doesn't mean it's not still effective. Think back to how sports teams use Time Outs. A team does not think it's an artificial process; it's simply a tool they use to regroup and get their act together. It's a form of deciding, not sliding into what is happening to you in the moment. More specifically, when you call a Time Out, you decide to *value the relationship* over who's right or wrong.

Using Time Out is one of the best ways to counteract the Danger Sign of escalation, and it helps prevent the others. Let's read on for additional ways to neutralize them.

Handling Negative Emotions

We believe that one of the great secrets of success in relationships lies in knowing how to handle three distinct challenges: what to do when you are upset, what to do when your partner is upset, and what to do when your partner gets upset because you are upset.

First: what can you do when you are upset with your partner? Much of what we cover in upcoming chapters addresses this, but we'll give you a preview here. The simple version is this: try to calm yourself down so that you can make your point effectively. The more calmly you speak, the better you will be heard. Pick a moment to respond when there's a better chance that your partner will be open to hearing your thoughts and feelings. Speak for yourself only, and don't talk about what *you* think your partner is thinking: "I am concerned about . . ." or "I feel anxious (or upset, angry, frustrated, etc.) that . . ." are good ways to start. This doesn't guarantee that your partner will take in what you're saying, but speaking for yourself in a relatively calm manner will always work better than raising your voice or attacking your partner with broad statements.

Next: what do you do when your partner is upset? The most common but worst thing to do is to get upset right back at them, or even get upset about them being upset in the first place. Those things will only invalidate your partner and lead to escalation. Instead, try to calm yourself down and listen to their concerns with an open mind. Show your partner that you care about what they are upset about. Don't pull away.

Now onto the third scenario: when one partner gets upset and then the other gets upset that the first is upset. When this happens, not only does the first partner not get a chance to talk about what they're upset about, but also they get blamed for getting upset in the first place. If you tend to get upset that your partner is upset, or you are the partner who is upset about something, and, in voicing your concern, you see that your partner is getting upset about you being upset, it's a good time for a pause or Time Out (remember to use the phrase or signal you two decided on together). You can say something along the lines of, "This is one of those times where we are both getting upset. Let's take a Time Out and find a time where we can both really listen to each other." Then follow your suggestion and find a time to have the conversation in a constructive way.

SHORT-CIRCUITING ESCALATION

All couples escalate from time to time, but some couples steer out of the pattern more quickly and in a way that leaves much less damage in their wake. In Chapter Two, we offered a pretty intense example of escalation by a couple named Jill and Reese. By contrast, here is an example where two partners, Maria and Estevan, are able to de-escalate rather quickly. Like most couples, many of their arguments are about everyday events.

MARIA: *(annoyed)* You left the butter out again.

ESTEVAN: *(irritated)* What's the big deal? Why are these little things so important to you? Just put it back.

MARIA: *(softening her tone)* They are important to me. Is that so bad?

ESTEVAN: *(calmer)* I guess not. Sorry I wasn't nice about it.

Estevan and Maria begin the process of escalation but quickly steer out of it. When escalation sequences are short-circuited, it is usually because one partner decides to cool things down and says something to de-escalate the argument, thus breaking the negative cycle. Often this takes the simple humility of choosing to soften your tone and put down your sword. Although in our culture we don't talk a lot about humility and the grace that accompanies it, there are few things more powerful for making wonderful things happen in relationships.

> *Although in our culture we don't talk a lot about humility and the grace that accompanies it, there are few things more powerful for making wonderful things happen in relationships.*

For her part, Maria softened her tone rather than getting defensive. For his part, Estevan makes the decision to cool things down by acknowledging Maria's point of view. Softening your tone and acknowledging your partner's point of view are potent tools you can employ to defuse tension and end escalation. Often that's all it takes. Really!

If you or your partner feel like you just can't soften your tone, a Time Out can help you both reset. The larger point is this: you can *decide* to not let damaging arguments devolve into a runaway train.

If you escalate things often as a couple, it probably means one or both of you have a hard time giving up on the need to win. "Winning," however, means losing when it comes to your relationship. It's in your best interest, and your relationship's, to soften things when you disagree and work together as a team to address a problem.

COUNTERACTING INVALIDATION

In Chapter Two, Reese got upset that Jill missed her doctor's appointment, and he accused her of being like her "useless father." She retaliated by saying he's a slob, just like his mother. Not surprisingly, this toxic exchange did not bring them closer together.

One of the strongest ways to counter invalidation is to tune in to what your partner is getting at and then show you care. In other words, the strongest counter to invalidation is validation. The key is to show respect for, and acknowledge, your partner's viewpoint or feelings as genuinely as you can.

Here's how the conversation could have gone if both Reese and Jill had shown respect for, and acknowledged, each other's viewpoint.

REESE: *(angry)* I am angry that you missed the doctor appointment again. I want you to be around with me in the future!

JILL: *(surprised)* It really upset you, didn't it?

REESE: It did. I want to know that you're going to be healthy long term, and when you miss an appointment that I'm anxious about, I really worry about you.

JILL: I understand why it would make you worried when I don't take care of myself.

Remember Maria and Estevan's exchange in Chapter Two, when Estevan was not very sympathetic about her being upset about feedback she received at work? Here's how that conversation could have gone so much better—if Estevan had showed some empathy,

MARIA: *(with a tear)* You know, Dan's evaluation of me felt completely unreasonable.

ESTEVAN: That must really tick you off.

MARIA: Yeah, it does. And I also get worried about whether I'll be able to keep this job. What would we do?

ESTEVAN: I didn't know you were so worried about losing your job. Tell me more about how you're feeling.

In both examples we replay the same issues, but with very different outcomes for both couples. In each there is respect and care for each other's feelings and character. There is validation.

By *validation*, we mean that the partner hearing the concern shows respect and understanding for what is being shared. It's important to note, though, that you don't have to agree with your partner to validate their feelings. In the heat of the moment, you may have to remind yourself of this, and that's okay.

Our research shows that invalidation is one of the very best predictors of future marital problems and divorce, but that the amount of validation doesn't say as much about the health of a relationship as the amount of *invalidation* does. That doesn't mean that validation is unimportant, but it does mean that stopping invalidation is more crucial. Remember what we said previously: the negatives can be overwhelmingly powerful and hard to make up for.

One final point. Even the most humble and validating partners will find themselves unable to de-escalate from time to time. But all isn't necessarily lost even when you lose your cool—so long as you're still willing to acknowledge it. When you've blown it, try saying something like, "Let's do that over. We can do better than that," or simply, "How about a do-over?"

RESISTING NEGATIVE INTERPRETATIONS

Another tried-and-true way to counteract escalation and reduce the frequency of negative communication patterns is to reframe your interpretation of events. This isn't easy, especially if you've spent years automatically assuming the worst. We know it's challenging to be more objective when you're convinced of the truth of your perceptions. But remember that only you can control how you interpret your partner's behavior (and, by extension, act). Negative interpretations are like weeds with long roots; to rid your relationship of such perceptions, you have to get ahold of the root and pull the weed out.

The first step is to open yourself to the possibility that your interpretation of things your partner does might be both wrong and overly negative. Second, push yourself to look for evidence that contradicts the negative interpretation you usually make. That's very difficult, because humans are geared toward collecting evidence that proves what they already believe. (Remember confirmation bias?)

For example, if you believe that your partner is uncaring, and generally see most of what they do in that light, look for evidence to the contrary. Does your partner do things for you that you like? Could it be that they do nice things because they are trying to keep the relationship strong? It's up to you to consider that, just maybe, others may see behavior you find objectionable as positive—or at least, less clearly negative.

Although sometimes a negative interpretation can be accurate, for the most part, we believe that people often have unfair, negative interpretations about what their partner does or why. Unless there is some truly accurate negative belief you have, we recommend that you *decide* to be a relationship optimist by assuming the best, not the worst, about your partner. That's one of the most positive things you can give to your relationship: affording your partner the benefit of the doubt. In truth, no one can ever really know someone else's motives or intentions, so it's important to verify your interpretation with the only one who knows the truth: your partner. Be curious and ask questions to verify or debunk your concerns, rather than being judgmental. Wouldn't it be nicer to see the good in your partner rather than infer the worst?

For High-Conflict Couples with Children

For those of you with children, the stakes of conflict management are even higher. Decades of research has documented strong links between parental conflict and negative outcomes in children. When regularly exposed to poorly handled conflict, kids become more sad, angry, and fearful, and are more likely to act out. This is one of the clearest and most consistent findings in the social science literature. It's also a reminder that children are usually more aware of what's going on between their parents or stepparents than the adults think. Of course, the effects on children are all the worse if the adults in the home get physically aggressive with each other.

That children can be harmed by how their parents handle disagreements has led many to conclude that these children would be better off if their parents split up. However, many of these children are hurt by *how* their parents fight, regardless of whether or not they stay together. In other words, these children don't really do that much better if their parents divorce because their parents still have not learned the skills to handle conflict in a healthy way.

Another downside to poorly managed conflict around children is that if parents regularly make negative interpretations of each other's motivations and behavior, their children can too easily learn to do likewise with their peers. Negative interpretation patterns thus raise the stakes for *everyone* in the home.

So, what can you do? Disagree, but not in a way that evokes any of these Communication Danger Signs. Try your best to model how to stay connected with someone even when you don't see eye-to-eye. If you cannot do that, you should get really good at taking Time Outs when arguments are escalating so you don't expose your children to toxic interactions. When you can, let your children see you and your partner making up. As far as your children's well-being is concerned, *coming back to some point of emotional harmony is more important than fully resolving the specific issue you were fighting about.* So, do your kids a favor: work together to manage your conflicts productively and with respect.

COUNTERACTING AVOIDANCE AND WITHDRAWAL: HOW TO NOT PLAY HIDE-AND-SEEK

If you notice a pattern of avoidance and/or withdrawal in your relationship, keep in mind it will likely get worse if you allow it to continue. That's because as pursuers push more, withdrawers withdraw more. And as withdrawers pull back, pursuers push harder. And on it goes. Furthermore, when important issues come up (as they inevitably will), avoiding dealing with them will only lead to damaging consequences. You can't stick your head in the sand and pretend that important or bothersome problems are not really there—in relationships as much as life.

If you are the withdrawer or avoider, you need to deal with whatever barriers are keeping you from engaging. The more you avoid and withdraw from difficult conversations, the harder communicating will get over time. Perhaps you withdraw because you feel your partner blames or criticizes you, or they share too much information too fast and you just can't process it. Or maybe their communication style is very different from the one you were raised with. In a calmer moment, share with your partner what triggers your instinct to withdraw and brainstorm ways you can make it safer to connect with each other. Let your partner know what helps you stay engaged on the tougher topics.

If you are the pursuer, try to back off the intensity a bit so you give your partner the chance to move forward. The more you can demonstrate to your partner that they are safe and any conversation will ultimately make things better, the smoother things will go.

Remember: you two are a team with a common goal of making it safe to connect. You will have much greater success if you work together to change or prevent the kinds of negative patterns discussed here.

As we will make clear in the chapters ahead, we are not suggesting that any given moment is always the best time to talk through an issue, particularly if one of you feels caught off-guard. In fact, it's often a good idea to ask and agree to find a good time to talk, ideally when both of you can provide your full attention (i.e., the kids are asleep). The larger point is that we want you and your partner to have control over the timing of your difficult conversations. If you can talk when things are a bit calmer, you will be in a better position to apply the skills you learn in this book. We are relationship optimists. We believe that people can learn to better recognize damaging patterns and handle conflict better.

In this chapter, we have described just some of the ways to reduce the Communication Danger Signs. In the rest of this book, we will cover many more strategies and skills you can try in your relationship. As the overall goal for learning what works for you, you won't do better than to be guided by the three keys: Do your part. Make it safe to connect. Decide, don't slide.

Like we said: change the dance, change your relationship.

Talking Points

1. Calling Time Out, in whatever form works for you, is one of the most powerful skills to learn when it comes to protecting your relationship.

2. Validation is a strong counter to invalidation, but invalidation is more harmful than validation is helpful.

3. Challenge your negative interpretations. Give your partner the benefit of the doubt and look for evidence to support more neutral or positive thoughts.

4. Do your part to calm yourself, soften your responses, and express how you feel respectfully.

Suggested Activities

Now we're going to ask you to think about these perceptions and negative patterns in a lot more detail. Please take a pad of paper and write your answers to these questions independently from your partner. When you have finished, we suggest you share them. However, if this raises a conflict, put off your discussion until you've learned more, in the next few chapters, about how to talk safely on tough topics.

1. Let's start with a general question: when you have a disagreement or argument, what typically happens? Think about the patterns we've talked about in this chapter as you answer this question.

2. Think about escalation. Has there been a recent example of it during an argument with your partner? What is one thing you could do to stop the pattern from happening the next time you have a conflict?

3. How do you feel when your partner invalidates you? If you invalidate your partner, identify at least one thing you could do to stop, reduce, or never get into this negative pattern the next time you have a conflict.

4. Think of a recent time when you assumed the worst about something your partner said or did. If you think about it now, can you see another interpretation of their behavior that may be less negative?

5a. Which partner in your relationship tends to withdraw the most? Why do you think you might withdraw? (For example, are you afraid of change, are you trying to control or perhaps feeling controlled, are you attempting to prevent intimacy, does conflict make you anxious?)

5b. Which partner in your relationship tends to pursue relationship issues? Think about why this happens: because the person is worried about the relationship, because the person wants more intimacy, or for some other reason?

PART 2

Teaming Up to Handle Conflict

4

When What You Heard Isn't What I Said

Understanding Filters in Communication

Have you ever noticed that what your partner hears can be so head-scratchingly different from what you were trying to say? You may say something you think is harmless, and suddenly your spouse is mad at you. Or maybe you ask an innocent question, such as "Where's the laundry basket?"—only for your partner to start complaining that you never do your share of household chores.

We've all experienced these moments where you think you're being clear, but your partner just doesn't seem to get it . . . or are you the one who doesn't? Or maybe you're sure you know what your partner said yesterday, only for them to say something that seems completely different today. However this kind of miscommunication presents itself, the results are predictable: misunderstanding and argument.

Like the rest of us, Crystal and Nate could relate to this common problem. One Thursday night, Nate got home and started surfing the news while waiting for Crystal. "I'm wiped," he thought. "I bet Crystal is, too. I'd really like to go out to eat and just relax with her tonight." Good idea, right?

Well, here's what happened (what they are thinking or hearing is in parentheses):

NATE: (*thinking he'd like to go out to dinner with Crystal, as she comes in the door*) What should we do for dinner tonight?

CRYSTAL: (*hears "When will dinner be ready?"*) Why is it always my job to make dinner? I work as hard as you do.

NATE: (*hears her response as an attack and thinks, "Why is she always so negative?"*) It's not "always your job." I took care of dinner the other night!

CRYSTAL: (*The negative cycle continues, because Crystal tends to feel she does everything around the house.*) Sorry, bringing home burgers and fries isn't "making dinner."

NATE: (*With frustration mounting, he gives up.*) Just forget it. If you're gonna be like that, I don't want to go out with you.

CRYSTAL: (*confused, as she can't remember him saying anything about going out*) You never said anything about wanting to go out.

NATE: (*feeling really angry*) Yes, I did! I asked you where you wanted to go out to dinner, and you got all negative.

CRYSTAL: What?! You never said anything about going out.

NATE: Yes, I did!

CRYSTAL: You're never wrong, are you?

Sound familiar?

Let's examine how this communication misfire happened. To start, Nate wasn't as clear as he could have been in telling Crystal what he was thinking. This left a lot of room for interpretation—and interpret Crystal did. She assumed that he was asking—no, telling—her to get dinner on the table as she walked in the door. Rather than interpreting "What should we do for dinner?" as a sincere question, she assumed there was a deeper subtext, that is, that he was *really* asking when she was going to start making dinner.

It's possible her stressful workday primed her for suspecting the worst in Nate's question. But even under better circumstances, this kind of miscommunication is all too frequent in relationships. Many of your biggest arguments have no doubt started with one of you misunderstanding what the other meant, with the misunderstanding itself being what then drives the angry words. What is it that gets in the way of clear communication?

The answer, in a word, is *filters*.

Filters change what goes through them. A furnace filter takes dust and dirt out of the air. A filter on a camera lens alters the properties of the light passing through it. A filter on your inbox gets rid of spam before it reaches you.

As with any other filter, what goes through our "communication filters" is different than what comes out. When what you say (or what you intended to say) is not the same as what your partner heard, then a filter is at work. Our main point here is a simple one: *filters are one of the leading causes of miscommunication in relationships.* The good news is that by understanding your filters, and then working to counteract them, you can immediately improve your level of communication. Here's how it works.

Filters are one of the leading causes of miscommunication in relationships. The good news is that by understanding your filters, and then working to counteract them, you can immediately improve your level of communication.

FIVE KEY FILTERS

We all have many kinds of filters packed into our heads. These affect what we hear, what we say, and how we interpret things. They are based on how we are feeling at the moment: what we think, what we have experienced in our life, our family and cultural background, and all of the other elements that influence our thinking. Here we'll look at five of the most powerful filters affecting clear communication:

1. Distractions
2. Emotional states
3. Beliefs and expectations
4. Differences in cultural style
5. Self-protection

Distractions

When you say something to your partner, do you have their attention, or don't you? Both external and internal factors in your environment can affect your ability to pay attention. External factors are such things as noisy kids, a hearing problem, cell phone notifications, or background noise at a party. Internal factors include feeling tired, thinking about something else (like work), or planning what you still have to do this evening.

There are a couple of reasons why we believe that this type of filter is more of a problem than ever before. First, people seem to be busier and busier, working more hours and having less, or taking less, time for leisure. Statistics consistently back this up. In a 2019 *Harvard Business Review* article titled "Beware a Culture of Busyness," the author noted that "an analysis of Gallup data by Harvard Business School's Ashley Whillans found that the percentage of employed Americans reporting that they 'never had enough time' rose from 70% in 2011 to 80% in 2018." A quick survey of friends and family likely reveals the problem has gotten even worse since.

Whether all of this busyness is being driven by people's desire for more stuff, a need to work more just to get by, a culture where activity is equated with achievement, or the increasingly blurry lines between work and home, the sheer number of hours many of us devote to our jobs has seemingly never been greater. That said, our busyness isn't all work-related. Since the new millennium, technology has intruded into nearly every aspect of our lives, with serious repercussions when it comes to focus. E-mail, texting, social media, streaming services, video games, and the like can be helpful or fun, but they also prime people to compulsively monitor their devices. Social media and online streaming services have been expertly engineered to make us crave a new hit of engagement or news update.

No matter the motive or platform, our constant flitting back and forth between this and that makes it very hard to pay attention to things that really matter. The culture we swim in induces a kind of mass attention deficit disorder. (For example, while you've been reading this chapter, have you paused to check your email, respond to a text, or check social media? Bet so.)

All of this results in filters on our attention and our ability to communicate well with those we love the most. We need to make the time for connecting, and when communicating, we need to make sure we can give each other our full attention. Set aside time to turn off the world, slow down, and talk about whatever without distraction. If you have something important to raise, make sure you check first that it's a good time for your partner to talk. So go ahead and ask just that: "Is this a good time to talk?"

Emotional States

Moods are powerful filters. For example, a number of studies demonstrate that we tend to give people more benefit of the doubt when we're in a good mood and less when we're in a bad mood. If you are in a bad mood, you are more likely to perceive whatever your partner says or does more negatively, no matter how thoughtful they are trying to be.

Have you noticed that sometimes, when your partner is in a bad mood, you get jumped on no matter how nicely you say something? (We know that you never do this, so we won't ask if you ever notice how your moods affect your mate.)

The best defense against allowing a filter to damage your relationship is to acknowledge it when you're aware that it's present.

> *The best defense against allowing a filter to damage your*
> *relationship is to acknowledge it when you are aware that*
> *it's present.*

Here's an example of what this looks like. Marta just got home after a stressful day at work. It's dinnertime, and she's in the kitchen cooking pasta. Ricardo just got home, too. He's sitting in his favorite chair reading the mail.

RICARDO: This bill for the phone company got missed again. We better get this paid.

MARTA: *(snapping with anger)* I'm not the one who forgot it. I'm a little busy right now if you can't see. Why don't you do something helpful?

RICARDO: I'm sorry. I should have seen you were busy. Rough day?

MARTA: Yes. Very. I don't mean to snap at you, but I've had it up to here. If I'm touchy, it's not really because of anything you've done.

RICARDO: Maybe we can talk about it after dinner.

MARTA: Thanks.

Without using the word *filter*, Ricardo and Marta acknowledged one was there. Marta had a bad day and was on edge. They could have let this conversation escalate into an argument, but Ricardo had the good sense to see that he had raised an important issue at the wrong time. He decided not to get defensive, instead choosing to become gentle with Marta in her frustration. Marta responded by telling Ricardo, in essence, that she had a filter deployed—her bad mood. Knowing this helped him react less defensively to her sharp tone. When both partners take responsibility for noticing a filter, and then gently acknowledge it, escalation may well be diverted.

Many kinds of emotional filters can exist in any one person. If you are angry, worried, sad, or upset about anything, it can color your interpretation of what your partner says as well as your response. Ricardo's response was helpful because it opened the door for Marta to clarify her emotional filter and allowed them to de-escalate and be clear with one another.

Beliefs and Expectations

How you think and what you expect in your relationship can create many different types of filters. We have a whole chapter on handling expectations (Chapter Thirteen), but here we want to focus on how powerfully expectations and beliefs can affect how we see others.

Studies in the fields of psychology, medicine, and law consistently demonstrate that people tend to see what they expect to see in others and in certain situations. No one's immune to this tendency, including you. It takes some humility to accept that you don't always get it right in how you size up others or their motivations.

Our expectations not only affect what we perceive but also can influence the actual behavior of those around us. For example, if you believe that someone is an extrovert, they are more likely to sound like an extrovert when talking with you, even if they are usually introverted. We "pull" behavior from others consistent with what we expect. In part, this is why so many old habits and communication patterns come back with full force during the holidays, when you are around the family you grew up with (especially if you do not regularly see them). Everyone's got their expectation filters working, and everyone is reacting to the mix.

Here's an example of how this filter can present itself in conversation between a couple. Heather and Selena had some free time and wanted to do something fun. But, like so many times before, they couldn't decide what to do. What should have been a straightforward conversation about their desires turned into yet another dance of assumptions that left them both feeling emotionally disconnected and frustrated. Note how each partner acts as if they can read the other person's mind:

HEATHER: (*really wanting to go bowling, but thinking that Selena is not interested in going out and doing anything fun together*) We have some free time tonight. I wonder if we should try to do something.

SELENA: (*thinking that she would like to get out but hearing the tentativeness in Heather's voice and thinking she really doesn't want to go out*) Oh, I don't know. What do you think?

HEATHER: Well, we could go bowling, but it could be league night, and we might not get in anyway. Maybe we should just stay in and watch a movie.

SELENA: (*thinking "Aha, that's what she really wants to do."*) That sounds good to me. Why don't we make some popcorn and watch Netflix?

HEATHER: (*She's disappointed, thinking "I knew it. She really doesn't want to make the effort to get out and do something fun."*) Yeah, OK.

In this conversation there was no escalation, invalidation, or withdrawal. Nevertheless, the couple did not communicate well due to the filters involved. Heather's (unverified) belief that Selena doesn't like to go out colored the entire conversation so much that the way she asked Selena to go out led Selena to think Heather actually wanted to stay in.

Differences in Cultural Style

Everyone has a different style of communicating, but each can lead to filtering. Perhaps you are much more expressive and your partner is more reserved. Maybe one of you talks very fast, the other more slowly.

Styles are determined by many influences, including culture, ethnicity, and type of upbringing—even what region of the country you grew up in. For instance, coauthor Howard grew up around New York City and coauthor Scott grew up in Ohio. When they first started working together, it would stress Scott out to go into a

New York electronics store with Howard (They both like and still like gadgets). Seeing something one them liked, Howard would ask what the best price was. "Gee, the price is right there on a sticker," thought Scott. "What are you doing?" Each was accustomed to a whole different way of living.

Sometimes such style differences are rooted in family backgrounds and can become powerful filters that distort communication. Karla and Tim came from very different families and cultures. Tim's family has roots in Italy and has always been very expressive, whereas in Karla's family, whose roots are in Japan, even a slightly raised voice could mean someone is angry.

The result was that in many conversations, Karla would overestimate the intensity of Tim's feelings, and Tim would underestimate the depth of Karla's feelings. Take this exchange, for example:

TIM: What did it cost to get the muffler fixed?

KARLA: Four hundred and twenty-eight bucks.

TIM: *(intense, getting red quickly)* What?! That's insane. There's no way it costs that much!

KARLA: *(lashing out)* Stop yelling at me! I've told you over and over that I can't listen to you when you're yelling!

TIM: I'm not yelling at you. I just can't believe it's that expensive.

KARLA: Why can't we talk calmly like other people?

TIM: Lets pause for a moment, I'm not upset at you. I'm upset at the car shop. And you know I can get pretty excited. I'm not trying to say you did anything wrong.

KARLA: *(calming down)* Well, it feels that way sometimes.

TIM: Well, I'm not upset at you. I'm sorry I reacted so strongly. Let me give that place a call. Where's the number?

You can see that they did a great job of de-escalating the situation. One partner figured out that there was a filter distorting the intended message and took corrective action. Couples from different backgrounds often face more challenges, but it's not these differences that matter most—it's how the differences are handled. Talking about these differences without fighting is key. We touch on aspects of cultural differences again in Chapter Thirteen on expectations and Chapter Fourteen on beliefs, values, and life experiences.

Self-Protection

Fear is the big enemy of secure and warm attachment, so it's no surprise that people will go to great lengths to avoid rejection, whether real or perceived. Accordingly, we know a filter is operating when our fear of rejection stops us from saying what we truly want or feel. Even a question as simple as "Wouldn't you like to go see that new movie with me?" can reflect a fear of rejection. Instead of expressing our desire directly ("I'd like to see that new movie; want to go?"), we often hide it because directly speaking of it reveals more of who we are, and that increases the risk of rejection. This may not matter a lot when it comes to movies, but when it comes to feelings, desires, and expectations in marriage, a lot of misunderstanding can result.

Think of this filter as causing you not to know each other as well as you otherwise might. As we discuss in more detail in Chapter Five, when this filter is operating, you may not say what you really feel or need in your relationship for fear of a negative reaction that leads to being hurt. The more self-confidence and self-esteem you feel, and the more secure each of you feels in your relationship, the safer you will feel to clearly and respectfully talk about what you want and need in your relationship. This is yet another reason why making it safe to connect is one of the three essential keys to a strong relationship. If you don't feel secure, you won't be able to communicate honestly, much less bond on an intimate level.

MEMORY MATCHING

Some of the biggest arguments partners have are about what was actually said or done in the past. How often have you wished that you had an audio recording of a previous conversation? This happens to all of us. These differences in memory occur so often because of the variety of filters that operate in all relationships. Any of the filters we've discussed can lead to differences—and arguments—about what was actually said or done in the past.

One great nonmarital example happened when a NY Mets player was quoted in the papers saying something negative about a teammate, who understandably got upset and confronted his teammate, who denied saying the comment. A video recording of the interview confirmed the quote and the first player said, "But that's not what I meant." Having a recording is not nearly as useful as you think (but it could be fun for others to watch).

Read again the conversation between Nate and Crystal in this chapter. Notice that they ended up arguing about what was actually said at the start of the conversation. He truly thought he asked her out to dinner, but because what he said was vague ("What should we do for dinner tonight?"), it provided an opening for her filters to activate their powers of distortion. She truly thinks he told her to get dinner on the table, but it's not what he meant.

We recommend two things to save your relationship from such fruitless arguments about the past. First, don't assume your memory is perfect. Have the humility to accept that it isn't. There are countless studies in the field of psychology that show how fragile human memory is and how susceptible it is to distortion by motivation and beliefs. Your memory is simply not as accurate as you tend to think it is. Confident and correct are different things. Accept that both of you have filters and that there is plenty of room for you to say or hear things differently than what was intended. That's one important way to do your part.

Second, when you disagree, don't persist in arguing about what was actually said in the past, even if it was only five minutes ago. You will get nowhere. Most of the time you are arguing about a small upsetting event, not the real issue between the two of you (we have much more to say about events and issues in Chapter Seven).

Shift to talking about what you each think and feel about the issue, now, in the *present*. Though it's hard to do, the most effective path out of arguments about memory is to say something like this: "I'm not sure what I said exactly, but I want to tell you what I meant to say, OK?" Listen carefully and nondefensively when your partner clarifies something in this way. Something very artful is happening, and you don't want to miss it.

The two most essential things to remember about filters are that (1) everyone has them and (2) they are not intrinsically good or bad. The goal is to recognize your filters before they can do any damage. When you acknowledge and deal with them, you can see your partner in a much clearer light, opening up pathways to intimacy-enhancing communication.

Talking Points

1. We all have filters, and they are constantly affecting what we say and hear.

2. The most common filters are distractions, emotional states, beliefs and expectations, differences in cultural style, and self-protection.

3. Recognizing and acknowledging your filters will go a long way toward improving your communication and your relationship.

Suggested Activities

Of all the filters discussed, the two that will benefit from the most self-reflection and possible changes in what you do are distraction and cultural style.

Distraction

In this era, a lot of our attention is captured by social media, the internet, video streaming, and all the other ways we are glued to our devices for hours each day. We are distracted from giving our attention to what really matters. All of these things can distract or add to opportunities for miscommunication. On our death beds no one will be saying, "I wish I spent more time on . . ." (fill in the blank for what you love to watch). Most people say they wish they had spent more time with family, partners, and friends. So, check you phone use once in a while, and for one week, try to note how you are using your time. Ask yourself if you are focusing on what's most important to you.

Cultural Style

Filters are often affected by your own background, including how you were raised; your ethnic, racial, and cultural background; your family growing up, your community; and so forth. These factors can influence how you interpret what others are communicating. Take some time to think about how all these factors affect how you communicate with others, especially your partner. And give some thought about what you can do to bridge any divides you see where you each may have filters in how you communicate with the other—and how you can do your part to keep the lines of communication open and clear.

5

What's Love Got to Do with It?

A lot, as it turns out.

Couples enter our office for many different reasons, but one of the most common complaints we hear is that the love a couple once felt is waning for one or both partners. The classic line from too many Hollywood relationship dramas, "I love you, but I'm not *in love* with you anymore" seems to capture how they say they feel.

When we dig a little below the surface, however, things aren't always what they seem. What they call *love* is often what we'd more accurately describe as passion. The excitement and erotic attraction partners once experienced and relied on—possibly too much—no longer registers as strongly as it once did, or even at all, and it scares people into thinking that their relationship might be doomed. Each partner will usually insist that friendship and commitment is still there. But that loving feeling is, well, gone.

This experience is completely normal for most couples who have been together for some time, arguably even expected. Rare is the couple whose fires of passion burn just as fiercely as when they first started dating or got married. Raising kids and climbing the ladder at work has a way of dousing the flames.

Passion feels wonderful, indeed, but it doesn't last forever in the form it originally took. It waxes and wanes over time, depending on each partner's personality, expectations, and life experiences. That's not to say that you can't recapture it in some way when the feelings aren't as intense as they once were. But in our view, something as fickle as passion should not be the basis of a healthy long-term partnership.

Don't get us wrong: passion is exciting and important. Without a doubt, it can bring couples together physically and emotionally. But even when it wanes, the couple's underlying love and attraction can still be nurtured so that the romance doesn't disappear. As we'll see, love travels through many phases and iterations in all long-term relationships; in fact, its ability to transform itself in so many ways is one of its most wonderful qualities. Because successful relationships rely on this miraculous, mercurial thing called *love*, let's try to understand what it looks like, and thrives on, in everyday life.

LOVE IN THE REAL WORLD

Love can take several different forms. It's an emotion, a drive, a state of mind, and a spiritual connection. Love is an ineffable "felt sense" that registers somewhere in our mind-body and hatches when triggered by the right person. It can even create changes in our neural chemistry; fMRIs have shown that it can resemble the high people get from cocaine. (Talk about high-potency stuff!) When someone invokes the word *love*, they could be thinking about infatuation, romantic attachment, commitment, passion, or affection. The love someone has for their child, for instance, is obviously different than the love two teenagers who just met have for each other. It's complicated. For purposes of this chapter, we are concerned with the feeling of romantic love.

Love is an ineffable "felt sense" that registers somewhere in our mind-body and hatches when triggered by the right person.

We know that the passionate, euphoric feeling, when our experiences of pleasure are heightened in the presence of our beloved and even linger in their absence, cannot be sustained indefinitely. The "love cocktail" of dopamine, oxytocin, serotonin, and various endorphins that flood our brain when we fall in love literally gets reabsorbed over time with increasing familiarity.

This means that to keep the good vibes going, we need to cultivate deep, long-lasting connections in a different way—one that isn't dependent on that fragile, druggy state that is often the strongest at the beginning of a relationship, when passion (and lust) are running high. One that's based on more mature and durable qualities like attachment, trust, safety, intimacy, fidelity, respect, kindness, healthy sacrifice, and compassion.

Love doesn't always feel sublime, but that doesn't mean we don't still love. Sometimes it feels comfortable, sometimes fraternal, sometimes treacherous, sometimes challenging. Sometimes it goes dormant or can even feel painful. But nothing in life feels more desirable and life affirming than loving another and feeling their love in return. Love gives our lives meaning. In the end, when people look back on their life, it's love that matters most.

We're not just saying this, either. The research unequivocally agrees. It turns out that people who are in loving relationships actually are healthier and live longer than those who are alone. To offer just one of many examples, consider the Harvard Study of Adult Development, one of the longest and most highly regarded studies on American aging, which followed a cohort of 268 Harvard graduates and their descendants for some *eighty* years. "When we gathered together everything we knew about [study subjects] at age 50, it wasn't their middle-age cholesterol levels that predicted how they were going to grow old," explained the study's current director, Dr. Robert Waldinger, during a 2016 TED Talk on the study's findings. "It was how satisfied they were in their relationships. The people who were the most satisfied in their relationships at age 50 were the healthiest at age 80."

Love cannot be designed, only hatched. But when that happens, something near-miraculous occurs. The love of another can give you the strength to survive whatever challenges you face over the course of your life. Love is the energy that motivates us to do the hard work of keeping our relationships healthy. It's what enables us to make sacrifices without resentment and to grow beyond our own personal needs. Over the years we've come to believe that there may not be a science to *falling* in love, but there is a science to *staying* in love. We may not be able to prescribe with whom or how you should fall in love (and why would we want to?). But when people use the tools in this book, they really work to sustain a lifetime of love.

Love is the energy that motivates us to do the hard work of keeping our relationships healthy.

LOVE STYLES

You may have noticed that things you do for your partner out of love sometimes backfire. This can be distressing, even if it's completely normal. People have different ideas about how to express their love, and the unfortunate result can be that their bids of affection don't land on their partner the way they intend. What's worse, these expressions of love are often experienced as the opposite!

Consider the woman who loved buying her partner gifts to show how much she cares, while her partner thought she was just trying to buy her love or prime her for sex. Or the wife who frequently expressed her worry and concern to show her husband how much she cared, while the husband felt burdened by her constant anxiety. How tragic! What's clear is that people show their love in many different ways, depending on what feels good to them. They assume the same holds true for their partner. Not necessarily!

There are many ways of expressing love, and each may hold a different meaning for someone. Some of us respond to words of love and appreciation, others, to physical touch. Some people like the feeling of just being alone together without talking, and some appreciate sharing activities. Some people feel loved when their partner takes a task off their plate or helps with chores. We know of cultures that teach strict interpersonal boundaries as a show of love and respect, and others where crossing boundaries demonstrates involvement, interest, and love. This list of possibilities—and opportunities for misunderstanding—can seem endless.

The Five Love Languages

Gary Chapman's influential book, *The Five Love Languages*, provides useful guidance on safely navigating varied expressions of love. Chapman suggests that there are five ways romantic partners commonly express and receive love. Although all of these languages should be part of every relationship, a person often emphasizes one primary language over the others. Problems can arise in relationships when partners speak different languages, because they're not interpreting the love being offered in the way it's intended. Here are the five love languages Chapman emphasizes:

- Words of affirmation (expressing affection through words of appreciation and compliments)
- Acts of service (things you do for your partner)
- Gifts (buying and giving presents)
- Quality time (giving your partner your undivided attention)
- Physical touch (showing physical affection)

How do you express your love? How about your partner?

Truth is, there are many ways to demonstrate love and support, not just one way that says it all. Often people focus on what's missing as the primary love style they desire most, when in fact if the other expressions of love were missing, they would see how important they each truly are. All of these ways of demonstrating love are wonderful and shouldn't be minimized, even if they don't exactly hit the nail on the head.

In Chapter Ten, you may be surprised to notice that these various caring expressions are not just ways of demonstrating your love but also ways of showing your support—showing that you are there for your partner, that you are thinking of them and listening to what they need and what feels good to them. Nothing feels more nurturing than feeling that your partner is taking you in, learning what your needs are, and offering that to you in the ways that matter most.

KEEPING ROMANCE ALIVE

The beautiful thing about long-term relationships is that for most people, it's the only relationship where romance, passion, and intimacy can be shared. You choose the person with whom you exclusively promise to express these feelings. This is why it's so important to not let your romantic feelings fade by ignoring or injuring your relationship. Romance can soften a rough day, drawing you closer together and fueling the love between you. It's so important to nurture these feelings on a daily basis, even when "that lovin' feeling" seems like it's faded.

In our experience, it's easier to access than you may have been led to think. One of the most harmful misconceptions about romance is that it can only arise spontaneously and in the heat of the moment. This simply isn't true. Even if a person isn't feeling amorous at a particular moment but knows deep down that they love their partner, with a little effort they can open themselves to expressing their love more freely.

It's completely possible to act romantically even if the underlying feeling isn't present at the moment. Loving words and behaviors can stimulate (pun intended!) your partner and you to re-create those romantic feelings, even when the initial motivation comes from a conscious decision rather than a spontaneous urge, because when you act in loving ways, the feeling often follows naturally. What's more, the positive response you get from your partner can make you both feel closer and like you want to keep the good times rolling.

After a day of chasing your kids around, grinding away at work, and completing the never-ending tasks necessary to keep your household running, romance can be one of the last things on your mind. It's all too easy for couples to slide into a relationship where you feel more like roommates, not romantic partners. We get it. Be that as it may, you still have a choice to *slide* into romantic doldrums or *decide* to keep the romance alive with sensitive gestures that make your partner feel loved.

You have a choice to slide into romantic doldrums or decide to keep the romance alive with sensitive gestures that make your partner feel loved.

The Three Components of Love

According to Robert Sternberg, love has three main components: intimacy, passion, and commitment. When received in various combinations, people experience different forms of love. For example, passion without intimacy or commitment is what he calls "infatuation," whereas people feel "romantic love" when there is passion and intimacy but no commitment. Intimacy with neither passion nor commitment is what he calls "friendship," and "fatuous love" (as in love at first sight) involves passion and commitment, but no intimacy. Most people are seeking what he calls "consummate love," the complete and deeply satisfying kind of love one experiences when all three components are present.

The longer you postpone acting in romantic ways, the harder it is to overcome the invisible emotional barriers that seem to get in the way. So why not dive in and give it a try?

COMMIT TO COMMIT

Here's a fascinating statistic: love-based marriages are less stable than arranged marriages, which have lower overall rates of divorce.

What does this tell us? For one, marriages by choice are presumably easier to leave by choice. As a result, they are more precarious. Partners can't rely only on that euphoric, often-fleeting state of being "in love" to sustain themselves over the long term. The expectation that feeling in love will last for a lifetime, or that love will conquer all, turns out to be a belief that's hard to maintain. (You'll learn more about expectations and the challenges they can create in Chapter Thirteen.)

If love is expected to conquer all, and if love comes solely at the whim of Cupid's arrow, then falling out of love seems likely to happen unless there is something else we can count on. That something is commitment. We may not have as much control as we'd like over who we fall in love with, but we do have control over keeping a loving relationship healthy and strong.

As you'll see in Chapter Sixteen, commitment is perhaps the most precious thing you can give each other—an unequivocal sign of love. It's the epitome of deciding, not sliding. Even better, it creates a virtuous and self-sustaining cycle: in committing to the long term, you give each other the space to stumble and repair, and ultimately deepen your love, time after time. In turn, this love will deepen your commitment.

We can't help but love how it all works.

TO LOVE MEANS TO LISTEN

We can't overstate how important it is to be able to convey your love in ways that are appreciated by your partner. To do this, though, you have to know them intimately. How do they express and receive love? What are their vulnerabilities, what makes them feel secure or insecure, what do they need and long for, what makes them tick, what makes them withdraw, what makes them feel safe, what intimidates them? If you want a love that can weather the inevitable ups and downs you and your partner will face, you need to be receptive to what they say and do so that you can support them in the ways that matter most to them. (The same goes for them!) To do this well you have to listen with your eyes, your ears, and most of all, with your heart.

In the words of the great Buddhist monk Thich Nhat Hanh, "to love means to listen." One of the most profound ways to demonstrate your deep and abiding love for your partner is to dedicate yourself to knowing them inside and out. Everyone wants to be seen and understood for who they truly are—not for who you want them to be. This is how you build trust and intimacy.

This capacity to truly *listen*—to perceive and experience another human being wholly—comes exclusively through the act of loving. It reflects a selfless desire to take in and understand the essence of another person in the fullness of their being. It invites you to learn who your partner truly is, without ego or filters that can distort what you see. This is the gift of connection that love bestows.

This kind of intimate knowing is what allows for mistakes and vulnerabilities to be shared, for differences of opinion to be safely expressed, and for compromise, forgiveness, and interpersonal growth to occur. It is what makes people feel close to each other and express intimacy in every way, emotionally and physically alike. And, importantly, it is what will enable you to know how to avoid saying things you know will upset your partner so that productive conversations can occur. By "listening" with all of your senses, you can understand the best way to engage in safe sharing. Feeling heard and understood can heal old wounds, resolve conflicts, and pave the way for productive problem solving.

This is the kind of listening we want you to cultivate when we describe the Speaker Listener Technique in Chapter Six.

Talking Points

1. Love is felt when it strikes; it is not something we can design or control. What you can control is what you do to keep your love alive.

2. Love is not a singular concept; there are many stages, dimensions, and expressions of love.

3. Like plants that grow with regular sun and water, love and romance must be nurtured in order to thrive.

4. Love fuels a partner's desire to work at their relationship; at the same time, working on the relationship fuels their love.

5. Love thrives in conditions of safety, trust, respect, and compassion, under the umbrella of commitment.

Suggested Activities

1. How do you know you love your partner? Where in your mind and body do you feel it?

2. Can you trust that knowledge even when times are tough?

3. How do you take responsibility for nurturing the love you have for your partner?

4. Do you ever doubt your love? What can you do to reignite it? What are some discrete things you can do to nurture and protect the love you want to feel?

5. Love grows into different forms after the initial infatuation subsides. How would you describe the love you feel right now? In what direction would you like it to grow?

6. Does your love style mesh or clash with your partner's? If your styles conflict, how can you better accommodate each other's needs?

7. Pay more attention to the love you express than the love you receive. Be the lover you want to be rather than waiting for your partner to inspire it.

8. How often do you tell each other you love them? What would happen if you told each other every day?

6

Talking Without Fighting
The Speaker Listener Technique

Communication is the lifeblood of a good relationship. It keeps good connections flowing and helps couples safely overcome the disagreements they experience day-to-day. In fact, in our years of conducting workshops, we've consistently found that strategies for communicating well are the single most valuable tool participants take away.

That said, understanding how important communication is and being able to do it well are very different things. Every couple we've talked to agrees that good communication is a very important goal for their relationship, yet most couples have never learned how to communicate well when it counts most.

That's where we can help.

STRUCTURE CAN BRING EMOTIONAL SAFETY

For your relationship to grow and enable you to talk as friends, reveal your inner feelings, and handle unavoidable conflicts, you need to work together as a team. This means *deciding* to keep damaging patterns—escalation, invalidation, avoidance and withdrawal, and negative interpretations—from surfacing (or, when they do occur, quickly defusing them).

83

One way to do this is to use agreed-on strategies and techniques to help you work through important conversations in a way that's productive and safe. We call this adding structure to your interaction. Structure can bring some degree of predictability and order to potentially chaotic and emotional topics. As such, it's one of the best tools for regulating the inevitable negative emotions we all experience in marriage, for talking without fighting about important issues and for feeling safe to express emotions about sensitive topics.

There are many places where you already take the principle of structured communication for granted. For example, in almost every sport there are rules that define what's OK and what's not OK, what's in bounds and out, and when the action starts and when it should stop. Without the structure that the rules provide, all you would have is chaos. In a similar vein, our approach enables you and your partner to use agreed-on rules to level the playing field. Both of you can listen, and both can be heard.

With adequate structure, you can manage conflict and talk about sensitive issues while reducing your chances of damaging your relationship. When less is at stake, or when emotions are running low, you don't need much structure. But at other times, a bit of structure can help you proceed through treacherous waters without damaging your relationship, and maybe even bring you closer.

With adequate structure, you can manage conflict and talk about sensitive issues while reducing your chances of damaging your relationship.

Enter the Speaker Listener Technique.

THE SPEAKER LISTENER TECHNIQUE

The Speaker Listener Technique offers couples an alternative way to communicate when issues are hot or sensitive, or likely to get that way. Any conversation in which you want to enhance clarity and safety can benefit from this technique.

The main reason the Speaker Listener Technique is so popular is because it's so simple and effective. When using this tool to talk about difficult issues there are two overarching rules. First, separate out discussing an issue from solving the issue. In other words, ban problem-solving and just focus on understanding your partner's perspective. That does not mean agreeing or disagreeing with each other but hearing each other out. Second, show your partner that you are listening—that you are focusing on what they are saying. When listened to in this way, many people feel that they are being "seen" by their partner.

Many couples we work with have reported using this skill to talk though difficult issues, years after taking our programs, when their natural way of dealing with issues is not working. They report engaging the technique when needed. This is why we ask you to give it a thorough tryout in your own relationship so it might become a tool in your back pocket, so to speak, to engage when your natural way of talking about issues is not working. It's not for use all the time, but for when you need it or it can help. Most couples can decide whether to go out for Thai food without this technique, but fewer can handle emotionally sensitive issues about money, sex, or in-laws, for example, without the safety net that such a technique can provide.

If you decide it's not for you, so be it. If you have another (productive!) way of talking when in conflict or when it's hard to be vulnerable, that's great. If you do not, though, here you go.

THE SPEAKER LISTENER TECHNIQUE

Rules for Both of You

1. *The Speaker has the Floor.* Use a physical object to designate whose time it is to talk. We're pretty concrete; we have actually given couples pieces of linoleum, so when someone says

they have the "Floor," they really mean it! You can use anything, though: the TV remote, a pen, a book, whatever. The point is that you have to use some specific object, because if you do not have the Floor, you are the Listener. As Speaker and Listener, you follow the rules for each role.

2. *Share the Floor.* You share the Floor over the course of a conversation. The Speaker is the first one to hold the Floor. After the Speaker talks, you switch roles and continue, with the Floor changing hands regularly.

3. *No problem-solving.* When using this technique, you are going to focus on having good discussions, not on trying to come to solutions. When you focus on solving a problem, you are much less likely to *really* hear what each other thinks about that problem.

Rules for the Speaker

1. *Speak for yourself. Don't mind read.* Talk about *your* thoughts, feelings, and concerns, not your perceptions of the Listener's point of view or motives. Try to use "I statements" and talk about your own point of view and feelings. "I was upset when you forgot our date" is an "I statement"; "I think you don't care about me" is not.

2. *Don't go on and on.* To help the Listener listen actively, it's important that you keep what you say to manageable chunks. You will have plenty of opportunity to say all you need to say.

3. *Stop and let the Listener paraphrase.* After saying a bit, stop and allow the Listener to paraphrase what you just said. If the paraphrase was not quite accurate, you should politely and gently restate what you meant to say in a way that helps your partner understand. This is not a test! You want to be sure your partner understands you as well as they can.

Rules for the Listener

1. *Paraphrase what you hear.* Part of your role is to paraphrase what the Speaker is saying. Briefly repeat back what you heard the Speaker say, using your own words, to make sure

you understand what was said. When you take the time to do this, you show your partner that you are listening. If you truly don't understand some phrase or example, you may ask the Speaker to clarify, but limit yourself to just asking for explanations.

2. *Don't rebut. Focus on the Speaker's message.* While in the Listener role, you may not offer your opinion or thoughts. This is the hardest part of being a good Listener. If you are upset by what your partner says, you need to edit out any response you may want to make and *pay attention* to what your partner is saying. Wait until you get the Floor to make your response. You will have your chance, and when you do, you'll want your partner to extend the same courtesy to you. When you are the Listener, your job is to speak only in the service of understanding your partner. Any words or gestures to show your opinion are not allowed, including making faces!

When using the technique, the Floor is serving a crucial role. The Floor indicates whose message is in play. Although the Listener will also speak even when the Speaker has the Floor, they are speaking only in service of listening by paraphrasing. When the Floor switches, the conversation shifts from being tuned to the one partner's station to being tuned to the other's station.

Before showing you how this technique works in a conversation, we want to give you some ideas about what good paraphrases can sound like. Suppose your spouse says to you, "I had a really tough day. My boss really got mad at me for telling a client I thought we could give them a better deal. Ugh!" Any of the following might be an excellent paraphrase:

"Sounds like you had a really tough day. That stinks."

"So, your boss criticized how you handled a client."

"Bad day, huh? I'm so sorry to hear that."

Any one of these responses shows that you have listened and reveals what you have understood. A good paraphrase can be short or long, detailed or general. At times, if you are uncertain of how to get a paraphrase started, it can help to begin with "What I hear you saying is . . ." Then you fill in what you just heard your partner say. Another way to begin a paraphrase is with the words "Sounds like you think [feel, want] . . ."

When using the Speaker Listener Technique, the Speaker is always the one who determines if the Listener's paraphrase was on target. Only the Speaker knows what the intended message is. If the paraphrase is not quite on target, it is very important that the Speaker gently clarify or restate the point and not respond angrily or critically. Remember that you and your partner may be dealing with filters that make it difficult to paraphrase accurately.

If the Speaker wants to ask a question, the most structured way to handle it is to ask the question and then pass the Floor to the Listener. The Listener should paraphrase the question to make sure they heard it clearly, and then answer the question. We recommend you practice Speaker questions this way, at least at the start. After you get comfortable with the flow of the technique, you can decide later how to customize it for the two of you.

When you are the Listener, be sincere in your effort to show you are listening carefully and respectfully. That means waiting your turn and not making faces or looking angry. Even when you disagree with a point your partner is making, your goal is to show respect for their perspective. The goal here is not to agree or disagree with what your partner is saying but to understand and let your partner know you are listening. This is one of the most important points we will make in this book. *Paraphrasing is not agreeing. It is simply listening well.*

Paraphrasing is not agreeing. It is simply listening well.

To go even further, try to put yourself in your partner's shoes and see things the way they do. This is pretty hard to do, especially if emotions are running hot and there's a strong disagreement between you both. Although none of us can make ourselves truly feel what another is feeling, we can try a bit harder at crucial moments to imagine what our partner is thinking and feeling, and why.

THE ART OF LISTENING

Genuine listening involves active participation and receptiveness. It requires you to give your partner the space and freedom to share their feelings, without interrupting, advising, judging, self-referencing, or redirecting. It involves making eye contact and giving your partner your full, undivided attention, setting your phone down, and temporarily putting your own needs aside. It also means adopting a stance of sincere curiosity, and maybe asking follow-up questions that suggest you'd like to learn more (as long as these questions don't come with an underlying agenda).

This is why paraphrasing is so crucial to the Speaker Listener Technique. Putting what you heard into your own words shows your commitment to communicating respectfully. It also enables your partner to know if you did or did not quite understand what they meant to say so that they can further clarify their meaning. Versions of this type of communication are used in many fields where it is crucial for the listener to have understood what the speaker intended. Airplane pilots and air traffic controllers do it (such as confirming the elevation they are changing to), people taking your order at restaurants do it (so, let me read that back to you, you want . . .), and so on. Simple forms of active listening like this are used everywhere, and for good reason. It helps ensure that the message sent is the message received.

When you genuinely listen to your partner in this way, anger, tension, and fear melt away, and it becomes safe for them to share their true feelings. They can then relax their guard and freely admit their needs, fears, and vulnerabilities. This is how intimacy grows.

Remember, *to love means to listen*. Try it and see for yourself!

USING THE SPEAKER LISTENER TECHNIQUE

Here's an example of how this technique can transform a conversation that's going nowhere into a real opportunity for communication. Peter and Tessa are in their mid-forties, with four kids ages two to ten. For years they have had a problem dealing with issues. Peter consistently avoids discussing problems, and if cornered by Tessa, he withdraws by pulling into himself.

Despite this, they know they need to communicate more clearly and safely on tough topics. So they recently agreed to try the Speaker Listener Technique, with the hope that its more structured way of interacting can help them. They have been practicing it during low-stakes conversations so they'll be prepared when a more emotionally challenging exchange comes up.

A good opportunity soon presents itself while they are discussing their son Jeremy's preschool enrollment, a loaded topic at the moment. When Tessa brings up the issue, they initially find themselves defaulting into an-all-too predictable pursuit-withdrawal cycle. But they eventually hit pause, remembering to try out the Speaker Listener Technique. Let's see what happens.

TESSA: I'm really getting tired of leaving Jeremy's preschool up in the air. We have to deal with this now.

PETER: (not looking up from the TV) Oh? I'm not up for this now.

TESSA: (walking over and standing in front of the TV) Peter, we can't just leave this decision hanging in the air. I'm getting really ticked off about you putting it off.

PETER: (recognizing that this would be a wise time to act constructively and not withdraw) Time Out. I can tell we need to talk, but I have been avoiding it because it seems like talking just leads to us fighting. I don't want that. Let's try that Speaker Listener Technique we've been practicing.

This is not a "normal" way to talk, yes, but it is a safe way to communicate on difficult issues. Each person will get to talk, each will be heard, and both will show their commitment to discussing the problems at hand. If you tend to withdraw, this technique can help you move constructively toward your partner when they are pursuing conversation. Why? Because the very act of engaging in this process will neutralize your partner's belief that you don't care about the relationship.

Let's return to the conversation. Keeping in mind the rules of engagement, Peter picks up the piece of carpet they use to indicate who has the Floor, and the conversation proceeds.

PETER (SPEAKER): I've also been pretty concerned about where we send Jeremy to preschool. I'm not even sure this is the year to do it.

TESSA (LISTENER): You've been concerned, too, and you're not completely sure he's ready.

PETER (SPEAKER): Yeah, that's it. He acts pretty young for his age, and I'm just not sure how he'd do, unless the situation was just right.

Note how Peter acknowledges that Tessa's summary is on the mark before moving on to another point.

TESSA (LISTENER): You're worried that he wouldn't hold his own with older-acting kids, right?

Tessa is not quite sure she has understood Peter's point, so she makes her paraphrase tentative.

PETER (SPEAKER): Well, partly that's it, but I'm also not sure if he's ready to be away from you that much. Honestly, part of what I think I'm reacting to is that this transition was very hard for me when I was a kid. I had a lot of trouble in elementary school because I was so young. Maybe I'm overreacting, but I still feel pretty anxious about it.

Note how Peter gently clarifies. He's moving forward in the conversation, rather than backward. In general, whenever the Listener says (or implies) that they need clarification, the Speaker should use their next statement to restate or expand on what they are trying to get across.

Tessa (Listener): So, you're feeling torn about him needing me a lot. But really more important, this brings up things you felt really vulnerable about as a kid, and that makes it that much harder.

Peter (Speaker): Yes. That's right. Here, you take the Floor. *(He hands Tessa the piece of carpet.)*

Tessa (Speaker): Well, I appreciate what you're saying. Actually, I hadn't realized your feelings were that deep about this. I was worried that you didn't care about it.

As the Speaker now, Tessa validates the comments Peter has made.

Peter (Listener): Sounds like you're glad to hear that I'm concerned, and you were afraid that my not wanting to deal with it meant I didn't care about you.

Tessa (Speaker): Yes. This really helps a lot to understand you. I agree that this is not an easy decision.

Peter (Listener): It's making you feel better that we are talking this through.

Tessa (Speaker): Big time. It also confirms something I'd thought anyway: that if we did put him in preschool this year, it would have to be just the right place. We'd both have to feel really good about it.

Peter (Listener): You're saying that it would have to be just the right preschool for it to be worth doing this year.

Tessa (Speaker): Exactly. I think it might be worth trying if we could find a great environment for him.

Tessa feels good that Peter is listening so attentively and lets him know it.

PETER (LISTENER): So you would try it if we found just the right setting.

TESSA (SPEAKER): I *might* try it; I'm not sure I'm ready to say I *would* try it.

PETER (LISTENER): You're not ready to say you would definitely want to do it, even with a perfect preschool.

TESSA (SPEAKER): Right. Here, you take the Floor again.

To their credit, their practice is really showing through. They are both doing an excellent job following the rules of the technique and showing concern and respect for each other's viewpoints. Couples can have discussions like this on difficult topics, even when they disagree. The keys are to make the discussion safe and to show respect for your partner's thoughts, feelings, and opinions. With practice, the process can become far more natural than it may seem to be at first.

Another reason this technique is so powerful is because of how quickly, and safely, it enables true feelings to surface. It's only because they are talking safely here that they get to two key pieces of information. One is that Peter is more deeply affected by this subject because of how it was handled when he was a child. The other is that Tessa was starting to make a negative interpretation about Peter's avoidance, thinking that maybe he just didn't care about her.

In summary, the Speaker Listener Technique can make a fraught discussion feel much safer, and in a way that makes each partner more willing to broach sensitive themes. We've seen this play out hundreds of times with couples. This does not always happen, of course, and there are other ways to increase intimacy and closeness in your relationship (and we'll get to almost all of them in later chapters). But it is one of the most powerful approaches we know of. It offers protection against the Communication Danger Signs by countering them. In this example, Tessa and Peter are able to come closer together on an emotional level while discussing an issue that could have all too easily driven them farther apart. Being able to feel comfortable and connected with your partner even when you're dealing with difficult issues is a huge achievement and a sign that your relationship is built to last.

> *Being able to feel comfortable and connected with your partner even when you're dealing with difficult issues is a huge achievement and a sign that your relationship is built to last.*

So the next time things get heated, why not follow Peter and Tessa's lead and give the technique a try?

FOR THE SKEPTIC AT HEART: COMMON QUESTIONS AND OBJECTIONS

- **"It's so artificial."** Probably the number one criticism we get about this technique is that it doesn't feel "natural," that it's not a normal way for people talk to one another. Very true. Note, however, the assumption embedded in this criticism: that how we naturally talk to one another is superior to ways we've learned to talk with one another. If you have children, you already know how often you show that you don't really believe that. There are many "natural" ways children communicate with others (hitting, scratching, biting, screaming, etc.), ways that you try to help them overcome by teaching them principles and rules for how to treat others.

  If you and your partner "naturally" engage in the negative behaviors we call Communication Danger Signs, we'd ask, what's so great about being natural? Maybe you should try being unnatural for a bit. It might feel a lot better.

- **"It goes so slowly when we talk like this."** Yes, it does. That's a big part of why it works. However, think about the staggering amount of time couples waste fighting about the same issues, over and over, without the partners really hearing one another. This technique may seem to be on the slow side, but it could lead to the fastest conversation you've ever had about a difficult topic in your relationship.

- **"We have trouble sharing the Floor."** So, one or both of you tend to hang onto the Floor once you have it? We have a simple suggestion to solve this: add a rule that you will switch roles after every three or four statements are paraphrased by the Listener. This ensures that each of you will know that your turn to talk is coming up soon.

Although it may be frustrating to have to pass the Floor when you are in the middle of building a point, rest assured, you will get the Floor back quite soon. Too often, people feel they have to get everything in before the door shuts, while their partner is finally listening. Don't try to get so much in that you make it unpleasant for your partner to keep the door open.

You can think about this as a trust issue: if you want your partner to listen to what *you* have to say, give them the courtesy of listening to what *they* have to say. If you listen respectfully to them, it's much more likely they will extend the same respect to you.

This is a simple point, although as we've said elsewhere, simple is not always easy. Share. Take turns. It's not magic; it's being polite. It's about honoring your partner.

- **"I really hate rules."** Many of you can relate to this one. Some people really dislike structure more than others. Some people feel truly confined when trying to follow these kinds of rules. We value that input. Remember, though, we do not recommend talking like this when you are just being together as friends and talking about things that aren't difficult. So most of your conversations shouldn't be bound by the constraints we suggest here.

The main point in this chapter is that every couple needs to have a productive way to talk through difficult topics. If you have another way, or develop another way, you'll do fine. But you need *something*.

- **"What if my partner isn't interested?"** Some of you will inevitably discover that your partner isn't as committed to working on these issues as you are. It's unfortunate, but not insurmountable. We feel strongly that any change in yourself (or your partner) will have a positive effect on your relationship. This means that any effort you make to bring safety and structure to your communication can still be helpful, and may even encourage your partner to become an equal participant as they comes to feel validated and accepted by you.

Our confidence in the usefulness of this technique for most (not all) couples is based on many years of research. Along the way we've had several crucial findings: (1) couples can learn how to do this, (2) couples who practice the technique for some period of time (see our recommendations about the need for practice) show improvements in their communication five years later, and (3) couples say this technique is the single most useful thing they have learned in our workshops.

Find out for yourselves what works for you. As we said before, the real key here is that the two of you need some way to talk safely about those subjects that are hard to talk about. The Speaker Listener Technique is one powerful, relatively simple way. There are others. You need only one. If you don't have one already, try ours.

Want to Hold Hands?

We sometimes recommend that couples hold hands, even when talking about problems, as a way of saying to each other, "We may disagree and we are struggling with this issue right now, but we are still a team and there for each other." It's very hard to be mad or mean when you are touching your partner lovingly. It may seem silly, but this works for some couples.

By holding hands as they talk and hugging afterward, couples nonverbally tell each other something very important: "We can disagree and argue, but we will not allow these tensions to crack the foundation of our relationship and threaten our long-term vision of our future together. We love each other and are there for each other no matter what!"

So, for some conversations, you may want to try holding hands while using the Speaker Listener Technique. If you are both open to it, give it a try.

A FINAL WORD ON THE IMPORTANCE OF PRACTICE

Practice is everything with the Speaker Listener Technique—and not just because it will help you get better at it. Often we find that couples who practice regularly incorporate the key aspects of the rules into their style of talking more generally, whether or not they are formally using the technique. We think this is because regular practice fosters a new communication mind-set, one that naturally steers clear of Communication Danger Signs. You are also practicing respect. There are two viewpoints in any important talk, and both need to be heard if an amicable resolution is going to be reached.

Among couples who are adept at this technique, there is a mutual understanding of when conversations are getting touchier, and they learn to shift into a modified version of the technique as needed. For example, they might not use a physical object for the Floor, but they begin a careful turn-taking process—again, because they've practiced. So even if you don't think you want to communicate this way very often, practicing these skills for some time can produce big benefits.

In sum, the Speaker Listener Technique is one of the most powerful tools we have found for two people to transform a conversation. Following some version of the structure can help any challenging or important conversation go better, with both partners feeling heard and both partners having an opportunity to express their own views. It is one of the great ways to make it safe to connect.

Talking Points

1. You can choose to use the Speaker Listener Technique to successfully work through any conflict or sensitive issue.

2. Talking safely about sensitive or deep issues promotes feelings of intimacy that come from knowing you can share who you are *and* be accepted by your partner.

3. Our research shows that couples can benefit greatly when they use a structured approach to handle conflict. Agreed-on rules like the Speaker Listener Technique add some degree of predictability, which reduces anxiety and avoidance, helping both of you win rather than lose when dealing with conflict. Rather than fight against each other, you can work together to fight negative patterns.

Suggested Activities

The Speaker Listener Technique does not work miracles, but it does work well. You're likely to be a bit unsure at the start, but as we've discussed, if the technique is going to be useful, you have to practice. You both need to learn the technique well enough that the rules can be followed automatically when you have something really difficult to discuss.

Starting Out: Practice with Easy Topics

Practice this technique a few times a week for ten minutes or so each time. For the first week, try the technique only with *non-stressful* topics that are nothing about any conflict or issue between the two of you. Pick whatever you want to talk about that will be easy to use for practicing the structure of the technique. That's your goal right now, not conquering some ongoing issue or problem. Learn the technique and get comfortable with a style of how the two of you want to use it.

Some topics you might try using for practice could include you each sharing something you are excited about, or even something you are a bit stressed about as a person—as long as it's not stress about or with your partner. Or you could talk about your favorite vacations; interests such as sports, books, or movies; or something you heard in the news; and so on. Your goal is to practice honing a new skill. If the topic you practice with is getting in the way of the goal of practicing, shift to another topic and table that first topic to another time, for when you are getting comfortable using the technique.

The more the two of you practice the Speaker Listener Technique, the easier and more comfortable you will feel when you use it—and the more successful your conversations will be when it matters.

Moving On to Conflictual Topics

1. After you have had a few successful practice sessions about low or no-stress topics, choose an area of minor conflict to discuss. Sometimes couples are bad at knowing what will and will not trigger a fight. So, if things get unexpectedly heated, drop it. (The issue won't go away, but you can deal with it after your skills are more finely honed.)

Practice several discussions in which you both exchange some thoughts and feelings on an issue that matters. Don't try to solve problems; just have good discussions. This means that your goal is to understand each other's point of view as clearly and completely as possible.

Problems are sometimes solved in the process because all that was really needed was for both of you to understand where the other was coming from. You'll learn and practice problem-solving in Chapter Eight.

2. When you are doing well with smaller issues, move up to tougher and tougher issues. As you do, remember to stick to the rules. The technique works if you work at it.

7

Controlling the Home Fires
Handling Issues and Events

We are often mystified that so many of our biggest fights seem to start over the smallest things (think toilet seat up, toothpaste cap off). In fact, you may not even recall what sparked your latest fight. Think for a moment. Can you say what started it? This is completely typical. Even if your fights are really about deeper issues, on the surface most appear to be conflicts over the day-to-day happenings of your lives, aka "the little things."

Have you ever seen a wildfire raging out of control? The all-consuming inferno can be a frightening sight. However, a fire that's under control can be a necessary and useful tool. Many wilderness areas rely on controlled burns to destroy dry wood and brush and to prevent out-of-control fires from starting in the first place. When clear boundaries are set and careful controls are in place, the danger can be minimized. Fire can even create a pleasant experience; a fire in your living room fireplace, for example, can be warming and romantic and provide light and warmth.

That's a lot like how relationships are for most of us. There are, at times, explosions of energy touched off by a tiny spark, leading to an out-of-control blaze of conflict. At other times, well-handled conflict, with clear boundaries and a safe discussion leading to resolution, can provide light and warmth and cause increased feelings of intimacy and closeness.

We call the sparks that incite conflicts *events*, which are the everyday happenings that we react to. We call the blazes that are triggered by events *issues*, which are the deeper, ongoing problem areas that all couples face. Not handling these issues well all too often fuels destructive conflicts.

All couples experience events, and all couples have issues. What is damaging for the two of you is when events regularly touch off unresolved or hidden issues that have not been adequately dealt with. In this chapter, we'll go even deeper in helping you understand some of the conflicts that affect you—and what to do about them.

ISSUES AND EVENTS

When we ask people what they argue about the most, the top two responses are consistently money and children. In a study from our research center, the top three areas that couples reported led to conflicts were money, sex, and communication. Other common conflict areas include in-laws, recreation, alcohol and drugs, religion, careers, and housework. These are all in the category of what we call *issues*.

It makes perfect sense that couples cite these issues as the source of their conflicts. And yet, most arguments don't actually start with a discussion over them. Have you ever sat there thinking, "Hmm, I think I'll start a fight with my partner about money at, say, 7:30 tonight. Yeah, that's right. That's a plan." Of course not! That's not how fights start. Things heat up when some event triggers an unresolved issue. An example will help you see what we mean.

Rachel and Gregg have a serious money issue. One day, Rachel came home from work and put her credit card statement down on the kitchen counter as she went to the bedroom to change. Gregg took a look at the statement and became livid when he saw a charge for $150 from a local clothing boutique. When Rachel walked back into the kitchen, tired after a long day at work, she was looking for a hug or a "How was your day?" Instead, the conversation went like this:

GREGG: What did you spend that $150 on?

RACHEL: (*very defensive*) What? None of your business.

GREGG: Of course it's my business. We agreed that we're spending too much. This isn't helping us get out of debt.

RACHEL: If you'd have the guts to ask for a raise, we wouldn't be having problems with money.

And just like that, they were thrown into a huge new argument about money.

It didn't come out of thin air, even if it may have seemed that way. It happened in the context of an event: Gregg looking at the credit card statement and seeing that Rachel had spent $150. Because money is such a hot issue for them, just about any money-related event could have triggered an argument about it. Given their current stress about money, even a small event is enough to trigger negative emotions, at virtually any time. Add to this combustible situation several Communication Danger Signs (Chapter Two), and it's no surprise Rachel and Gregg had a wildfire on their hands.

Regulating Negative Emotions: A Life Skill

One of the most important skills for someone to learn in life is how to manage negative emotions. So much of how life will go for a person depends on how well they can do this. All of us need to know what to do when we are upset and when our partner (or someone else) is upset (often at us). A person who is unable to control their responses will go through life reacting with anger, sadness, and hostility, depending on the whims of the events they experience. Psychologists call the process of maintaining control *negative affect regulation*; you can call it *remaining calm*.

(*continued*)

When it comes to your relationship, the ability to regulate your negative emotions when you are upset and when your partner is upset is essential. Anger is contagious, and when you lead with anger your partner will invariably respond in kind. Alternatively, when someone is angry at you it's likely that you'll feel attacked. And if you feel attacked, you will either counterattack or become defensive. This is why it's so important to learn how to interrupt this cycle in the first place, such as by channeling your anger into more constructive communication, like a statement or request. Or, if you're unable to do that, at least have the good sense to call a Time Out to give yourself some breathing space.

It's equally important to learn how to respond rather than react if your partner is angry with you. What's the difference between responding and reacting? When you respond, you are taking a moment to consider what to say rather than immediately jumping back at your partner. You are being deliberate. When we react, though, our blood pressure goes up, our heart pounds faster, we're flooded with the stress chemical cortisol, and our rational brain shuts down. Our bodies are preparing us to fight, flee, or freeze because we sense danger, and so we lash out. These automatic, hair-trigger responses come from our "animal brain," meaning they are not mediated by thought. Remember how your parent or first-grade teacher would insist you "Think before you speak"? This is exactly what we mean. And when you're angry, it's very hard to do.

The good news is that with practice we can learn to recognize when we are becoming agitated, how to interrupt our impulse to (over)react, and instead make a thoughtful choice about how best to respond. In a word, this is what is meant by being mindful. Mindfulness simply means the ability to witness the thought, sensation, or feeling you are having as if from a distance, and then redirecting your attention to something more grounding, like your breath or the present moment. When you focus on your breath you are squarely in the present moment; you're not ruminating about past gripes and you're not projecting anxiously into the future. And, returning to the present creates a fertile space in which to replace your negative or destructive thoughts with a more constructive response, one that you've taken a moment to first consider.

When using your breath to calm down, it's best to take long slow breaths, elongating the exhale through your mouth. This also has the benefit of slowing down your runaway thoughts, rapid heartbeat, and too-fast speech, giving you better access to your thinking brain. There are hundreds of apps that teach mindfulness meditation, making it easy to learn and practice. Like anything else, the more you practice it, the more easily you can access the skill when you need it most!

Here's a metaphor from Mother Nature that many couples find useful. Have you ever visited Yellowstone National Park? Issues and events work like the famous geysers that dot the park. Underneath the park are caverns of hot water under pressure, and unresolved issues in your relationship are like these underground pockets of steam and heat. The more troublesome issues contain the greatest amount of heat in the form of negative emotions. The pressure keeps building up when you aren't talking about your issues in a constructive manner. Then the smallest events, sometimes so small they are embarrassing to mention, trigger a sudden eruption in your relationship. (To extend the metaphor even further: most couples also have an Old Faithful. You know, one big issue that keeps coming back time and time again.)

This leads us to another one of the most important points in the book: most couples deal with issues only in the context of the events that trigger them. In other words, the only time an issue gets their attention is when they are fighting about it—which of course is the least likely time that it will get thoughtfully resolved.

Most couples deal with issues only in the context of the events that trigger them. In other words, the only time an issue gets their attention is when they are fighting about it.

For Rachel and Gregg, there was so much negative energy stored up around the issue of money that it easily combusted. They never sat down and talked about money in a constructive way, when no event had occurred. Instead, they argued about money when a check bounced, a large bill came due, or the hot water heater broke. They never got anywhere on the big issue because they spent their energy dealing with crises caused by the events. These are not moments anyone is likely to handle things well.

What about you? Do you set aside time to deal with issues that you disagree about before events can trigger them? You're not alone if you usually don't. It's hard to be proactive, and it's especially hard to decide to talk about a conflict area when things are going well. But we all pay a price in the form of eroded love and happiness if we go through life just waiting for the next fight to erupt. As Scott (coauthor) often says, "There are many important times that we damage our relationships by sliding instead of deciding."

You aren't effectively managing the ongoing, recurrent problems and struggles you have together by letting them slide, as if they will magically go away by themselves. Events tend to come up at inopportune times: when you're ready to leave for work, you're coming home from work, you're going to bed, you're heading out to relax, the kids are around, friends are set to come over, and so forth. Call it Murphy's Relationship Law. The solution is to *decide* that you will deal with the difficult stuff, and then set a time and place to do it.

You can either let your issues control you, or you can learn to control your issues!

When events frequently drag you into issues and conflicts, you start to feel like you're walking on eggshells. You can become hyper-vigilant, constantly checking to make sure you haven't accidentally disturbed the peace. If you feel anxious most of the time about conflicts breaking out, you'll have a very tough time keeping the feeling of safety and security in your relationship. Remember, it's crucial to make it safe to connect. The good news is that by applying the principles of this book you can restore the relaxed and comfortable feelings that drew you together in the first place.

HIDDEN ISSUES: THE DEEPER THEMES

Most of the time the issues triggered by events are very clear, because they are related to challenges we deal with every day: money, chores, children, and so on. In the case of Rachel and Gregg, his looking at the credit card statement touched off the issue of their finances (specifically, how precarious they were). That's not hard to figure out. But at other times, you'll find yourselves getting caught up in fights around events that don't seem to be attached to any particular issue. Or you find you aren't getting anywhere when talking about particular problems, as if your relationship were a car stuck on ice, spinning its wheels.

In our experience, hidden issues are often to blame for the really frustrating or destructive arguments couples have. For example, one of the biggest sources of argument between a couple we worked with, Samantha and Tim, revolved around the amount of time Tim spent talking with his mother and his willingness to take calls from her at any time. Samantha constantly expressed her frustration that Tim was "bringing his mother with us," including on date nights. She said it annoyed her. But once we really examined things, she admitted that the *real* issue was that she felt she wasn't important to Tim and that he didn't care about her.

When we say issues are often hidden, we mean that they are usually not being talked about openly. Hidden issues are very important to address because they reflect the unexpressed expectations, needs, and feelings that, if not attended to, can cause great damage to your relationship.

Hidden issues reflect the unexpressed expectations, needs, and feelings that, if not attended to, can cause great damage to your relationship.

We see several types of hidden issues in our work with couples: *control and power, caring, recognition, commitment, trust,* and *acceptance.* There may be others present in your specific relationship, but these six are the most common.

Although we call these *hidden* issues, that doesn't mean they're any less important than problems that are out in the open. On the contrary, they reflect deeper themes between the two of you and the values you each hold when it comes to your relationship. Sometimes you don't even realize how strongly you hold these values until an event in your relationship triggers a hidden issue to surface. The intensity of your response can be a sign of the value's importance, helping you realize that you need to take it seriously.

Here's a short summary of the first five issues. Acceptance, the final issue, is important enough to warrant its own subsection.

- **Control and power.** Control is intimately intertwined with status and power. Who decides who does the chores or how to spend family funds? Are your needs and your desires just as important as your partner's, or is there an inequality? Is your input important, or are major decisions made without you? Who's in charge? Do you feel controlled?

Control and power issues can surface in your relationship whenever decisions come up—even small ones. A power struggle can result over just about anything. In many relationships, it is the person who says no to things—no to sex, no to spending money, no to going places—who has the real power in the relationship. In communication, it can be the withdrawer, the one who refuses to talk about the issues, who really controls what is going on. Regardless of the source of hidden issues of power and control, it's important to resolve them. In the words of noted psychiatrist James Hollis, when power prevails, love fails.

- **Caring.** Concerns over caring are often triggered when people feel that their partner isn't meeting their emotional needs. This can be an especially challenging issue to uncover because caring behavior is often tied up in symbolic acts. That is, actions that one partner thinks indicate caring (making a special meal, being present for certain events, etc.) may be interpreted completely differently by their partner, who may not give them the same weight. Given the high possibility of misunderstanding, you should try to give your partner the benefit of the doubt if they don't seem to care enough about something that's important to you. Clear, level-headed communication is critical here (as always!).

- **Recognition.** Whereas issues of caring involve concerns about being cared for or loved, recognition issues are more about feeling valued by your partner for who you are and what you do. Does your partner appreciate your activities and accomplishments? Do you feel that your efforts in your marriage are ignored?

Issues about recognition are especially common in relationships where one partner is the primary breadwinner and the other runs the household. When we work with couples like this, we often hear that each feels unrecognized and unappreciated for the primary role they play, and their partner focuses instead on the help they're not getting or minimizes what the other does. In both these cases, partners may try hard to get recognized for what they bring to the family, but eventually give up if their mate fails to express appreciation.

People like to say that they don't think it's necessary to thank their partner for the things they're usually expected to do. Our response to that is, *why not?* How much nicer would it be if you thanked your partner each time they put dinner on the table or took out the trash? How long has it been since you told your partner how much you appreciate the things they do?

- **Commitment.** Commitment themes reflect anxiety about how stable and enduring your relationship is and how well it will withstand the challenges that naturally come along. The key here is each person's sense of the long-term security of the relationship: are you going to stay with me?

One couple we worked with, Tyler and Will, had huge arguments about separate checking accounts. Whenever the bank statement arrived, Will would complain bitterly about his having a separate account.

Not unsurprisingly, the real issue for Will wasn't the money. It was commitment. He had been married once before, and his ex-husband had had a separate account. He decided to leave Will after eight years of marriage, which was easier to do because his ex-husband had squirreled away thousands of dollars in this account. Now, when the separate statement for Tyler's account would arrive, Will associated it with thoughts that Tyler could be planning to leave him. Tyler was planning no such thing, but because Will rarely talked openly about his fear, Tyler wasn't really given the opportunity to alleviate Will's anxiety by affirming his commitment. The issue kept fueling fast-burning conflicts about money when spending events came up.

When your commitment to one another is secure, it brings a deeper kind of safety to your relationship than that which comes merely from good communication. This is safety that comes from the lasting promise to be there for one another, to lift one another up in tough times, to cherish each other for a lifetime.

- **Trust.** Trust can be triggered as an issue whenever your partner questions your motives, values, or standards. Whether real or imagined, this questioning leaves you feeling judged, fueling a desire to defend yourself. As we've discussed throughout this book, trust is a fundamental pillar of a healthy relationship, and a relationship without it can't survive for long. To trust, however, is to be vulnerable, which is why it can be so hard for some partners to do, especially if their trust has been violated in the past.

This is why some partners insist they must know who their partner is talking to, going out with, or working with at all times. While their concerns may come from an understandable place, it's not an acceptable excuse. If you've given them no reason to doubt you, they must learn to trust you—or you them—if your relationship is going to be sustainable. (Which is why we have a chapter dedicated entirely to the topic of trust and how to regain it.)

Acceptance: The Bottom Line

There's one primary issue overlaying all the others we've talked about here: the desire for acceptance. Sometimes this is felt more as a fear of rejection, but the fundamental issue is the same. At the deepest level, people want to feel accepted and avoid rejection in their relationships. This reflects the deep need we all have to be respected, connected, safe, and freely accepted by our spouse.

A fundamental fear of rejection drives so many other hidden issues. Unfortunately, the fear is valid. Marriage involves imperfect people who can deeply hurt one another. You can see this fear of rejection come up in many ways. For example, some people are afraid that if they act in certain ways, their partner is going to reject them. Often people ask for something indirectly because they don't want to risk becoming more vulnerable by expressing their desires more openly. For instance, this person might say, "Wouldn't you like to have sex tonight?" rather than "I would like to have sex tonight." When a self-protection filter causes you to phrase your desires in this way, your worries were triggered by the fear of rejection.

There are a number of other ways in which people act out their hidden issues of acceptance and rejection. Consider the example of Craig and Shira and the arguments that come up with his yearly hunting trip.

The couple has been married for seventeen years and have two kids. There are few things they don't handle well. They talk regularly about the more important issues, which keeps their marriage running pretty smoothly. However, there is one problem they've never really handled: once a year, every year, Craig goes hunting with his friends. The men rent a cabin in the mountains and virtually disappear for two weeks.

The following argument about this event is typical. This year it happened at night while Craig was packing to leave early the next morning.

SHIRA: I really hate it when you leave for this trip every year. You leave me to handle everything by myself.

CRAIG: (feeling a bit defensive) You knew when we got married that I did this every year. I don't know why you have to complain about it every time.

SHIRA: (going on the attack) I just don't think it's very responsible to leave your family alone for so long. The kids need you around more than that. They get very irritable while you're gone.

CRAIG: (He's thinking, "Why do we have to do this every year? I hate this argument." He's getting angry.) I do a lot with them. You need to deal with this better—I'm not about to give this trip up.

SHIRA: (angrier herself) If you cared more about your family, you wouldn't have this need to get away from us for two weeks every year.

CRAIG: (*getting up to leave the room, feeling disgusted*) Yeah, you're right. You're always right.

SHIRA: (*yelling as he walks out*) I hate it when you talk to me like that. You can't treat me like your dad treats your mom. I won't put up with it.

CRAIG: (*shouting from the other room*) I'm not like my father, and you aren't telling me what to do. I'm going, I'll keep going every year, and you might as well get used to it.

What's really going on here? Getting ready for the trip is the event. They have this same nasty argument every year, usually the night before he leaves. It's as much a part of the tradition as the trip is. Neither likes it, but they haven't found a way to handle the situation differently.

You can see many of the hidden issues being triggered for Craig and Shira. Deep down, she worries whether Craig really cares about her when these trips come up. He knows how she feels and yet he goes anyway. She feels lonely when he leaves, and this is hard to handle because she sees him looking forward to being gone. She wonders if he's delighted to get away from her. She feels nearly abandoned, reflecting some commitment issues that also get triggered. Her focus on the kids is a smokescreen for her real concerns.

Craig likes to be in control of his life, so that's one hidden issue triggered here. "No one's going to tell me what to do!" Also, as they argue unproductively, a caring issue comes up. He feels she's calling into question his devotion as a husband and father. He sees himself as very dedicated to the family and just wants this two-week period each year to be with the guys. He gives her plenty of advance notice and doesn't think that's asking a lot.

You can see acceptance underneath it all as the most basic hidden issue driving the issues of power, caring, and commitment in their argument. Neither believes that the other accepts who they are, and that is very confusing. After all, they really do have a great relationship, and each generally feels good about the other. Yet the need for acceptance is so basic for all of us that it can get triggered by almost any event or issue—if we let it.

Signs You're Dealing with Hidden Issues

You can't handle hidden issues unless you can identify them. On that note, here are four common signs that hidden issues may be affecting your relationship:

- **Wheel spinning.** When an argument starts with you thinking, "Here we go again," you should suspect hidden issues are at play. You never really get anywhere on the problem because you often aren't talking about what really matters—the hidden issue. We have all had these arguments in which we've said everything so many times before, only for the process to repeat itself yet again.

- **Trivial triggers.** If a disagreement blows up into a fight that seems entirely out of proportion with the matter at hand, you may be dealing with a hidden issue. Even the most minor transgressions (not putting down the toilet seat, lack of interest in a family recipe, etc.) can become powerful symbols of control, power, and (lack of) caring.

- **Avoidance.** When one or both of you are avoiding certain topics or levels of intimacy, or feel walls going up between you, you should suspect hidden issues. This is often accompanied by the avoidant partner accusing the other of wanting to start an argument or by deflecting their reason for not talking onto something else.

- **Scorekeeping.** Scorekeeping—keeping a tally of who owes who what, or who did what—is a sign you and your partner are actively working against each other, rather than being a partnership that takes the good with the bad. In this situation, it's highly likely there are important underlying issues the two of you aren't talking about.

Handling Hidden Issues

What can you do when you realize hidden issues are affecting your relationship? Apart from recognizing when one may be operating, the first step is to start talking about it constructively. This will be easier to do if you are cultivating an atmosphere of teamwork using the kinds of methods we've presented thus far, such as the Speaker Listener Technique. When dealing with hidden issues, it's very important to focus less on problem-solving and more on hearing each other's thoughts and feelings. There is no more powerful form of acceptance than really listening to the thoughts and feelings of your mate. This type of validation is critical to emotional intimacy in relationships.

Keep in mind that oftentimes you don't *solve* hidden issues; rather, you soothe them through mutual understanding, respect, and acceptance. These deep feelings are part of who you are, your view of the world, and the result of your life experiences. They are not necessarily things that need to be "solved," but to be worked through. When you really hear each other, what has in the past been frustrating—and perhaps caused confusing filters to go up during many of your interactions—can turn into opportunities to know one another more deeply. This is the essence of connecting safely.

Oftentimes you don't solve hidden issues; rather, you soothe them through mutual understanding, respect, and acceptance.

Working through those tough issues can help couples strengthen their sense of commitment. Couples who soothe each other's concerns come to understand each other's emotional triggers and learn to handle them more gently. When you experience your partner behaving toward you with care and sensitivity, you develop a greater sense of trust, which deepens your connection.

When conflicts flare up in the context of events, it can be unclear what led to the amount of frustration or hurt you each feel. When this happens, it's often because there are issues underneath the surface that are driving the bus that's rolling right through your connection together. You can handle the things underneath the surface best if you are working toward making it safe to connect.

Talking Points

1. Events are day-to-day happenings in everyone's life that can spark conflict about deeper issues.

2. Issues are underlying areas of conflict that are also part of everyone's life.

3. Hidden issues are even farther under the surface and can blaze out of control when not recognized and addressed. Of the six types of hidden issues, acceptance, or the corresponding fear of rejection, may be at the root of all other issues we face.

Suggested Activities

Take some time with these activities as you consider possible hidden issues that might be fueling conflicts you have about issues or events.

What Are Your Hidden Issues?

Think about the biggest hidden issues in your relationship. In addition to the hidden issues listed here, there may be some issue you'd like to add. Consider each issue and to what degree it seems to affect your relationship negatively. Also evaluate how hidden they are or aren't. Do you acknowledge what might really be at hand when an event triggers an argument?

- Power and control
- Caring
- Recognition

- Commitment

- Acceptance

Talking About Your Hidden Issues

Plan some time together to talk directly about a particular hidden issue. Name what it is, and share your thoughts about it respect-fully. For most couples, there are ones that repeatedly come up. Identifying these can help you draw together as you each learn to handle those issues with care. Also, as you discuss these matters, you'll have an excellent opportunity to get in more practice with the Speaker Listener Technique.

We want to remind you, again, that you may not be able to "solve" hidden issues. Instead, use this talk time to understand each other's point of view and learn how to respect and support each other when these sensitive issues come up.

8

New Perspectives on Problems and Problem-Solving

Many couples believe there is something wrong with their relationship if they have problems that are not readily solvable. This belief can be very damaging to a relationship. One of the pathways to unhappiness, breaking up, or divorce is believing (falsely) that there is something seriously wrong with your relationship because you haven't resolved all your problems. All couples have issues, even the happiest ones. We tell you this in hopes it can help you adjust your expectations to be more in line with reality. For most problems the key to overcoming them is not the problems *themselves* but how couples handle them.

For most problems the key to overcoming them is not the problems themselves but how couples handle them.

You and your partner will be much happier if you can work together to resolve them in a way that satisfies both of you. That's the focus of this chapter. We present a straightforward approach to problem-solving that can help you through those times when you really need practical, workable solutions.

Most couples in our solution-oriented society do not take the time to discuss each partner's thoughts and feelings about issues before working on solutions. That is rushing things, and the solutions tend not to work. We suggest, instead, that couples use the Speaker Listener Technique to build understanding before trying to solve the issue or problem at hand.

Most couples in our solution-oriented society do not take the time to discuss each partner's thoughts and feelings about issues before working on solutions

NO GETTING AROUND HAVING PROBLEMS IN LIFE

Although the nature of the problems changes for couples over time, all couples encounter problems. There are some problems that are likely to remain much the same over the long term. For example, let's say personality differences lead to fairly frequent conflicts between the two of you. Perhaps one of you is more compulsive and super organized, and the other more carefree. Or one of you is super-shy and the other the life of the party. Such differences are often what attracts partners in the first place, but they can also become sources of conflicts over the details of life. These kinds of problems are not likely to go away over time. What does tend to change in great relationships is that the partners develop the ability to accept one another in spite of the differences.

In contrast to these kinds of problems, some are very specific and need real solutions. Maybe it's July, you've moved to a new neighborhood, and you disagree about whether or not your children should go to the school down the block or to the new charter school a few miles away. That's a problem that requires a real decision right now. The ideas in this chapter are ideal for such situations, when the two of you need a little extra structure to deal with the problem most effectively.

You have a choice when dealing with any problem. Either you will nurture a sense that you are a team working together against the problem or you will operate as if you are working against each other. Here's a trick you can use: think of the problem as separate from yourselves and that you're teaming up to find the best solution. For example, you like it warm but your partner likes it hot. Approach the problem as trying to find the optimal temperature that accommodates you both. This principle holds with all problems, great or small. How you handle problems is a decision—it's up to you!

Why the Big Rush?

Many well-intended attempts at problem-solving fail because couples don't take the time needed to understand each other's concerns. This is particularly true when one partner is upset about something. All too often, we want to fix what's wrong—and all too often our efforts wind up making our partner even more upset. It's critical that you take the time to listen first and then decide if resolution makes sense. How can you make a wise decision if you haven't heard and considered all of the relevant factors?

Two major factors propel couples to rush to solutions: time pressure and conflict avoidance.

Time pressure. We live in a "give-it-to-me-now" world of instant solutions to problems and desires. This might work fine when it comes to wanting a certain brand of shaving cream or a particular color of draperies at the store, but it's not how relationships work. When it comes to the problems with which most couples struggle, hasty decisions are often poor decisions. You may have heard the expression "You can pay me now or pay me later" in regard to car maintenance, and it's all the more true when dealing with problems in relationships.

(continued)

Conflict avoidance. Sometimes people rush to solutions because they can't stand to deal with the conflict. Phillip is concerned that his wife, Jennifer, devotes a lot of time to a job that doesn't pay. An issue for Jennifer is that she does not feel supported by Phillip for the important work she feels she does.

They never get anywhere when they discuss the issue, though, because they just tip their toes into it and half agree on some lame solution like paying down their credit cards or putting more in their retirement account without any discussion of the stress this causes Phillip or the threat to a deeply meaningful endeavor Jennifer has devoted so much energy to. The root of this dynamic for them is avoidance of conflict that leads them away from grappling with the real issues and being more connected by addressing it.

What they do is what a lot of couples do most of the time. When an issue does come up, and they are not just arguing, they throw out quick ideas on solutions that will go nowhere.

HANDLING PROBLEMS WELL

When the first edition of this book was published, Howard had the honor of appearing on the *Oprah Winfrey Show*. At one point in his conversation with Oprah, Howard explained, "We have estimated that as many as 70 percent of the problems couples face don't need problem-solving as much as a good, open talk." Howard braced himself for disagreement, but the opposite happened: Oprah went a step further, declaring that she thought the true figure might be 80 percent or more!

We can't speak for Oprah, but we still believe a good, open talk can do wonders for a relationship. To that end, the first phase of our two-part problem-solving process, the Problem Discussion phase, is often all that is needed to reach mutual understanding. The second round, the Problem Solution phase, is for when you need to make a decision that requires a concrete solution. It's a bit more comprehensive and includes a series of steps we call the ABCs of Handling Problems.

Much like the Speaker Listener Technique, our approach to solving problems here is also structured. In other words, it involves a specific set of steps. We think of this structure like a scaffold around a building under construction: in both situations, you need support to complete the project. Full discussion clarifies all of the underlying issues, decreases chances that Communication Danger Signs will rear their ugly heads, and increases the feeling of teamwork. Solutions flow naturally from working together against *problems* rather than working against *each other*.

Here's an outline of the process:

I. Problem Discussion

II. Problem Solution

    A. **A**genda Setting

    B. **B**rainstorming

    C. **C**ompromise and Agreement

    D. **D**o It: Implementation

    E. **E**valuate and Refine

Those are the basics. Now let's dive in.

Problem Discussion

The most important step in solving a problem together is understanding each other. This step is often skipped, and that makes it far harder to make progress. Building a basis of understanding makes it more likely you can work together to come up with a solution that addresses what each of you care about.

Lay the Foundation to Work as a Team

Understanding starts with creating a safe atmosphere of mutual respect and acceptance. Therefore, we strongly recommend having a respectful conversation about the issues giving you trouble before trying to solve a particular problem. In the Problem Discussion step, you are laying the foundation for a solution to come. Whether the problem is large or small, you should not move on to Problem Solution until you both understand where the other is coming from. We recommend using the Speaker Listener Technique for this step to facilitate the kind of productive discussion that's needed before you attempt to find solutions. Or, if another technique helps you talk through your issues, use it instead.

As we discussed in Chapter Six on the Speaker Listener Technique, sometimes couples are concerned that this process will feel slow or overly structured. Our response now—as then—is that there are times when going slower and having a more formal structure of give-and-take as you speak your mind is exactly what you need. You'll waste far more time trying to quickly dispatch challenging issues with unworkable solutions. When you've put all the relevant facts and feelings on the table, you've laid the foundation for working as a team.

We mentioned Phillip and Jennifer previously. Phillip was feeling tremendous financial strain and was pushing Jennifer to give up a low-paying job she loved to earn more money. Whenever money came up as a problem, they'd argue, with all of the danger signs rearing their ugly heads. One evening, they used their Time Out strategy and decided to follow the problem-solving model just described. They had a great discussion using the Speaker Listener Technique with each expressing their thoughts and feelings. This led to a breakthrough that enabled them to roll through the rest of the steps and get to a solution. They each felt heard on something they'd known or thought they'd been saying for a long time.

Phillip talked about his growing fear about what their future might be like, financially, and how that might impinge upon their plans for having kids. He felt Jennifer really heard him this time, and took his worries seriously. Likewise, Phillip stopped pushing Jennifer to change and listened to how and why her time invested in the charity meant so much to her. Their situation is a great example where the Problem Discussion phase of problem-solving is almost the whole ballgame for getting anywhere on some type of resolution.

Being Clear About What You Are Upset About

Often we complicate our communication by expressing so much anger and general frustration that our real message can be lost in the shuffle. In *A Couple's Guide to Communication*, the authors discuss an effective way to ensure your message will be clearly heard by your partner: the XYZ statement. This can be very valuable whether you're problem solving or just need to assert yourself clearly. When you make an XYZ statement, you put your gripe or complaint into this format:

"When you do X in situation Y, I feel Z."

When you use an XYZ statement, you are giving your partner usable information: the specific behavior, the context in which it occurs, and how you feel when it happens.

For example, suppose you had a concern about your partner making a mess at the end of the day. Which of the following statements do you think gives you a better shot at being heard?

> "I can't believe you expect me to clean up after you. You're such a slob!"

> "When you drop your pack and jacket on the floor [X] as you come in the door at the end of the day [Y], I feel frustrated [Z]."

Or let's say you were angry about a comment your spouse made at a party last Saturday night. Which statement is better at getting your point across?

"You are so rude in front of my friends."

"When you said that what I did for work wasn't really that hard [X] to John and Ted at the party last Saturday [Y], I felt very embarrassed [Z]."

Let's be real on this. Your partner is not going to love hearing you express a concern really well, as in the two XYZ examples. The value of the technique is relative to the alternative that is destructive.

When you're upset and angry, it's easy to blame your partner and to say hurtful things you might not even mean. When you use an XYZ statement, however, you're speaking for *yourself* and expressing *your own* feelings rather than pointing fingers at your partner.

"I felt embarrassed" is a true statement about how you felt. No one can argue with that. "You are so rude" is a character assassination that your partner can easily take issue with. It is your opinion, not your truth, and no one likes to be negatively labeled. Be careful when describing your feelings not to make "disguised" I-statements: "I feel you are so rude" is simply a personal attack disguised as your own feeling.

In their book *Getting to Yes*, Roger Fisher and Richard Ury suggest that most arguments break down because people argue about their positions rather than their underlying interests. A position is a firm resolution or action plan, and an underlying interest is the reason behind it. When trying to solve problems, leading with your interests is much more likely to facilitate good communication and seeing eye to eye.

Problem Solution

As we mentioned previously, for addressing many issues a Problem Discussion is often enough. But if you find yourselves still grappling for a resolution, the following steps can take you there.

Agenda Setting

The first step in the Problem Solution phase is to set the agenda for your work together. The key here is to make it very clear what you are trying to solve at this time. Often your discussion will have taken you through many facets of an issue. Now you need to decide what to focus on. The more specific you are here, the better your chances of coming to a workable and satisfying solution. Many problems in marriage can seem insurmountable, but they can be cut down to size if you follow these procedures. Even a great rock can be removed in time if you keep chipping away at it.

Let's say you've had a Problem Discussion about money, covering a range of issues, such as credit card problems, checkbooks, budgets, and savings. The problem area of "money" can contain many smaller problem areas to consider. So take a large problem such as this and focus on the more manageable pieces, one at a time. It is also wise to pick an easier piece of a problem to work on at first. We suggest setting the agenda in the form of a question that you work together as a team to answer, for example, "How can we make sure we have time next week to create a budget?" It's often important to include a time frame to make tasks more manageable.

For example, Barb and Fred had some complex money problems to address. Too much debt on credit cards without any attempts to actually pay the balances down, not enough money at the end of the month, no savings for a rainy day, with some spending habits by each that were not helping. Common stuff. They chose to work through a series of Problem Solution steps that were focused on very tightly defined agendas. In their first effort, they focused on solving a problem framed by this question: "What could we do differently in the next few weeks to a month about our spending, such as going out to lunch or buying fancy coffees daily?"

From their discussion about all the issues about money, they both acknowledged how they each loved to go out to lunch or go to Starbucks on the drive into work. That acknowledgment was a meeting of the minds. After brainstorming and working through the following planning steps, they decided they would each try to cut back on going out to lunch at work and on coffee runs. They both agreed that all this spending added to quite a bit, and they each agreed to limit their spending in this category to $150 a month. That might seem to you like a huge amount or a small amount. It seemed right to each of them and would, in fact, be way less than the hundreds of dollars they were currently spending in this way. Of course, for this agreement to work, they both agreed to keep receipts or tallies and show their efforts.

Note that they set their agenda to solve one very specific, but meaningful part of their money problems. That focus gave them a much better chance at succeeding in working together to reign in this spending.

Brainstorming

As far as we know, the process referred to as brainstorming has been around forever. However, it seems to have been refined and promoted by NASA during the early days of the US space program. NASA needed a way to bring together the ideas of many different engineers and scientists when grappling with solutions to the varied problems of space travel.

There are several rules regarding brainstorming:

- Any idea is OK to suggest.
- One of you should write the ideas down as you generate them together.
- Don't evaluate the ideas during brainstorming, verbally or nonverbally (this includes making faces!).
- Be creative. Suggest whatever comes to mind.
- Have fun with it if you can. This is a time for a sense of humor; all other feelings should be dealt with in Problem Discussion.

If you can resist the temptation to comment critically on the ideas, you will encourage each other to come up with some great stuff.

Compromise and Agreement

In this step, the goal is to come up with a *specific* solution or combination of solutions that you both *agree* to try. We emphasize *agree* because the solution is not likely to help unless you both agree—sincerely—to try it. We also emphasize *specific* because the more precise you are about the solution, the more likely you will be to follow through with it.

Although it is easy to see the value of agreement, some people have trouble with the idea of *compromise*. Obviously, compromise can sometimes mean giving up something you wanted, which can feel more like lose-lose than win-win. But it's important to remember that you're *giving to*, or investing in, your relationship each time you make a change that takes into account your partner's needs. And this is ultimately a win for you.

When you reach an agreement, we like to call the result *Plan A*. This is your best guess at finding a solution that meets both of your needs given the information at hand. Plan A also implies an openness to reviewing and revising the plan again later if new information comes in. It implies there could be a need for Plan B.

Once Plan A is agreed on, we recommend writing it down because people often recall conversations differently. A good agreement should be clear and specific, stating who is responsible for what, and in what time frame, and even what contingencies (backup plans) are in place should things not go as planned. This safeguards against leaving someone high and dry if something unanticipated should occur.

What happens if you can't come to an agreement? Can you instead agree on a way to decide what feels fair? Maybe you'll take turns, draw straws, consult an expert or mediator and agree to their recommendation. Maybe you'll agree to disagree and pursue your different paths. Or maybe you'll agree to try both ways and decide which is preferable after seeing how they each work out.

There are very few problems that are so mutually exclusive that they can't be equitably solved if you're working as a team.

Do It: Implementation

There's actually a missing piece of information that even a good discussion and agreement can't address: What's going to happen when you try the agreement out? How does it work? How does it feel? How do people react? What happens next? These unknowns are exactly why an agreement must be seen as Plan A. Hopefully, when you implement a plan it goes as expected. But often there are new considerations that you can't anticipate until you experience something directly. Action creates new information. This information provides important feedback needed to evaluate and potentially refine or update Plan A.

Many times this action step requires you to do something that falls outside of your comfort zone. You've agreed to try an approach that wasn't exactly as you wanted it to be, and you're required to change. Change can be hard! Change often occurs through action first—you can't always anticipate how something will feel until you walk the talk. Once you implement your plan and see how it feels, you can then assess if your Plan A worked as expected or requires revision.

Evaluate and Refine

It is just as important to follow up on how the solution is working out as it is to devise the original plan. Hopefully, Plan A was successful and worked as expected. But over time and experience, things might need to be updated and revised. Problem Solving is a dynamic process that in essence should be an ongoing feedback loop, adapting and adjusting as new information comes in. Perhaps your solution worked out well financially, but emotionally it didn't sit well with one of you. Perhaps your plan to go on vacation was upended because one of you got sick. Perhaps the punishment you agreed on for your child backfired because it caused a different issue to arise. Many things can go awry even with the most well-thought-out plans.

This is why it's always important to feed new information back into the original solution and have a follow-up conversation to evaluate how well it worked out. This is also why viewing a solution as Plan A can make an agreement easier to enter into: you know it can always be revised if it doesn't work out well. No two individuals and no two relationships are alike. Couples who follow the ABCs of problem-solving are in effect customizing their decisions to best reflect the nature of their unique partnership. There is no single best solution for all time and all people, just as there is no guarantee that one solution will stand the test of time. But you each can do your part to keep moving forward, and this model can help.

WHEN IT'S NOT THAT EASY

We'd like to tell you that this model always works well, but there are times when it doesn't. What do you do then? In our experience with couples, there are a few common difficulties that often come up when dealing with problems. Here we'll make some suggestions for handling them.

Cycle Back Through the Steps

You can get bogged down and frustrated during any segment of the Problem Solution phase. If so, you need to cycle back to Problem Discussion. Simply pick up the Floor again and resume your discussion. Getting stuck can mean you haven't talked through some key issues or that one or both of you are not feeling validated in the process. It is better to slow things down than to continue to press for a solution that may not work. While you're getting used to the process, or when you're dealing with more complex and difficult issues, you might cycle through the steps several times.

Halfway Can Get You All the Way

The best solution you can reach in one problem-solving session may not always be the conclusive solution to a problem. At times, you should set the agenda just to agree on the next steps needed to get to the best solution. For example, you might brainstorm about the kind of information you need to make your decision. Say you were trying to decide together if you should move to another place to live, and if you should, when. This is certainly not a decision you can resolve in one sitting. There are too many things to consider and figure out. So perhaps early on, you brainstorm how you'll get to the next step. For example, what do you need to know to make the big decision? Which of you can find out what answers, and from whom? Divide and conquer.

When There Is No Solution

There are some problems that don't have solutions with which both of you will be happy. Suppose you've worked together for some time using the structure we suggest, yet no solution is emerging from your work together. You can either let this lack of a solution damage the rest of your marriage, or you can plan for how to live with your differences. Sometimes couples allow the rest of a good marriage to be hurt by insisting there must be a resolution to a specific unresolved conflict.

If you have a problem area that seems unsolvable, you can set the agenda in Problem Solution to protect the rest of your marriage from the fallout from that one problem area. You would be literally "agreeing to disagree" constructively. This kind of solution comes about from both teamwork and tolerance. You can't always have your partner be just the way you want them to be, but you can work as a team to deal with your differences. As we covered in Chapter Seven, accepting some aspect of your relationship that you wish was different is one of the most powerful ways to do your part.

In this chapter, we have given you a very detailed model for solving many of the problems that will inevitably arise in your relationship (and, if they can't be solved, some advice for accepting them). We don't expect most couples to use such a structured approach for minor problems. We do expect that most couples could benefit from this model when dealing with more important matters, especially those that can lead to unproductive conflict. This is one more way to add more structure when you need it most to preserve the best in your relationship.

Talking Points

1. All couples have problems; the key is in how you handle them. Teamwork is the best path to a great relationship.

2. Talking about your issues before trying to solve them will lead to better solutions that are more likely to stick. Understanding your partner's point of view is the key to finding the best solutions.

3. Problems and disagreements offer great opportunities to enhance a couple's sense of identity as a team, founded on honor, respect, and acceptance.

Suggested Activities

There are two separate assignments for this chapter. First, we want you to practice making XYZ statements. Second, we ask you to practice the problem-solving model presented in this chapter.

XYZ Statements: Constructive Griping

Here are some typical negative statements couples often make to each other. Practice turning these into XYZ statements: when you do X in situation Y, I feel Z. We've given you a couple to get started.

You never listen to me!

XYZ: When you won't turn off the TV after I say I'd like to talk to you about something, I feel hurt and resentful.

You're such a slob!

XYZ: When you leave your dirty clothes on the bed instead of putting them in the hamper, I feel angry and taken advantage of.

Now you try these:

1. You're never affectionate with me.

2. You always want to do things your way.

3. I always have to tell you everything ten times.

4. You never pay attention to me.

Bonus exercise: XYZ statements work equally well to recognize your partner's positive behaviors. Think of three things your partner does for you and make XYZ statements about them. Then share them with your partner!

Problem Area Assessment

The following is a simple measure of common problem areas in relationships; we have used it for years in our research and clinical practices.

Consider the following list of issues that all relationships must face. Please rate how much of a problem each area currently is in your relationship; write down a number from 0 (not at all a problem) to 100 (a severe problem) next to each area. For example, if children are somewhat of a problem, you might write 25 next to Children. If children are not a problem in your relationship, you might enter a 0 next to Children. If children are a severe problem, you might write 100. Feel free to add other areas not included in our list. Be sure to rate all areas before comparing lists. When talking about issues start with lower-rated problems and as your skills improve move up to higher-rated ones.

Problem Inventory

_____ Money	_____ Recreation
_____ Jealousy	_____ Communication
_____ Friends	_____ Careers
_____ In-laws (or other relatives)	_____ Alcohol and drugs
_____ Sex	_____ Children (or potential children)
_____ Religion	
_____ Time together	_____ Household chores
	_____ Other

Practice Problem-Solving

When practicing this model, following these instructions will maximize your chances of success.

1. Set aside time for a couples meeting, or if you have set one already, use this time to get some experience with this model.

2. Pick a problem to solve together. Start with a topic that's very low in conflict before tackling some of the more challenging issues.

3. We recommend that you set aside time to practice the Problem Discussion and Problem Solution sequence several times a week for a couple of weeks. If you put in this time, you'll gain skill and confidence in handling problem areas together.

4. It's important to not talk about issues, conflicts, or problems just before falling asleep. Not only will your arguments be less fruitful just before bed, but you'll probably sleep worse, and the next day's conversations will probably not go much better.

9

Ground Rules for a Great Relationship

To finish up this first part our marriage-strengthening journey, focused on productively dealing with conflict and talking without fighting, we will now introduce a series of tried-and-true relationship rules that have stood the test of time. Just as there are different ground rules for different sports, no two couples are alike, and we want you to choose the rules that work for *both* of you. If all the rules we suggest feel right for you, that's great. But if not, using what works is a totally fine option. The idea is to use the rules to help you both control difficult issues in your relationship, rather than allow the issues to control you.

As we have learned in previous chapters, the choices you consciously *decide* to make during arguments can make the difference between being happy and connected or distant and angry. You know that *sliding* into conflict without a moment's thought all but guarantees a bad outcome, one that probably could have been avoided. You also understand various strategies for talking safely without fighting, for solving problems, and for preserving and restoring positive connections. Our hope now is to offer some overarching ground rules for nurturing a great relationship and protecting it from the destructive effects of conflict.

As we've repeatedly stressed, creating an environment of emotional safety—making it safe to connect—is critical to working through the inevitable differences that arise between two people, and for feeling free to open up and be vulnerable. In our work over the years with couples, companies, and organizations, we've found that having ground rules is an essential component in any sensitive dialogue, because it allows the participants to hear what's being said without feeling afraid or getting defensive—that is, to feel safe. Ground rules make the path to resolution that much smoother by reducing friction between both parties.

GROUND RULE 1: AGREE ON EFFECTIVE GROUND RULES FOR YOUR RELATIONSHIP

People have different ways of expressing their needs and preferences, just as people have different triggers and vulnerabilities, so what feels safe and effective for one person may not feel that way to the other. For example, some people might find that raising voices for emphasis is a natural way to make a point, and others would find that to be intimidating. The first person, then, might ask that a ground rule be "no yelling," and then partners would need to discuss whether or not that is reasonable given each other's natural predilections.

There are many small annoyances that can build up and get in the way of having productive conversations. That's why it's important to agree on terms that you both feel you can adhere to. No one should ever feel strong-armed into playing by rules that don't make sense to them, so remember not to shortchange the discussion by agreeing to something you can't follow through with. Your word should be sacred, and you both need to trust that the ground rules will be followed.

GROUND RULE 2: ENSURE PHYSICAL SAFETY

This may seem like a nonissue to some, but to others who fear that their partner might have physical outbursts when discussions get heated, it is very important that the physical environment feel and be safe. This is particularly important when discussing emotionally charged, sensitive topics. There should never be any aggressive physical contact, "in your face" yelling, or throwing things.

Even the physical location should feel safe. For example, for difficult conversations perhaps it feels best to be somewhere where no one else is around and you can give each other your undivided and private attention. Perhaps you want to be out of earshot of your children. It might be optimal to be in a place where one of you can easily leave if the conversation doesn't go anywhere despite your efforts, or in a neutral location where no triggers or upsetting memories are attached. Ideally, the physical environment should enable you to give each other your full attention, with minimal or no other distractions or diversions (cell phones, children, TV, etc.).

GROUND RULE 3: ESTABLISH EMOTIONAL SAFETY

All of these ground rules—in fact, this whole book—are about keeping the emotional environment safe. Yet emotional safety still bears mentioning here, again, because of its critical importance. If you don't feel emotionally safe you simply won't be open to having a productive conversation. Your stress hormones will set in and you'll feel afraid, defensive, angry, or closed down—states that will prevent you from listening to your partner with an open mind. Feeling emotionally safe means that neither of you will resort to name-calling, real or implied threats, "below the belt" remarks, or other means of intimidation. It may also mean keeping the volume levels under control and respecting each other's personal space, and not interrupting and interjecting while your partner is speaking. Telling your partner that you love them and have their best interest at heart (and reminding them of that throughout the conversation) is always helpful and sets the tone for having a compassionate and open-hearted dialogue. Holding hands or touching each other tenderly can be another. It's very hard to say something mean to someone while you're holding their hand. Try it!

If you don't feel emotionally safe you simply won't be open to having a productive conversation.

When you feel loved and respected, you're far more inclined to be emotionally generous and open to compromise. Commit yourself to being as kind and loving as you can during difficult conversations. The goal is not to win an argument, but for both of you to understand each other fully and work together as a team.

GROUND RULE 4: USE TIME OUTS

This simple ground rule, discussed in detail in Chapter Two, can help you counteract the Communication Danger Signs (escalation, invalidation, withdrawal and avoidance, and negative interpretations). It's a way to prevent the two of you from damaging your relationship when you know that's likely to happen, or may already have started to happen. As we emphasized in Chapter Two, it is important that you not only agree to use Time Out or something like it but also on the specific signal indicating it's time for a Time Out.

In any case, it is important that you both know what the other is trying to do when you hear the signal. Remember that even though one of you may call Time Out more often, it's something that the two of you are doing together. Otherwise, it can look as though one partner is just avoiding the other, and as we have explained, that just fuels more escalation and anger.

Detouring Around Dangerous Conditions

Scott and Nancy were driving with their son Kyle, age four, in the back seat. They were arguing about whether or not it was illegal to make a left-hand turn across double yellow lines. After listening for several minutes to the discussion, Kyle, having absorbed the PREP techniques since birth, piped up and said, "That's not healthy arguing!" Scott and Nancy stopped, looked at each other, and ended up laughing about it. If you learn how to take a Time Out, as taught here, you don't have to depend on your children, neighbors, or others to help you rein it in when things get heated.

GROUND RULE 5: USE THE SPEAKER LISTENER TECHNIQUE

We can't say it enough: it is extremely important for every couple to have at least one good way to talk when it's hardest to do so. With this ground rule, you are agreeing to use more structure when you need it. There are many times during a heated discussion when you may not need a full-on Time Out but could benefit from the safety structure can bring. Remember, talking without fighting is the key to relationship success.

For example, suppose that you wanted to talk about a problem such as how money is spent in your household. You know from your history that these talks usually get difficult. You would be wise to follow this ground rule, raising the issue in this way: "I'm pretty concerned about money right now. Let's sit down and talk using the Floor." This sort of statement cues your partner that you are raising an important issue and that you want to talk it out carefully. However, it also shows that you are consciously deciding to keep your conversation from derailing. It shows you are being mindful—that you care.

There are other times when things have already escalated and a Time Out might have helped, but you decide to skip right to using the Speaker Listener Technique. The point of this ground rule is that the two of you have made a decision to handle difficult or sensitive topics more effectively and with increased structure, rather than to use old, destructive, and mindless modes of communication.

GROUND RULE 6: SEPARATE PROBLEM DISCUSSION FROM PROBLEM SOLUTION

Too often, couples rush to agree to a solution, and the solution fails. It makes no sense to hurry when doing so only moves you backward. Discussion and solution are different processes. Whenever you start to solve an issue, stop and ask yourself, "Do I really understand my partner's perspective? Do I feel understood?" If either answer is no, you are probably not ready to move to solutions. This ground rule is a simple reminder of the need to talk first and solve second.

You now have lots of tools to help you do this, and setting up your ground rules is a perfect place to use the Speaker Listener Technique and/or the ABCs of problem-solving. If you set this as your **A**genda, you can **B**rainstorm together which rules might work best for your relationship, agree on those that would be most useful and effective (**C**ompromise and **A**greement), and then go ahead and implement them when you have a disagreement (**D**o it: Implementation). How well did they work? Which ground rules weren't particularly effective? (**E**valuate and Refine). This brings you back to the beginning, where you discuss what did and didn't work, brainstorm new possibilities, agree to a revised set of ground rules, and implement those the next time around.

For more on separating out discussion from solution, and problem-solving steps, see Chapters 6 and 8.

GROUND RULE 7: YOU CAN WAIT FOR A BETTER TIME TO TALK—BUT MAKE SURE YOU TALK

Each partner should feel empowered to bring up a topic to talk about in a nice way at virtually any time. But the person who hears this request should also be able to request (unless it's an emergency) to postpone the discussion to a better time. That said, that partner has to take responsibility for making the conversation happen in the near future.

The purpose of this ground rule is very important: it ensures that you will have an important or difficult talk at the time you both agree is right. How often do you begin talking about a key issue in your relationship when your partner is just not ready for it? Most couples talk about their most important issues offhandedly or at the worst times—dinnertime, bedtime, when it's time to get the kids off for school, as soon as you walk in the door after work, when one of you is preoccupied with an important project or task—you get the picture. These are times when your spouse may be a captive audience, but you certainly don't have their attention. Choose the time wisely.

This ground rule assumes two things: (1) you each are responsible for knowing when you are capable of discussing something with appropriate attention to what your partner has to say and (2) you can each respect the other when they say, "I can't deal with this right now."

Your response to this may be, "Isn't this just a prescription for avoidance?" That's where the second part of the ground rule comes in. The partner who doesn't want to talk takes responsibility for making the discussion happen in the near future. This is critical. Your partner will have a much easier time putting off the conversation if they have confidence that you really will follow through. We recommend that when you use this ground rule, you agree that you'll set up a better time within twenty-four to forty-eight hours.

GROUND RULE 8: HAVE WEEKLY COUPLE MEETINGS

Most couples do not set aside a regular time for dealing with key issues or problems. It's hard to get most of us to do this because of the fast-paced lives so many of us live. Nevertheless, the advantages of having a weekly meeting time far outweigh any negatives. First, this is a tangible way to place high priority on your marriage by carving out time for its upkeep. We know you are busy, but also that if you decide this is important you can find the time to make it work.

Second, following this ground rule ensures that even if there is no other good time to deal with issues, you at least have this one regular time. You might be surprised at how much you can get done in thirty minutes or so of concentrated attention on an issue. During this meeting, you can talk about the relationship, talk about specific problems, or plan for what's coming up.

A third advantage of this ground rule is that having a weekly meeting time takes much of the day-to-day pressure off your relationship. This is especially true if you are snared in the pursuer-withdrawer trap. If something happens that brings up a gripe for you, it's much easier to delay bringing it up until another time if you know there *will* be another time. Pursuers can relax. You'll have your chance to raise your issue. Withdrawers can relax during the week, knowing that events will not trigger issues. We also find that withdrawers, who of course have things they want to talk about, too, may actually start looking forward to meetings, because such meetings are a safe place to talk without fighting.

You may find it tempting to skip the meetings when you are getting along well. Don't succumb to this urge. For example, Roberto and Margaret had set aside Wednesday nights at nine o'clock as a time for their couple meeting. If they were getting along really well during the week and Wednesday night rolled around, each would begin to think, "We don't need to meet tonight. No use stirring things up when we are getting along so well." Then one or the other would say, "Hey, let's just skip the meeting tonight; things are going so well."

What Roberto and Margaret came to realize is that things were going so well partly because they were regularly having their meetings! After they canceled a few, they noticed that more conflicts would come up during the week. They had given up their time to deal with issues and reverted to the uncertainty of dealing with things "if and when." They decided that "if and when" was not placing the proper importance on their marriage, and they got back to the meetings, recognizing small events or issues that needed to be discussed even when there had not been big conflicts.

GROUND RULE 9: MAKE TIME FOR FUN, FRIENDSHIP, AND SENSUALITY

Just as it's important to have time set aside to deal with issues in your relationship, it's also critical that you protect your positive times together, keeping conflicts and tough talks at bay. You can't be focusing on issues all the time and have a really great marriage. You need some time when you are together relaxing—having fun, talking as friends, making love, and so forth—when conflict and problems are off-limits. This is such a key point that we've devoted whole chapters (coming up) to these essential ways to connect.

For now, we'll emphasize two points embodied in this ground rule. First, *make time* for these great things. After all, they're what brought you together in the first place. Second, if you're spending time together in one of these ways, don't bring up issues that you have to work on. And if an issue does come up, table it for later, when you schedule a time to deal with issues constructively. Having fun together, even when there are conflicts or unresolved issues to work out, is not the same as avoiding or subtly forgiving a wrongdoing. It's just a "time out from distress": a time to focus on the very things that cement your relationship together. You can still make love or laugh together when issues come up, so don't short-change the good stuff!

Talking Points

1. Relationships need ground rules to level the playing field and ensure both partners communicate fairly.

2. Rules are not one-size-fits-all; customize them to fit the needs of your own relationship.

3. Safety—emotional and physical—is the number one ground rule and must always be respected.

4. Structured approaches to conflict resolution (the Speaker Listener Technique, the Problem Discussion/Problem Solution model) naturally incorporate ground rules, which is what makes them so effective.

5. Time Outs are not about avoidance or withdrawal; they are used to protect and preserve a healthy relationship. But each partner must make sure they aren't being overused (or abused).

Suggested Activity

Your activity for this chapter is very straightforward: discuss these ground rules and begin to try them out. You may want to add some others or modify them in some specific manner to make them work better for you. That's fine. The key is to agree on your own ground rules and then practice using them to give them a chance to work in your relationship.

PART 3

Enjoying Each Other

10

Staying Friends and Having Fun

"I'm marrying my best friend."

You've probably attended a wedding ceremony where the bride or groom declared this sentiment, or maybe you've heard a friend say it to you when telling you about their plans to marry. And it's often true. When you ask couples what attracted them to each other as they were getting to know each other, the response may well be that they were having so much fun together, that it felt like they were hanging out with their best friend.

Early on in relationships, as partners prioritize doing fun, exciting things together, friendship comes easy. But marriage is not always synonymous with fun and friendship, particularly as the years go on. Negotiating about money, kids, and other stress-inducing family issues doesn't always bring out the friendliest disposition in you and your partner. In the heat of an argument, your partner can feel like your enemy, or at least nothing close to your best friend. Sometimes we even stoop so low as to use our partner's vulnerabilities against them, insulting them about some insecurity they shared during a moment of closeness.

It's hard to imagine why we would treat the person we love most in the world as poorly as we sometimes do. In fact, research shows we will often treat strangers more positively than the people closest to us. Keep in mind the relationship mathematics discussed previously: one zinger that is hurled in anger can erase five or ten positives. Enhancing and protecting—or, if need be, restoring—fun and friendship goes a long way in keeping love alive.

There are many reasons couples drift apart. Sometimes insensitive comments will build up over time and create walls. Sometimes the automatic routines that characterize modern domestic life make things feel boring and predictable, and the joy of being together erodes. Sometimes spouses can begin to feel more like roommates or co-managers rather than lovers.

Doing things that friends do with your partner can all too easily become your last priority, but it's not inevitable. In this chapter we'll offer you the perfect antidote to these unfortunate tendencies. We'll show you how you can *decide, not slide*, to carve out time for fun and friendship and protect that time from conflict and stress.

FUN IS RELATIONSHIP FUEL

When was the last time you and your spouse went out together and had some fun? For too many couples, the answer is "way too long ago." Fun plays a vital role in the health of a relationship, yet many couples put having fun together on the back burner of their relationship priorities.

Having fun is a kind of skill—an easy one to master, but a skill nonetheless. When you're young and relatively free of responsibility, you don't have to think a lot about having fun; it's simply what you do, a naturally built-in part of life. But as time goes on, and there is competition for your time, it becomes more like a skill—or it needs skill to be kept strong.

How to Have Fun (Again)

Fun takes planning and a willingness to say yes. If it's been years since you regularly had fun, it's going to take some mental adjustment to fully embrace it. You may have to train yourself to relax. That's OK and to be expected.

If you are raising children, you might find lots of things you do with them as being fun—but it's still *family* fun. For purposes of keeping your connection strong as a couple, we want to focus on things the two of you can do together that are fun for both of you. Things you do that tend to relax you both, together. This could be almost anything, no matter how trivial it might seem. Even shopping for a new couch can be fun if you're in the right mind-set and you enjoy each other's company. One couple told us that walking down the center aisle of Home Depot holding hands was a lot of fun for them. It's not everyone's cup of tea, but it was theirs. More power to them.

Laughter Is the Best Medicine

"Humor is just another defense against the universe," said Mel Brooks in a 2018 interview with *The Atlantic*. It may also be a defense against an unhappy marriage. Recent research suggests that partners who laugh at the same kinds of jokes may be more likely to stay together. In a 2016 article, researchers found that "there is significant positive association between the humor styles of married partners." A paper by Jeffrey Hall published a year later came to a similar conclusion. In an interview published by his university (the University of Kansas), Hall explained, "People say they want a sense of humor in a mate, but that's a broad concept . . . That people think you are funny or you can make a joke out of anything is not strongly related to relationship satisfaction. What is strongly related to relationship satisfaction is the humor that couples create together."

This makes intuitive sense. If you think about your closest friends, the ones you can talk to about anything, chances are you laugh at the same kinds of stuff. Humor fosters intimacy,

(continued)

which fosters friendship, and so on in a virtuous cycle. Few feelings are as deeply comforting as the feeling that someone else "gets you."

What's one way to start laughing together? You guessed it: having fun! So, if you and your partner are feeling a little laugh-deprived, it may be time to plan a trip to the comedy club or watch a stand-up special on TV. Have you ever watched a YouTube video of a baby belly laughing? We dare you not to laugh, too.

Tips for Having Fun

Let's take a moment to clarify what we mean by *fun*. Fun might be best defined as any activity in which the primary goal is for the two of you to enjoy each other's company, temporarily free from responsibilities of life. Here are some pointers that can keep you on the fun track.

Keep It Low Stakes and Low Stress

Nothing risks derailing a fun time out like overly complicated plans. The bigger the expectations, the bigger the chance things don't turn out as planned . . . and that you'll be left scrambling to make last-minute arrangements, a well-known source of stress and a common killer of fun. If you are working on increasing fun keep things simple. A dinner out at an unpretentious restaurant close to home is a better bet than trying to get a reservation at a trendy hotspot across town. Old and reliable is a good rule of thumb. The less pressure you and your partner put on yourselves, the more space you'll have to simply enjoy each other's company, not stress about things that could go wrong.

Once you get more confident in your ability to schedule fun, and your tolerance for complications gets a bit higher, you can consider activities that have more moving parts. But until then, beware of adding unneeded stress. It's best to have a list (written or not) of big and small things that work for both of you.

Separate Fun from Kids and Other Family Members

The point of fun is to help you and your partner reconnect in an enjoyable and low-pressure environment. Although kids are often enjoyable, they are rarely low pressure. Accordingly, you should plan your fun excursions away from kids and any other people in your life who might inhibit either of you from being at your most relaxed. Depending on your family dynamics, this may or may not include certain family members.

The same goes for friends you have as a couple. Doing a fun activity with another couple or several other couples can be a great idea. But if either of you have issues with someone in the group, it can negatively affect you or your partner's level of relaxation, a crucial ingredient of fun. It's hard to have or be fun when you're guarded or on edge.

Try Adding Some Excitement from Time to Time

Alicia and Joel were on the brink of divorce. In fact, Joel was planning to file without telling Alicia the week after they went to see coauthor Howard as part of a last-ditch effort to save their relationship. At the end of the session, Howard asked each of them to tell each other the scariest thing they could do together during the following week. Joel said riding a rollercoaster and Alicia said skydiving.

Howard instructed them to go ride the rickety old wooden roller coaster at a local amusement park and put aside all thoughts of divorce at least for that week. The scary ride, combined with Howard's advice that they focus on positive connections, worked. They decided to continue working on their relationship in and out of couples therapy. Joel never filed his papers.

There is evidence that engaging in activities that are novel and exciting—maybe even a little dare-devilish—can sometimes cause a type of spillover of energy into other types of emotions that are positive. The specifics of how this phenomenon works are a subject of debate in the psychology field. Some believe that when partners experience shared emotional excitement—especially if it has not happened in a long time—it can help rekindle a fading connection. Additionally, their willingness to try new things implies a level of each partner's dedication to one other. For Alicia and Joel, the roller coaster experience at the amusement park was a lot more fun than the one that had made up their marriage as of late.

Fortunately, you don't have to be on the brink of breaking up to shake things up a little.

Create a Fun Deck

1. Brainstorm a list of fun things. Be creative. Anything goes, so have fun coming up with ideas.

2. Write these ideas out on three-by-five cards to make your fun deck. It'll come in handy when you don't have much time to decide what to do but are ready for some fun.

3. Set aside time. Pick from the deck three things you'd enjoy doing. Hand these three cards to your partner. Each of you should take responsibility for making one of your partner's choices happen in the time you've set aside.

As you continue to use your fun deck over time, you can organize activities by time and amount of money the activity costs. What can you do for an evening date that is free? (*Possible answers: taking a walk, playing a board game, and having sex.*) What can you do for two hours during the day that costs under $30? (*How about seeing a movie?*) Making the fun deck a regular part of your relationship is a great way to bring some excitement into your dating life and relationship.

Go for it and, of course, have fun!

FRIENDSHIP: THE HEART
OF EMOTIONAL INTIMACY

There's nothing like a true friend. This isn't just a figure of speech. People who have at least one really good friend do better in almost every area of life, especially in their physical and mental health. Research consistently shows that the support, care, and acceptance friends provide buffer us from the trials and tribulations of life.

Despite the importance of having close friends, there are a lot of reasons to believe that friendship is on the decline in the United States. In 2021, a large study on friendship conducted by the Survey Center on American Life announced that 12 percent of Americans say they have no close friends. The figure was even worse among single men, inching up to one in five. Obviously, there is a lot of complexity underlying such statistics, which overlap with national discussions on things like the epidemic of "deaths of despair" (deaths from suicide, drug overdoses, or alcoholism).

What's our point? There is a dramatic decline in social participation and connection with others, a bitter irony given our supposedly highly connected, "always-on" world. Paul Amato and colleagues have shown much the same to be true when it comes to couples. Many seem to be becoming more isolated, as a couple, from society at large. Fewer are going out and participating in community groups or hanging out with friends. Friends circles are getting smaller. You can see, then, why the absence of *friendship* in a marriage or long-term partnership can potentially be detrimental to your health and well-being.

Great Expectations

In 1945, family scholars Burgess and Locke wrote *The Family: From Institution to Companionship*. Even though it was in a relative state of infancy compared to now, they saw the trend away from thinking of marriage and family in merely an institutional sense and toward expectations of companionship. This companionate view of marriage grew over time in wealthy economies toward viewing friendship as a core feature of good marriages. This trend gained an even fuller expression as the soul-mate ideology gripped the imagination of modern marriage. One's spouse was no longer expected to merely be a good life partner, but, in the more extreme versions of this view, the most perfectly matched best friend and lover.

That took things a little too far. Although Eli Finkel, in his book *The All-or-Nothing Marriage: How the Best Marriages Work*, noted that such super marriages may have become more possible than in eras past, he suggests that this expectation comes at the expense of leaving a lot of other couples less happy than they could be. The standard is high and not a great ideal to shoot for if you want lasting love. We believe that a lot of couples can have a great friendship at the core of their relationship without having unrealistic expectations about what that means. In fact, it's more possible if the expectations are reasonable. What's reasonable? You'll have to decide for yourself, but we'd argue it's reasonable to expect connection and emotional support, that you are both safe to connect as two imperfect, accepting friends in life.

So, how do you do that?

Like Old Friends, Just Different

One of the major mental obstacles to being friends while married is that it so often looks different over the course of a lifetime. When people are dating, engaged, or early in marriage, they are often in a younger and more carefree stage of life. It seems that couples either have more time earlier on, or they are better at *making* more time earlier on, largely because they are in the throes of romantic love. Couples who are falling in love seem to pay more attention to building and nurturing their friendship, whether it's through going out to dinner, hanging out with friends, traveling, walking and talking, or just watching a movie at home. What matters is simply enjoying being together.

During this phase of a relationship, it's natural to talk about the kinds of things friends talk about: movies and music, sports, religious matters, politics, life philosophies, current events, hobbies, quirks, the future, self-doubts, insecurities, that person you find odd at work, and thoughts about what each is going through at this point in life. It seems natural to want to learn everything there is to know about a new partner, and to dig even deeper as time goes on. And it generally feels safe to go to these places with each other.

And then, life starts to get in the way. The fervency of the desire to know all about what your partner is thinking and feeling wanes a bit as some of the newness wears off and other priorities apply pressure. This is perfectly normal, but waning needs waxing or else there will be a growing loss of connection.

Over time, your friendship will likely require the two of you to dig a little deeper to find activities that you both enjoy and can still do together. Sometimes, doing some new things can help create the opportunity to experience part of each other you have not yet found, or you thought was lost. Sometimes, you just have to do a better job keeping at doing the things that always worked well to bring you two together.

How to Talk Like a Friend

Here are some tried-and-true tips that can help you protect and enhance your friendship.

Don't Try to Solve Problems

Most of the time, when you are with a friend, you don't have to solve a problem. You may have a limited amount of time together, but there's no pressure to get something done. If you had a friend with whom most of your discussions were about problems between the two of you, how long do you suppose that friendship would last? Not long. That's why it's so important not to talk about matters of contention between the two of you when you're in friendship mode. Make those things off limits during time you've set aside to be together as friends.

Share Good News

When you receive a nice compliment at work, accomplish a personal goal, or execute a new recipe that turns out just right, you often feel compelled to call a friend and share the good news. (Or maybe the recipe turned out completely wrong—sounds like something to joke about with a friend!) That kind of friendship talk, when you just share the news of your life, is enriching. And when the talk is mutually engaging, you feel just as good whether sharing or listening to what your friend has to say.

Listen Like a Friend

Good friends relax, talk, and listen. Sometimes they even have arguments about things where nothing is at stake between them; it's all part of just being friends and enjoying the banter. You don't have to worry about feelings getting hurt or whether your friend will be offended by something you say, because relationship issues won't be at play.

As our friend and colleague Bill Coffin once observed, "A friend is someone whose face lights up when they see you and they don't have any immediate plans for your improvement." When you're talking as friends, you aren't trying to change one another. You can both relax and just enjoy being together. Even when you let your hair down and talk about something really serious, you don't want a friend to tell you what to do as much as you want them to listen to your heart. That's something you can give to each other.

When you're talking as friends, you aren't trying to change one another. You can both relax and just enjoy being together.

Offer Emotional Support

Talking to friends gives you an outlet that no other kind of talk provides. You can talk about your feelings, ideas, dreams, hopes, and goals, without fear of contradiction or conflict. You know your friend will listen, help you figure out how to reach your goals, and help you to the best of their abilities. When your partner can be that kind of friend, your relationship is all the stronger. If your partner shares something of a feeling, tune into that and show that you heard it. We all need a person in our lives who knows our story.

Outside Friends

This chapter makes a strong case for the importance of maintaining a deep friendship with your partner. But related to that is the importance of being there for friends outside your relationship, and for them to be there for you.

These goals shouldn't be seen as contradictory. Having close friends is strongly correlated with many positive life outcomes, including increased life expectancy. The opposite is also true: the Centers for Disease Control (CDC) says social isolation and loneliness increase someone's risk for a laundry list of negative outcomes, including heart disease and stroke, type-2 diabetes, depression and anxiety, addiction, suicidality and self-harm, dementia, and earlier death. The health agency estimates the cost of loneliness to the US economy to be about $406 *billion* per year!

This isn't just because friends can offer a sympathetic ear when you're in the midst of a conflict with your spouse. The evidence is rock-solid that having close friends is good for your well-being, full stop. So, whether you work through an issue you're having with your wife or compare thoughts on

(continued)

recent movie releases, when you cultivate friendship, you are strengthening yourself—and, by extension, your relationship.

We're not suggesting you say yes to every social obligation or request you get to hang out. That's obviously a recipe for burnout and relationship stress. You don't even have to say yes to most of them! But consider that friendship outside of your primary relationship needn't be an all-or-nothing proposition. Sometimes a ten-minute call checking in after a surgery or an email congratulating someone for starting a new job or having a kid is enough to keep a relationship going.

PRIORITIZING AND PROTECTING FUN AND FRIENDSHIP

We do not know exactly what works for the two of you for keeping a strong connection. We do know the most important strategies for making it possible for you to build it and keep it. The general principles apply equally to both fun and friendship.

Make the Time

To keep fun and friendship alive you need make the time to have fun together and to talk as friends. When it comes to having fun, some partners find it useful to schedule fun activities with their spouse and make these times non-negotiable. Remember, it's important to *decide, not slide*, because if the two of you are not committing to preserving time for fun and being together as friends, something else will choose how you spend your time.

Some couples may object that "scheduling fun" removes the possibility of spontaneity or serendipity, or that it risks making the relationship feel too stilted. In our experience, this objection just isn't warranted. For one, when you're a busy couple with kids (or even without them), moments of serendipity are few and far between! In fact, these moments are far more likely to arise during dedicated time together, even if you (gasp!) have to schedule it. How many things are there that are of great importance in your life where you don't schedule or build in time for it? We bet not many.

Marisa and Jared were eight years and two children into married life, and both were feeling increasingly disconnected from each other. There was always so much stuff that just had to be done. Their time to be together doing something fun or just relaxing had disappeared. This was no decision; it was just something they slid into. They otherwise were doing well as a couple and managed life as a team. But something was missing. So one evening after dinner, Jared spoke up.

JARED: You know, we don't go out and do anything much anymore, just the two of us. I miss that.

MARISA (SHRUGGING): I know. I want to do stuff. But it's hard now. The kids take up every second.

JARED: I know it's hard. That's why we never do it! But I think we should at least make an effort. This kind of time together isn't just going to appear. We're going to have to plan.

MARISA: You mean like a date night?

JARED: Maybe, sure. It could also be a little less formal. We could go out or stay in. I'm down with almost anything. We just have to make it happen. Like we do with everything else that matters to us.

MARISA: You're right. Pick some possible dates and let me check. I'll work on looking for a babysitter.

JARED: Yes. Let's do this.

That's an example of an exceptionally clear-thinking, easygoing, get-it-done couple starting to make a plan to make fun and friend time happen. We're not going to suggest that it's always that easy. But note the elements at work. Someone, either one, had to bring it up. And, hopefully, picked a good moment to raise the idea.

The message was totally positive and stressed its importance, and it didn't place blame on one partner (though it—reasonably—mentioned the circumstance, that is, that having two kids ate up a lot of time). They were communicating well and enthusiastic. And they started to make a plan. Will their plan be perfect and free from setbacks? No. But they made a decision to turn a corner. That's how this kind of change starts.

But that's not all you need to do to protect your friendship. You also need to talk like friends, even if it feels awkward or unnatural at first.

Sacred Date Night

Many couples have instituted a ritual into their weekly schedule called Date Night. Some have even commented that it has saved their marriage. One of the biggest pitfalls couples fall into is putting their relationship on the back burner with the belief that being together during routine family time will sustain the romance between them. Or, they believe that the children's needs should always come before their own.

We believe that a child's well-being is directly related to the health of the parents' relationship, which should always be on the front burner if their marriage is to remain strong. It's actually a source of security for children to know that their parents' relationship is a priority and not something they need to worry about. This is why we suggest making this time for yourselves—a time that is regular, set apart, and dependable throughout your lives together.

So go ahead: dress up for that date and find a sweet place where you can focus on—even flirt with—each other and remind yourselves how special you are.

Protect the Time from Conflict

One of the core philosophies of this book is that couples should control the times and conditions under which they deal with difficult and conflictual issues in their relationship. The strategies for handling conflict that we presented in the first part of the book are powerful tools, but the two of you didn't marry each other with the goal of being great at handling conflict.

You do have to handle conflict well, though, if you want to protect the more wonderful aspects of intimacy and connection in your marriage. That means setting time aside to deal with issues as issues. In fact, try not to work on problems (or argue about them) except at times you've agreed to deliberately attend to them. But do make those deliberate, focused, issue times happen because that takes the pressure off relaxing in so much of the other time you have together.

When problems intrude on fun and friendship time, use Time Out and come back to that issue later. This is one of the most powerful ways to make it safe to connect, giving you space to nurture the trust, safety, and acceptance that friendship thrives on.

You might be surprised how effective it can be for the two of you to agree that there are times together defined as "fun and friendship time" and that are off-limits for conflicts and issues. For example, you could decide that whenever you take a walk in your neighborhood, it's automatically fun time. Or you could go out to dinner and agree that "this is fun time tonight, OK?"

Some couples benefit by agreeing to try to make friendship their default. In other words, unless they both have decided it's time to work on an issue or problem, they are trying their best to stay in relaxed-around-you mode. By keeping issues in their place, you create room for the deepening of friendship and enhancement of fun between the two of you.

Just because you're not on a dedicated friendship outing doesn't mean you can't treat your partner as your friend during a regular day. This is true no matter how busy you both are. This could mean emailing news articles or texting jokes during the workday, listening to podcasts or music while you make dinner together, and so on. Although there's no substitute for dedicated blocks of fun and friend time, consistently sharing jokes or articles and the like is an easy, high-value way to reinforce your friendship bonds. Your partner will appreciate the effort—even if the jokes stink.

We can't think of anything more important for the long-term health of your marriage than for you to stay friends and share in fun experiences. Even if you start feeling distant, remember that your best friend is still in there, and it may take a little thought and effort to reconnect with them.

Talking Points

1. Friendship is at the core of long-lasting, happy marriages.

2. Enhancing friendship in your marriage is an investment that will pay off over time in relationship satisfaction.

3. Having fun comes naturally to everyone in childhood, but you may need to treat having fun as a skill to be practiced in the context of your busy, adult lifestyle.

4. Setting aside dedicated times to be friends and to have fun, and then protecting those times from conflict, can help a relationship grow closer.

5. Talking to your outside friends gives you an outlet that no other kind of talk provides. If you can be a good friend outside your relationship, chances are you'll be a great one inside it.

Suggested Activities

It's now time for some friendship and fun!

Friendship Talks

The idea behind friendship time is to have quiet, uninterrupted periods to just be together and talk as friends. You probably have lots of ideas for what to talk about during these special moments, but you can also use the following suggestions to help kickstart the process. Just remember to avoid all conflict issues and problem-solving. If something in the conversation triggers an issue, let it bounce off you or call a Time Out. Do your part to protect and preserve your time for positive connections.

- Talk about something you are excited about right now. This might be a book you are reading, a TV show you saw, a new restaurant in your neighborhood, or an idea you have.
- Talk about an event or something important from your childhood. You can reveal something about your family, schooling, friends—whatever jumps to mind. You can even retell a story but from a different perspective or with new insights.
- Discuss a current goal or something you've always dreamed of doing.

Fun Deck

Create your fun deck and go out and try some new fun things to do together. Add to your fun deck over time. Enjoy!

11

Being There
Supporting One Another in Life

When your partner is upset about something going on in their life, how do you handle it? How do you provide the support that your partner needs at these important times? Alternatively, when *you* are distressed, upset, or concerned about something going on in your life, how does your partner react?

These are the key questions we'll explore in this chapter. Along the way, we'll explain how the two of you can be there for each other whenever the challenges of life confront either of you. Our focus isn't on financial support but on emotional reinforcement and connection: how you react when your partner is upset or worried or stressed (and the issue isn't related to a conflict between the two of you). In our view, being able to productively give and receive support is such a critical part of healthy relationships it deserves its own chapter.

In Chapter Ten we talked about the importance of friendship in your relationship, and why it's essential that you regularly set aside time to talk and act as friends. Whether you're talking as friends or engaging in support talk, the same rule applies: it's important not to slide into talking about relationship problems. As you probably know from experience, when you're in the middle of conflict, you and your partner are much less likely to be as emotionally supportive of each other as you could be (to put it mildly!).

One critical research finding is that *believing support is available to you* is even more important than the support you actually use. For example, many of us have a good friend we talk, text, or email with only occasionally, but who we know is there for us 24/7. When we're going through a rough time, just knowing they are available is often enough to help us feel better. Ideally, you feel the same way about your partner.

WHAT UPSETS OR WORRIES YOU?

Unless you have been living an unusually charmed life, you and your partner have probably both experienced your fair share of stress, crises, illness, and other upsetting life events. Some were big and some were small, but no matter what, there were undoubtedly times when you were unable to be happily carefree. Such is life, to invoke an old but useful cliché.

Think about the things that you know your partner is concerned about right now—things that are on their mind that are causing worry, stress, or concern. Now consider the upsetting or troubling things that are on your mind. It they affect you enough, they may become what researchers call *stressful life events*. These include major happenings such as losing a job, having a child, the death of a relative, and so on. (Yes, even happy events like having a child or moving to a better job can be extremely stressful!)

Other common stressful life events and situations include the following:

- Concerns about a child (dealing with an illness, finding affordable child care, etc.)
- Job loss, problems at work
- Medical issues
- Conflicts with family and friends
- Financial worries

- Aging parents
- Politics or current events
- Losing something you care about

TYPES OF SUPPORT

Support is a many-splendored thing, and there are a variety of ways that you and your partner can support each other, which brings us to one of the most important points of this chapter: *what works best for one person is not necessarily what works best for another.* Sound familiar? Offering support is just like expressing love. Like most people, when you want to be helpful, your instinct is to offer the type of support that works best for you. But it's so important to learn what kind of support your partner prefers (or needs) and give that to them.

The hard truth is that even though you may be trying your best to be supportive, your partner may not sense it. In fact, difficult situations can sometimes become worse if your partner feels like you're not there for them when they want you to be; the same obviously applies when you're the one in distress. To that end, when you are stressed and in need of support, try to notice when and how your partner provides it, even when it's not what you might want or need. By paying closer attention, you can offer them more specific, constructive feedback once things cool down.

We want you each to learn how to give more support to each other—the right kind of support at the right time in the right way. It will also help, however, to recognize and be thankful for what your partner tries to do for you, an admittedly challenging task when you are stressed and anxious, but a worthy goal nonetheless.

What follows is a breakdown of six proven types of support. Whereas most support studies focus on support from all types of people in someone's life, here we draw from studies focusing on support among relationship partners. As you read the next sections, think about what your partner needs and what you give, and what you need and what your partner gives.

Being There

Being there for someone means being physically available, whether in person or by phone, text message, or email. Being there implies a sense of commitment, in that you and your partner are demonstrating that you can count on each other for the long term. It is one of the highest forms of doing your part. As many have said, "Showing up is 80 percent of life." Although it may suggest being there in a particular moment, it also means being present in a series of moments over time. Taken together, they will eventually blossom into a lifetime of support and love.

Here are some ways to be there for your partner:

- Saying things like "I am here for you"—and meaning it
- Just being there physically (not talking is fine)
- Telling your partner they can call, text, or email you any time, and responding if they do (with the understanding that you shouldn't be expected to immediately!)
- Holding and hugging your partner when they are hurt or worried
- Keeping your promises and commitments (i.e., "showing up")
- Leaving them notes

Doing Things

In the strongest marriages, partners provide support for each other and their marriage by *doing* things. For some people, this primarily takes the form of earning income to support their partner and family. Don't get us wrong: this is plenty important. However, this kind of support isn't our focus here. We are more interested in exploring concrete ways people can do things for their partner, lightening their load when they are struggling.

Here are some examples of specific tasks that one partner can do to support the other when challenging times arise:

- Doing more housework
- Picking up the kids
- Making dinner (or planning a delivery order)
- Doing the grocery shopping
- Assessing the chores your partner usually does during the day, and taking on one of those tasks

Offering Encouragement

In "Take Me out to the Ball Game," the classic baseball song sung during the bottom of the seventh inning, one of the rousing lines is "Root, root, root for the home team." This is excellent advice in relationships just as much as sports. By *offering encouragement*, we mean rooting for your own home team: your partner and your relationship.

For example, when your partner is getting ready for an important job interview or presentation, you can say, "You can do it" and "I have faith in you." This is rooting for your partner. When things are tough between the two of you, you can say, "We will get through this; we are a great team; we can do it." This is rooting for your relationship.

Here are some ways to encourage your partner:

- Sending an e-mail, text, or note saying something like:

  "You can do it."

  "Things will be fine."

  "We can work it out."

  "Keep it up!"

"You're the best."

"I believe in you."

- Cheering them on (or just being there) during important family or professional events

A close cousin to encouragement is appreciation, and it's no less important. In Chapter Eight we introduced you to the XYZ statements, and they are a great way to express your appreciation for the great things your partner does. We strongly encourage you to use them frequently to show your appreciation. Here are some examples of what this could look like:

- "When I came home and you gave me a hug, I felt loved."
- "When I read that article you sent me this afternoon, I really appreciated you thinking of me."
- "When I saw you working with Karla on her homework earlier tonight, I felt so appreciative of what a great mother you are."

Giving

Another common way partners provide support is through giving gifts of one sort or another. Giving flowers or candy on Valentine's Day is a classic example. This can be a nice gesture. But the problem is that some partners wind up giving gifts instead of *giving themselves* in ways that are meaningful to their spouse. Instead of making time to be friends, or doing housework, or showing up to important family events, they give a gift or provide material comforts. For most people, though, material things can never take the place of a partner truly being there to support them.

To support your partner and your relationship, you can give the following:

- Your time—which is also part of being there
- Your undivided attention

- Small tokens of love (such as gifts)
- Advice or opinions (though these are best given only when asked for)

Talking and Listening

Some experts suggest that emotional support is the most important form of support in terms of the benefits received, and that talking and touching (which we discuss in the next section) are the two most important forms of emotional support. To better understand why talking is so essential, let's look at the example of Molly and Cathy.

Cathy feels unsupported by Molly, but from Molly's point of view, she's doing all she can for the family by working over sixty hours a week just to stay on top of their bills. Cathy also works, though not for as many hours, and she does most of the housework. Both feel exhausted and like they cannot do another thing.

Is this true? Probably not. Even if Molly is tired, she can still make a good-faith effort to be supportive in ways that don't involve being the breadwinner. Although Cathy may well wish that Molly takes responsibility for more of the chores around the house, what would have the greatest impact on Cathy would be for Molly to take some basic steps to give her more emotional support in life.

Eventually Molly was brave enough to ask Cathy what she could do to help her feel more supported in the things that weigh her down. Cathy responded that it would be great if Molly could call or text her from time to time during the day and ask her how her day was going. This would help her know that Molly was thinking of her and that she cared. She also explained to Molly that, very often, all she wanted was for Molly to listen to her talk about what was on her mind, especially when she was upset or anxious about something.

Being available to talk and listen is such a powerful way to show support and, ultimately, bring you and your partner even closer together. With that in mind, here are some ways to talk (and listen) supportively:

- If your partner asks to talk, make the time. Schedule it if you have to, like you would any other essential task.
- If your partner seems upset but does not say anything or indicate that they would like to talk, nicely say something like "It seems to me you're upset; would you like to talk?" Avoid saying, "You're upset—what's wrong?" In other words, offer the opportunity to talk safely, rather than pushing your partner to talk. (The exception would be if your partner is experiencing high levels of psychological distress or is being harmful to themself or others. At that point, pushing the other to talk is likely needed, as well as seeking outside professional help—see "Getting More Help" at the end of the book.)
- Focus on your partner.
- Pay attention; do not multitask.
- Let your partner know you are listening, especially if you are not face to face, by saying things like "Uh-huh" or "Okay."
- Do not interrupt.
- Make sure your partner feels understood.

We really can't overemphasize the importance of listening. Remember that giving advice, especially when it's offered to be supportive, is one of the most common causes of relationship conflict. Have you ever given your partner what you thought was sage advice, just to have it all backfire? If you have, you know exactly what we're talking about. Most of us have great advice to give—or so we think. However, when your partner is looking for another form of support (or none at all), advice giving can come across more negatively than you intend. Wanting to give solutions as a form of support is similar to wanting to solve relationship problems quickly—an effort that, as we talked about previously in this book, is often doomed to fail.

A Partner Nudge

Sometimes, when we are stressed, we get stuck and have trouble coping well in the moment. We are not talking situations in which either of you are stressed because of the other or because of a relationship problem. The skill we describe here is for situations when one of you is stressing out or anxious about a personal matter or challenge (e.g., something at work or an issue with a friend) and is stuck in an unproductive strategy to cope in that moment.

The partner nudge is a way for the supporting partner to help their loved one move from an unproductive strategy to a productive one. It's a form of support timed just right for the moment. It is a team-based strategy that you need to work on together. It only works when both of you have developed acceptance for being able to help each other in this way.

This skill comes from the work of our colleague, Sarah Carter, and the creative team at PREP, Inc.

Here are the ingredients for a successful nudge.

The nudge giver has to notice what is happening, notify their partner in a calm manner about what they are seeing, and suggest an alternative to the unproductive strategy their partner is stuck in. A nudge is not a push, a criticism, nor is it advice. It is just a suggestion—and invitation to move to be better strategy, with an offer to help make that happen if fitting.

The receiver of the nudge has to recognize that their partner is attempting to help them get to a more effective strategy. They need to try to gain perspective in the moment by considering what their partner is noticing. Then, the receiver needs to be prepared to try to pivot to a better coping strategy.

Two quick examples will highlight the potential power of this skill.

(continued)

Gina notices that Paul is pacing and upset about changes coming up at work. He's obsessing and stuck in the anxiety he is feeling. Gina says, "Hey, I can see you are really upset. Want to go for a walk with me?" He accepts this idea and gets how it's much better than pacing and obsessing to himself. She cares and he knows it.

Ashley has been struggling with a nagging health problem that her doctor cannot seem to pinpoint the cause of. Zach notices that she's distracted and seems stuck in her worries. Zach says, "Hon, I can see you're biting your lip and you seem a million miles away. Are you worried about your next appointment? There's nothing we can do about it tonight, but would it help for us to do something to shift your focus off of that to something you enjoy? I'm happy to help any way I can." Ashley says, "I know you are right. I'm just sitting here shriveling up with my thoughts. Maybe it would help me relax a little if we played cards."

This skill can take many forms and be a powerful way to leverage your care for each other. It works best if you have both talked about it and that you are each trying to work out how best to do this.

Touching

From the Beatles to Diana Ross to Lady Gaga, over the years countless pop stars have sung about the glories of holding hands. The reason is obvious: holding hands is one of the most powerful but simple ways to be supportive and loving.

This loving act often comes naturally, but at times, in even the best of relationships, partners have to remind themselves to reach out and touch their loved ones in physical ways when they are upset, whether it's by holding hands, hugging, or something else. When your relationship is not going well, touching may feel particularly awkward—but arguably it's even more important at those times. In a set of classic studies many years ago, Harry Harlow and his colleagues at the University of Wisconsin demonstrated the importance of touch to living and thriving. These researchers showed that without touch, monkeys developed serious problems and in some cases even died. Everyone recognized that what was true for Harlow's monkeys was especially true for humans. We need to be connected, and one of the most fundamental ways to know that we are is to touch and be touched. Touch is vital for our personal survival as well as for our relationships.

As you are probably aware, there is chemistry behind almost everything you feel. It is now widely understood that the chemical oxytocin is fundamental to feelings of attachment. It's a chemical famous for flooding a woman's body at the time of birth, which helps in both managing stress and boosting rapid attachment between mother and child. Although women have more oxytocin than men and may be more affected by it, men have it, too. Physical contact, including and especially sex, causes a lot of oxytocin to be released in the bodies of both women and men. People also call oxytocin the cuddle hormone. Holding hands, hugging, sitting close together—really simple stuff—can make a big difference in your sense of connection and your bodies' abilities to fight stress. When times are tough, the tough get hugging.

When times are tough, the tough get hugging.

Here are some ways to touch supportively:

- Give a hug.
- Hold hands.
- Give a gentle massage.
- Sit next to each other.
- Have your partner lean on you.

- Have your partner rest his or her head on your shoulder.
- Cuddle on the couch.

ENHANCING SUPPORT

Partners must make support a priority if they want to nurture a relationship that is safe and secure. Remember, however, that support starts with you. *You* have the power to ask what your partner wants or needs. You have the power to be there, to encourage, to listen, to help, to touch, and to give. You have the power to shift the distance between you by reaching out in any of a number of supportive ways. To paraphrase Gandhi, "Be the change you want to see in your relationship." Some tips for helping you do this are offered next.

Will you decide to use your power for good? (We hope that you will!)

Make the Time for Being Supportive

If you know your partner is going through a tough time, make a point of periodically checking in. This doesn't have to be complicated. It can be as simple asking how your partner is doing or if they want to talk. Even a text or email can be enough to show that you care. In other words, look for opportunities to support your partner. It might seem paradoxical, but the most effective ways of being supportive don't really take that much time. They do take thoughtfulness and action, though. Remember: a partner's perception that that they are supported is just as powerful as the support they actually receive. So if they have evidence they are supported, it goes a long way. You can do this.

Be Open to and Appreciative of Your Partner's Supportive Acts

There may be times when your partner needs support but the type you provide isn't what they want. If this happens, accept that although your intentions are good, you need a different approach, and then change course. Here's an example of what this looks like:

Liz: *(feeling upset about learning that her friend's boyfriend broke up with her)* I'm really worried about Marisol and how she's going to handle this. She really thought Will was "the one." I can see how much she's hurting.

Matt: I don't know. I think he just wasn't that into her. And honestly, I never really liked him that much. Maybe she should call Dean, from your office. I think they'd be a good fit. *(a form of giving advice)*

Liz: I know you're trying to be supportive, but I'm very concerned about Marisol and just want to talk to you. Can you just listen to me now?

Matt: Oh. OK, so what happened with Marisol and Will?

Protect Your Time from Conflict

It's very important not to slide into talking about relationship problems when a situation calls for support. When one of you needs support, the last thing that you want as a couple is to have conflict drive you apart. A little awareness and discipline can help you be protective of those times, because when one of you is stirred up about something it's too easy for some event to trigger an issue. This may be particularly true when both of you feel the need for support at the same time and perceive the other to be unavailable or self-absorbed. If a problem comes up during a support-related conversation or interaction, decide to Pause and talk about it safely, call a Time Out and talk about the issue later, or let the event bounce off you. Then make the decision to continue moving closer, doing what you can to support your partner.

Make every effort to make your supportive interactions count, and do not let the times you feel that your partner does not come through for you overwhelm the times they do. As always, try to fight the power of the negatives: the tendency for the negatives to count more than the positives in your relationship. Make sure you regularly show appreciation for your partner's supportive acts.

If you can do much of what we recommend in this chapter, your partner should never have to worry about you being there.

Talking Points

1. One of the greatest gifts you can give to each other in life is to be there for each other when times are challenging. Providing support to one another in ways that are effective and meaningful can make all the difference during a difficult time or when under stress.

2. Friendship talk revolves around the things you and your partner are excited about; support talk is what you give to your partner when they are upset.

3. There are six types of support: being there, doing things, offering encouragement, giving (the right things), talking and listening, and touching.

4. The support you typically give may not be the support your partner needs (and vice versa).

Suggested Activities

As you tackle these activities, think about times when you want some help or support from someone in your life.

What Type(s) of Support Do You Want?

Take out a piece of paper and write down each type of support. Then rate on a scale of 0 to10 (with 0 being never and 10 being all the time) how often you typically need or desire each type of support when you are upset. Then repeat the process for the types of support you typically provide when your partner is upset. Compare notes.

Next, write down your answers to the following questions and then share them with your partner:

- How do you let each other know you need support?
- What kinds of touch help, if any (hugging, holding hands, massage)?
- How do you let each other know that you need the other person just to listen?
- How can you tell when your partner is supporting you?

Practicing Support Talk

Have one of you pick a topic that you are concerned or upset about and that doesn't have to do with your relationship (so talking about being upset with your partner does not work here). Some examples: worries that your mom is losing her memory, concerns about the environment, concerns about a decision the city council made, concerns about an issue at work, and so on. This person talks, and the other listens.

This is not a relationship talk, though you might start talking about a personal concern and find that it quickly becomes a relationship concern; if this happens, pause and refocus on support talk only. Nor is this friendship talk, which is meant to be about fun and lighter things. That said, like the best friendship talk, talking about concerns in a way that's genuine and helps you and your partner feel listened to and understood, is a tried-and-true way to protect, enhance, or even restore intimacy.

12

Sensuality and Sex
The Magical Art of Touch

One of the most common reasons couples give for getting a divorce is that they have grown apart and "fallen out of love." As you might guess, we strongly believe that, by and large, this is a false premise—and that many of these supposedly love-deprived divorces can be prevented if the partners are dedicated enough.

When most people say they have fallen out of love or are in the process of doing so, often they really mean that the passion has faded away. As we discuss at length in Chapter Five, we feel that too many couples mistake passion for love. Although passion is an important element of love, expecting it to remain constant throughout a long relationship is, frankly, unrealistic. Nevertheless, with some work, it can usually be restored to a level that's satisfying. Although you obviously cannot make yourself instantly fall back in love, you *can* do your part to help those loving feelings return. One of the best ways to do this is to focus on your sensual relationship. (Not that your sexual relationship doesn't matter; more on that in a bit.)

When we offer this advice, many people's response is, "I don't feel close to my partner, and I do not feel like being sensual with them." If that's your feeling, we suggest it's actually the very best time to focus on the sensual because it can open the doors to other pathways toward increased feelings of connection and love. We believe that it is important to always remember that if you are partners, you are lovers, and you must nurture all that that means. After all, if you are in an exclusive relationship, this is the only person with whom you've committed to expressing your physical connection. And as we also learned in Chapter Five, if you don't nurture romantic feelings they can easily subside or wane over time.

SENSUALITY VERSUS SEXUALITY

What comes to mind when you think about the word *sexuality?* For many, the first thoughts are of sexual intercourse, orgasms, and all the pleasurable acts that may come before and after. Anything else? Now think about *sensuality.* What comes to mind? Usually, some pleasant experience that involves touching, seeing, smelling, tasting, or feeling—such as walking on the beach or being massaged with sweet-smelling oil. How about the roughness of a beard or the silkiness of hair? The smell of your partner? Chocolate? You get the idea. These are sensual experiences that heighten your senses and make connecting to your partner enjoyable. They are typically neither goal oriented nor explicitly sexual. Rather, they reflect feelings you have about being in love and attracted to your partner.

Sensuality includes physical touch or other senses but is not always associated with making love. Our definition includes holding hands, hugging, romantic talking, affectionate cuddling, nonsexual massages, kissing—all acts that provide sensual arousal and pleasure in nonsexual ways. We are amazed at the number of married couples for whom this very important distinction between sensuality and sexuality is blurry. We would like all couples to have an understanding, if not a ground rule, that there are times when a kiss, hug, or cuddle is not a prelude to sex, but rather is the main event itself. If expectations are not mutual and clear in terms of the role of sensuality, it can easily interfere with one's willingness to engage.

We would like all couples to have an understanding, if not a ground rule, that there are times when a kiss, hug, or cuddle is not a prelude to sex, but rather is the main event itself.

In the early stages of their relationships and into their early years of marriage, many couples tend to touch quite a bit. They hold hands, hug, kiss, and so forth. Over time, however, they tend to bypass the sensual and move more exclusively to goal-oriented sexual behavior. Less time and energy is spent on the playful, intimate, casual but sensual contacts that were once so commonplace. This leads to big problems, because it's the sensual connection that keeps partners from feeling as though they are growing apart. Over time, sex itself often becomes more a matter of performance than of intimacy. For some couples, the pattern progresses to the point that they become interested in sex only for sex's sake. Once sensuality drops out of the equation, couples have no way of physically connecting unless they have sex. That starts to put a lot of pressure on the sexual relationship. How many times have you wanted to be physically close without necessarily desiring sex?

Sophie and Brandon have been married for nine years. They used to spend a lot of time just cuddling, caressing, and talking about sensual and sexual things they'd like to do with each other. As time went by, they got busier with kids, work, and home—as most of us do. After a year or two of marriage, they had settled into a pattern of having sex about twice a week. Given time pressures and other cares of life, they devoted less and less time to sensuality. At night, in bed, one or the other would initiate sex, and they'd quickly have intercourse, usually finishing in about ten minutes—less if there was something good on TV!

They had become quite efficient when it came to making love—or rather, having intercourse. They didn't have or make a lot of extra time, so they made do. In fact, they were making do rather than making love. Their focus on sexual intercourse rather than sensuality led to dissatisfaction for both. "What happened to all those times we'd lay around for hours together?" Sophie wondered. "It seems like Sophie used to be a lot more responsive when we made love," Brandon mused.

The fact is, there needs to be a place for romance *and* for sensual talking and touching in your relationship—both in and outside the context of making love. Too many couples shortchange the sensual and just focus on sex. Sex without the overall context of romance, touching, and closeness can over time actually lead to less sex. Why? Because men and women need and value the sensual side of intimacy for pleasure, attachment, and arousal. Sensual experiences set the stage for better sexual experiences. Without the pleasure sensuality provides, joy and intimacy subside and sex can begin to feel mechanical.

Sex need not always be the goal of sensuality. The expectation that intercourse always follows can often make people avoid sensual touching. In fact, it's often nice to agree not to have sex, but to just enjoy exploring each other's bodies or the feeling of physical closeness.

Jessica and Jeff have been married for twenty years and have always enjoyed an active and satisfying sex life. But lately Jessica's sex drive has begun to wane. What she really longs for is to occasionally just cuddle and touch and fall asleep in each other's arms. Rather than just rebuff Jeff after a recent advance, she decides to explain why she's tended to avoid physical intimacy lately, and what she wants instead:

JEFF: Honey, I was thinking about you all day and couldn't wait to be in bed together tonight. I love touching you.

JESSICA: That's so sweet! But I'm really not in the mood right now.

JEFF: I understand. But it seems that you're not in the mood a lot these days. Is something up?

JESSICA: It's just that sometimes I like just cuddling and falling asleep in your arms without worrying it will lead to sex.

JEFF: I didn't realize you felt that way. How about if we play around for a bit or maybe I can just give you a backrub until you doze off.

JESSICA: I would love that! I love cuddling and feeling your touch. I just don't want to give you the wrong idea.

JEFF: I don't need to always have sex either. Would it help if I sometimes said that I'm not looking to make love?

JESSICA: Yes, that would be great. Or I can say that as well. Will it hurt your feelings?

JEFF: No. I don't ever want you to feel pressured or obligated. I do hope we can become close in other ways.

JESSICA: Me, too. It feels great and I love being close to you.

The Art of Sensual and Romantic Talking

One of the best ways to enhance your sensual relationship is the one most couples rarely use: sensual and romantic talking. We mean telling your spouse how attracted you are to her, how sexy they are, how much you love and care for them (one of the best ways to directly short-circuit a hidden caring issue). You can talk about what you'd like to do together the next time you are alone, how much you enjoy their touch, how much you love touching their legs or arms, or how you can't wait to be alone and touch under the table or have a lingering, soulful kiss during which time stops. We are all starved for romance!

There are a virtually infinite number of expressions of love and affection and caring and attraction: whispers while doing the dishes, text messages, e-mail, flowers, romantic dinners, and so forth. Some research has found that sensual and romantic talk when no sexual interaction is possible actually tends to lead to better sexual connection later on. Ah, the joy of anticipation!

Even if you're not quite in the mood, it can't hurt to try a little tenderness. Saying something loving isn't "fake" per se if you know deep down that the feelings are there.

LET'S TALK ABOUT SEX

Now that we've defined and made a case for the importance of sensuality, we can move on to the next and ultimate expression of closeness: sex.

Although there is no correct or even normal amount of sex that couples *should* be having, what is important is that some aspect of sexuality remain alive in couples where at least one partner desires it. Though intimacy can certainly be expressed in many different ways, the physical expression of love is key to maintaining a healthy bond.

If you're having plenty of sex and both of you are happy, great! You probably don't need any tips. But for those who feel you're not having enough sex, or the sex you're having could be improved, here are some suggestions for getting back on track.

WHEN YOU'RE JUST NOT INTERESTED (IN SEX)

Do either of you (or both of you) have difficulty just being interested in sex? If you both have little interest, it may be that this causes no great strain on your relationship. You might decide together to have a relationship with limited sex. But if only one of you has low interest and the other has higher interest, you have a difference that can cause a lot of hurt and resentment on both sides. It's all the more difficult for couples to cope with this if the physical relationship is one of their primary ways to feel connected.

Experts say there can be any number of reasons why so many people have low sexual desire or what researchers are now calling *erotic loss*. Apart from relationship issues, the list of possible suspects may include the following:

- Depression
- Side effects of medications (including antidepressants)

- Excessive alcohol use
- Chronic illnesses of many kinds
- Hormonal changes (e.g., with pregnancy, aging)
- Stress
- Sleep problems (nothing works well when you are not sleeping enough)
- Weight gain
- Body image

Most of this list has to do with your overall health, energy, age, and life stage. If you are tired, run-down, sick, and stressed, you're not likely to feel very interested in sex (which is why new parents and parents of young children are notoriously sexless). When you are coping with financial or parenting problems, it's hard to feel that your sexual problems are a top priority. With more dual-career couples and ever-present technology to distract us and sap our energy, erotic loss is becoming more and more common.

If any of these health-related concerns may be affecting you, see a doctor and/or a therapist. Be candid about your concerns so that they know what questions to ask you and what tests to run. If your sexual desire is fine but your partner is the one having more trouble being interested, be supportive and patient in trying to find what may help. Hint: it's unlikely that pressure and anger will help very much at all.

Once you've either ruled out health concerns or begun dealing with them the best you can, work together on the things that are under your control. Consider other causes for your differences or lack of interest.

Conflict

Mishandled conflicts can damage your physical relationship by adding tension and distance both in and out of the bedroom.

Let's face it: when you've been arguing and angry with each other, you don't usually feel like being romantic or sensual, much less making love. For most people, tension isn't compatible with enjoyable, intimate lovemaking.

Some couples find that their sexual relationship is temporarily enhanced when there is conflict followed by "make-up sex," but for most, poorly handled conflict adds a layer of tension that affects everything else in the relationship. (Note that it's one thing to enjoy make-up sex after a fight, but when it is part of a cycle of aggression, you may need more help. Please see "Getting More Help" at the end of the book.)

Work to handle conflict well—for example, by using the ground rules and other techniques we've been stressing. It's critical that you agree to keep problems and disagreements off-limits when you are being sensual or making love. Protect and preserve these precious times alone when you are nourishing your relationship.

Disconnection

Feeling close is the basis for sex for most people. If you don't feel connected, if you don't feel like you're friends, or if you don't feel emotionally safe and like you can be yourself, you probably won't feel like having sex. Making love involves being able to be vulnerable and exposed with each other, and desire is enhanced when your connection is strong. If you're feeling self-protective and closed down, it's hard to open up to your partner. Likewise, if you're feeling disconnected and distant, sharing sex can seem empty.

As we discussed in Chapter Ten, having fun together and being friends are key to a great relationship. But, it takes dedication to make the time to talk as friends and to have fun together. These enjoyable times are just the things that can make you feel relaxed and free with each other. Sex is all about feeling intimately connected—emotionally, physically, and spiritually. Supporting and accepting one another, having fun and feeling free to express yourself—these are key to feeling close and having the sex life you want to have. Build your positive, close relationship by using the ideas in this book about love, fun and friendship, and support. Get support from a therapist if you've been hurt by one another in ways that have damaged your sex life or your ability to connect emotionally in the way you would want to. It's worth getting the feeling back!

Performance Anxiety

Performance anxiety is anxiety about how you're "performing" when you make love. It may be an issue if someone frequently finds themselves wondering "Can I do this today?" or "How am I doing?" or "Is my partner enjoying this?" When you become preoccupied with your performance, you create emotional distance between you and your partner. You become focused on how you're doing rather than on being with your partner in the moment or pleasure you're feeling.

Many people report feeling distant when making love, as though they're just watching what's going on instead of participating. This kind of detachment can lead to the most common sexual problems people experience—often starting with sexual boredom and then leading to premature ejaculation and problems keeping erections, for men, and difficulty lubricating or having orgasms, for women. The focus on performance interferes with arousal because you are distracted from your own sensations of pleasure and from the pleasure you're sharing. You can't be both anxious and pleasantly aroused at the same time.

This isn't to say you shouldn't care at all about your performance. Doing your part means being a responsive lover and meeting your partner's needs (within reason and mutual consent, of course!). So you should care. But if your concern is getting in the way of your or your partner's enjoyment, it may be a sign you need to talk things through or perhaps get outside help.

COMMUNICATING DESIRES

The structured techniques we have been teaching you in this book can make talking about sensuality and sexuality easier. Many books about sex are available and may also make this talk less stressful. But before you turn to them, this current section may be helpful enough.

Sometimes people can feel shy or fearful about talking with their partner about sexual issues. They worry about hurting the other's feelings or things evolving into an argument. Often, couples don't have a comfortable language to use and are embarrassed to bring the topic up. We believe that talking about your needs, be they in the bedroom or in the kitchen, be they about lovemaking or about carpooling, are all part of maintaining a healthy relationship. Negotiating your sexual preferences is part of communicating well, and hey—talking about sex can also be fun!

You Should Know What I Like!

It's a mistake to assume that your partner will like whatever you like or that you can read each other's minds. Would you go out to a restaurant and order for your partner without talking about what they wanted? Of course not.

It's also too easy for some people to assume that their partner won't like the things they actually do like. Either way, you're making assumptions. And because many couples have trouble communicating about their physical relationship, it's really easy for these assumptions to take control. You don't know what your partner's expectations are until you ask—and vice versa.

We can't tell you how many couples we've talked with where someone expected the other to know what they like most when making love. It's as if people believe that it just isn't romantic or exciting if they have to vocalize what they want in the bedroom. As if saying it makes things awkward or unsexy. Far from it. Think of what you're missing by standing on (ill-advised) principle and not saying what you'd like!

We recommend that you communicate clearly about what feels pleasurable to you—ideally, while you are touching or making love. Your partner doesn't know unless you say something. We're not suggesting that you have a Speaker Listener discussion in the middle of lovemaking. (Though if it really excites you that much, let us know how it goes!) Talk together about what is sensual for each of you. What do you enjoy? Have you tried new things? Experimented with new sexual activities? What about acting out fantasies or talking about arousing activities you've enjoyed before? What is most arousing to you in your history with your partner? Are there new things that would be arousing and enjoyable to you that you're afraid to bring up? Remember, you're both consenting adults, and the key here is to discover together what is pleasurable to you both.

Couples who have the best sexual relationships have ways of communicating both verbally and nonverbally about what they like. Additionally, they usually have a genuine desire to please one another. That desire, combined with talking openly, leads to great lovemaking, which leads to great marriages. For these couples, doing your part has never been so easy—or so much fun!

Taking a Risk

Unless you feel safe and take emotional risks by sharing your feelings with your partner, your relationship will not be all it can be. This is especially true when it comes to talking about sex, one of the hardest topics for any couple to discuss, even couples who are otherwise happy and communicative. Couples who are having great sex are able to risk rejection and express wants, needs, desires, and fantasies. Doing this is hard, because your desires say a lot about who you are, so to express them is to risk being hurt. It requires vulnerability.

One strategy for facilitating a difficult conversation about sex and avoiding the fear of rejection is to "say no in the context of yes." What we mean is that you say yes to the spirit of the request while deferring on the particulars. Consider this conversation between Maddy and Joe:

MADDY (*taking a risk*): I've been feeling like our sex life is becoming kind of predictable. I was wondering if you'd like to try some new things.

JOE: Hmmm—what do you have in mind?

MADDY: I don't know. Maybe we could try a different position tonight?

JOE (*saying no in the context of yes*): I really like that idea but I'm so tired tonight. Can we try that over the weekend when I'm more rested?

Talking is just the essential first step toward improving your physical relationship. It helps to try some new ideas to break out of ruts, just as Maddy and Joe are attempting to do. Agree to surprise each other and try something new. Think of these forays as an experiment rather than as a failure if something doesn't go well. Great sexual relationships involve keeping things new and fresh, so don't be afraid to play. What's important is keeping it safe and fun.

PRIMARY PLEASURES: MAKING YOUR SENSUAL RELATIONSHIP A PRIORITY

We have developed a simple but powerful plan for romantic success that we've found to be helpful to many couples (see the box "Your Plan for Romantic Success"). Plans such as this one are highly likely to help couples move out of ruts, as long as both partners are committed and really follow through on what they've agreed to try to do differently. We suggest you try our approach for a few weeks and see if it enriches and enhances your marriage. See what works best and customize these suggestions to fit your particular relationship. You may find that other problems and stresses seem less urgent or are more easily resolved if you feel closer to each other and more loved.

Your Plan for Romantic Success

Here's a tried-and-true plan for bringing a more vital romantic spirit back to your lovemaking. We've suggested this plan to many couples, with (we're told!) great success. We suggest you take the time to customize this list to suit your own tastes and priorities as a couple. Have as much fun as you can!

- Take care of yourself.
  - Shower.
  - Brush your teeth.
  - Work out.
  - Get enough sleep.
  - Eat well.
  - Pay attention to your appearance.
- Be a great lover.
  - When having sex, kiss and touch sensual spots that your partner enjoys—the earlobe, neck, or whatever.
  - Try something new; marital sex is the place to explore all kinds of sexual activities.
  - Do not focus on orgasms or other outcomes; pressure is not an aphrodisiac. Instead focus on the process (e.g., lovemaking).
  - Read a book or article online about how to be a great lover.
- Focus on being romantic.
  - Call in the middle of the day to say "I love you."
  - Slip a love note into your partner's jacket pocket.

(continued)

- Surprise your partner with a small gift or a special night out.
- Make a playlist of favorite songs, love songs, or songs that are meaningful to the both of you.
- Go on a picnic to watch the sunset or sunrise—in a park or your own backyard.
- Book a room at a hotel for an hour or a night.
- Send a single flower or a bouquet, for no apparent reason.
- Go for a walk in the rain or snow or fog.
- Make dinner or breakfast in bed.
- Be sensual.
  - Touch your spouse erotically during dinner.
  - Hold hands wherever you go.
  - Read poetry, love stories, or erotica together or to each other.
- Take risks.
  - Initiate lovemaking at unexpected times and places.
  - Try making love in different places—on the floor, in the backyard, in the bathtub. (Please make sure you're both comfortable!)
  - Try a new position. Buy a book or go online to find new positions you can both agree to experiment with.
- Use your imagination; be creative.
  - Leave a note on the bathroom mirror suggesting a rendezvous at a specific time and place.

- Fill ten balloons with love notes and blow up lots more; tell your partner they have to pop them all to read them.
- Make a set of love coupons: for a full-body massage, a dance in the rain, a romantic dinner for two, champagne and cuddling by the fire, a kiss anytime anywhere, and so on.
- Be sensitive to your partner's rhythms and needs and wishes.
  - Find times to make love that are good for both of you.
  - Push yourself to initiate sex if your partner usually does.
  - Think about what is happening in your partner's life. Did they make a big presentation today, have to fire an employee, or take care of your children and their friends?

One final, important point: the most open mind in the world and a willingness to get creative won't ultimately matter if you don't make time for having sex a priority. It's sad but true: as their years together go on, most couples take less and less time for this very important kind of bonding. There's really no good reason for this. Sure, we all get busy, and there really are competing priorities (like changing diapers or going to work). But that only means that it's all the more critical that the two of you make time for this special part of your relationship. If you don't, it just won't happen, or it will happen less and less often.

The bottom line is that we believe, contrary to popular belief, that just about every couple can have a wonderful sensual and sexual relationship—even if they no longer feel that way. Too many people accept the harmful idea that once initial sexual passion wanes, sex naturally gets put on the back burner, never again to return. Only you and your partner can decide if this is true.

Talking Points

1. Couples need to protect their sensual relationships, as well as their sexual intimacy, by being more deliberate, communicating their needs and desires, and guarding intimate times from conflict.

2. Anxiety is a guaranteed way to stop arousal and decrease sexual pleasure.

Suggested Activities

Set aside specific times for sensual activities together. This works for all couples, regardless of whether they are engaging in sexual activity. Be sure you will not be interrupted. (This is the time for babysitters or voicemail!)

When you choose to be sensual together, talk about what's sensual for each of you and what you'd like to try doing to keep sensual experiences in your relationship. Here are some ideas:

- Give a massage to your partner.
- Share a fantasy you've had about your partner.
- Cuddle and hug as you talk to your partner about the positive things you love about them.
- Plan a sensual or sexual activity for your next encounter.
- Plan a wonderful meal together. Prepare it together and sit close together—share the meal.
- Spend some time just kissing.
- Take turns being the giver and receiver of sensual touch.

13

Why You Can't Always Get What You Want

Unraveling the Mysteries of Expectations

Relationships face all kinds of obstacles. Many come from the risks and pitfalls we discussed previously in the book. Many come from failing to nurture the great things that attracted the two of you as you fell in love. And others arise from the normal stresses of life, career, and family.

When shared or understood between two partners, expectations can be a source of connection. They can increase the sense that you are "on the same page" and living life as a team. But sometimes people unwittingly create their own obstacles because what they expect is unexpressed, unrealistic, or both. These expectations may be crystal-clear or entirely subconscious and unexamined. Either way, when they butt up against someone else's needs and expectations, some level of dissatisfaction is all but guaranteed to result. The question is, if this occurs, how will you and your partner address your feelings of disappointment?

Sometimes people unwittingly create their own obstacles because what they expect is unexpressed, unrealistic, or both.

This chapter will help you better understand, work through, and share your expectations for your relationship. Although we can't guarantee you will get what you want, we can help you express what you need (and as the Rolling Stones song says, maybe even get what you need).

HOW EXPECTATIONS AFFECT RELATIONSHIPS

Expectations affect every aspect of your life and relationship. You have specific expectations about minor things, such as who will take out the trash or who will pay the car insurance. You have expectations about common issues, such as money, housework, in-laws, and sex. You also have expectations about deeper, often hidden, issues: how power will be shared (or not shared), how caring will be demonstrated, or about the level of commitment in your relationship.

In general, you will be happy or disappointed in life depending on how well your perceptions of what is happening match what you expected—that is, whether what is happening falls short of, meets, or turns out better than what you think should be happening. It's not surprising, then, that expectations play a crucial role in how happy your relationship will be.

Think of the high bar at a track meet. The goal is to jump the bar at the greatest height you can manage. Some partners set their "expectation bar" too low and thus do not challenge their relationship to be the best it can be. Others set their bar too high, leading to disappointment. The bar we want to help you clear with this chapter is about better understanding, sharing, and addressing expectations that affect your relationship.

Meeting Your Partner's Expectations

Researchers Don H. Baucom and Norman Epstein have identified three major areas in which people have expectations about the way things "should be" in their relationships:

1. *Boundaries*. Where does the line around the couple go? When are you inside it, and when are you outside? How much independence is okay between the two partners?

2. *Investment.* How much time and effort does each partner feel the other should be putting into the relationship? This includes the sense of what each person thinks is the "right" way to show their investment.

3. *Control and power.* Who makes which decisions? Is power shared? How?

In their assessment, the authors noted something very important: differences between two partners' standards matter less than the ways in which they are addressed in the relationship. In other words, two people can be different but still work out a mutually acceptable way of meeting their standards.

Zoey and CJ have been married for just a year, and things have generally been going well. However, CJ has come to be upset about his wife's regular nights out with her friends. Like many young couples, they have different expectations about spending free time with friends, as opposed to together. This creates conflict for them, because they each hold expectations that they have not talked about and may not agree on.

Zoey goes out once a week with her longtime girlfriends, some-times to movies and other times to bars. On occasion her going out triggers a major argument, like this one:

CJ: *(feeling agitated)* I don't see why you have to go out again tonight. You've been out a lot lately.

ZOEY: *(obviously irritated, rolling her eyes)* How many times do we have to argue about this? I go out once a week and that's it. I don't see any problem with that.

CJ: Well, I do. All your friends are single, and I know they keep their eyes open for guys.

ZOEY: So?

CJ: So they're looking for guys, and you're married.

ZOEY: (*angered, feeling attacked and accused of being disloyal*) We don't go out hunting for guys. I don't like it that you don't trust me.

CJ: I just don't think a married woman needs to be out so often with her single friends. Guys notice a group of women, and you can't tell me your friends aren't interested.

ZOEY: (*turning away and walking toward the door*) You sound jealous. I have to leave now. I'll be back by eleven.

Zoey and CJ are arguing about differences in their expectations. He didn't expect that she'd still want to go out with her girlfriends so often after they got married. Zoey expected to cut back some of the time she spent with her friends, but not to stop seeing them altogether. These nights out mean a lot to her, and she sees nothing wrong with them.

In this example, you can't really argue that either person's expectation is outrageous. What's much more important is that their expectations don't match, which fuels conflict. The conversation also highlights the ever-present issue of subtext. What is CJ *really* worried about? Expectations can often be linked to hidden issues. When hidden issues get triggered by events, it's often because some expectation was not met. Either the partners have different expectations or the expectations of one or both are unrealistic or unreasonable.

CJ could be wondering if Zoey really cares to be with him, seeing as she still wants to go out regularly with her friends. Or he might feel insecure about how committed she is to him, as he seems to be implying. Zoey may believe that he's trying to control her. If they are not able to talk directly and constructively about such issues of trust, commitment, and power, it will undermine their connection.

WHERE EXPECTATIONS COME FROM

Expectations build up over a lifetime of experiences. Although our expectations have their base in the past, they operate in the present. There are three primary sources for our expectations: our family of origin, our previous relationships, and the culture we live in.

Family of Origin

Your family experiences lay down many patterns—good and bad—that become models for how you think the world and the people in it are supposed to work. Expectations were transmitted both directly by what your parents (or other caretakers and parent figures) said and indirectly by what you observed. Either way, what you expect results from something you've learned in the past. No one comes to marriage with a blank slate.

For example, if you observed your parents avoiding all manner of conflict, you may have developed the expectation that couples should seek peace at any price. If there's disagreement and conflict with your own partner, your past experience may have taught you that you're in dangerous territory. Or, if you observed your parents being very affectionate, you may have come to expect that same level of affection in your marriage and be disappointed if your partner doesn't show their love in the same manner. If your parents divorced, you may have some expectation in the back of your mind that marriages don't really last. In fact, research shows that often people whose parents divorced do have somewhat less confidence in the permanence of marriages. You get the idea.

Anna and Nico came from very different families. In Anna's family, her father made virtually all the decisions—even down to what kind of toilet paper to buy. Nico's family started out similarly, but his mother left his father because he was so controlling. Nico went to live with his mother. His mother taught him by her actions and words never to treat his own wife as if she were the help.

As you might imagine, Anna and Nico have some trouble making decisions. Anna deferred to Nico for many decisions, and he found this disturbing. He felt the pressure from all the responsibility. From his point of view, Anna's wanting him to make all the decisions not only was the wrong thing to do but also could lead to the marriage failing—just like his parent's marriage had. So Nico would try to get Anna to take more responsibility, while she tried to have him take charge. In his deference he saw himself as showing respect; she saw him as weak.

Because of their mismatched expectations, hidden issues were easily triggered. They were finally able to talk this through using the Speaker Listener Technique. This is just part of their talk, but you can see how they were able to get their issues on the table.

ANNA (SPEAKER): The key for me is that I've been expecting you to lead more, to make decisions, because that's what I grew up being used to.

NICO (LISTENER): So you've expected this from me because that's what you grew up to expect.

ANNA (SPEAKER): Exactly. I never really thought a lot about the expectation, but I can see that I've had it and that it's been affecting us.

NICO (LISTENER): So you're saying that even though you've had this expectation, you haven't really thought a lot about it before. Yet, you can see it's affected us negatively.

ANNA (SPEAKER): Yeah. That's just what I mean. (*She hands Nico the Floor.*)

NICO (SPEAKER): I can understand better now why you've pushed me to make all the decisions. I really want you to hear that it's not that I'm uncomfortable being responsible. But to me, sharing decisions is a way to show you respect.

ANNA (LISTENER): So, what had looked to me like you pushing off responsibilities was really you wanting to share the decision-making process with me.

Nico (Speaker): Yes. That's it. Because of my own background, I've thought that our marriage would be hurt if I just went ahead and took all the control. I thought it meant you didn't care about us because you didn't want to share in making decisions with me.

Anna (Listener): So you have had an expectation that was a lot different from mine, and that led you to worry that we'd have trouble if we didn't share in making decisions.

Nico (Speaker): And that's really been worrying me.

Anna (Listener): It really worried you because you weren't sure I cared.

Nico (Speaker): Exactly.

They had a much easier time dealing with decisions once they began to talk openly about their expectations. Because they had made it safe to connect on this one particular topic, they were in a much better position to negotiate other expectations they had for their relationship. They were working to set the bar in the same, agreed-on place, and then help each other get over it.

Previous Relationships

You also have developed expectations from all the other relationships in your life—most important, from previous dating relationships or a prior marriage. This is even more relevant today, when more people than at any other time are in families with partners who are not their spouse. You also have expectations about how much to kiss, what is romantic, how to communicate about problems, how to spend recreational time, who should make the first move to make up after a fight, and so on.

Suppose, for example, that your experience has been that whenever you began to open up, in prior relationships, about painful childhood events, your partner couldn't handle the closeness and broke up with you. After several such experiences, you might have developed the expectation that sharing past experiences is risky and causes people to pull away. On a deeper level, you may expect that people cannot be trusted with knowing the deepest parts of who you are. If you have such an expectation, you'll pull back and withhold a level of intimacy in your present relationship. A key dynamic of intimacy is that you can share things you feel vulnerable about and be heard and accepted.

Studies show that people who have come to expect that others can't be trusted have more difficulties in relationships. If you look at such a person's entire life, it will usually make sense why they developed such an expectation. Yet it can lead to trouble if the mistrust is so intense that they can't even allow someone they really love to get close. Part of making it emotionally safe to connect involves each person doing their best to be as accepting as possible when their partner shares their vulnerabilities. This is so critical to building closeness and overcoming difficulties in trust.

Cultural Influences

There are a variety of cultural factors that influence our expectations. Television, movies, social media, religious teachings, our ethnic backgrounds, what we read, and the communities we are raised in all powerfully shape our expectations. We explore some types of culturally relevant differences in more detail in Chapter Fourteen.

Although influences from social media bombard us every day, religious or ethnic backgrounds may have an even bigger impact for some people because they are often so concerned with fundamental questions such as right and wrong and how to remain connected to our in-group. For example, if you come from a culture where gender roles are more rigid and conservative, and you decide to marry someone from a background where gender roles are more fluid and egalitarian, some level of conflict is pretty much guaranteed. The good news, though, is that if you commit to meeting these challenges head on (decide, not slide), you can overcome many of them. Keep reading to learn how.

HANDLING EXPECTATIONS WELL

As discussed, expectations can lead either to massive disappointment and frustration or to deeper connections. If it's the latter you seek (and why wouldn't you?), we have four guidelines for handling expectations well. Couples who do the best in life are usually doing a good job on all four.

1. Be *aware* of what you expect.

2. Be *reasonable* in what you expect.

3. Be *clear* about what you expect.

4. Be *motivated* to meet your partner's expectations, even when you don't have the same expectations.

Be Aware of What You Expect

Unmet expectations can lead to disappointment and frustration in your relationship. Many times, what you expected and why you are disappointed are obvious. But not always.

Clifford Sager, a pioneer in couples therapy, argued that we don't have to be fully aware of expectations for them to affect our relationships. Many expectations are virtually unconscious and function automatically, but we ignore them at our (relationship) peril.

The best "hack" to help you identify unconscious expectations is to notice when you're disappointed in your partner's behavior, but you are not totally sure why. It's a tip-off that you believe an agreement has not been upheld, but you may not be fully aware of what you think the agreement was. More important, it may not be something the two of you have ever actually come to an agreement about. Your disappointment may be a red flag that you're carrying an unconscious expectation.

The best "hack" to help you identify unconscious expectations is to notice when you're disappointed in your partner's behavior, but you are not totally sure why.

Here's an example that captures how this situation so often plays out. Paul would get very sad when he'd ask his wife, Kat, to go boating with him and she'd defer, saying "That's OK; go ahead without me and have a great time." She would rather stay home and garden. He worked very hard during the week, and boating was his favorite way to relax. Kat didn't care for boating but really wanted Paul to feel OK about having a nice time without her.

Paul's disappointment and sadness was a clue that an important expectation was at work. In thinking about it, he realized that he'd expected that they'd share this very important interest of his, and he felt hurt that she didn't want to spend that time together. Once Paul became aware of his expectation and the reasons for his sadness, he was able to express what boating with her meant to him. She'd had no idea. She didn't love boating but was glad to come along occasionally once she knew it meant so much to him. She wanted to do her part.

Be Reasonable in What You Expect

It's important to point out that being aware of an expectation does not automatically make it reasonable or fair. Many expectations in relationships are just not realistic. Some unreasonable expectations are very specific. For example, is it reasonable to expect that your partner will never seriously disagree with you? Of course not. Yet, you'd be surprised just how many people expect this.

Sometimes, a person has a perfectly reasonable expectation that just is not reasonable for the relationship they are in. As a result, there are some layers to thinking through what is reasonable and unreasonable. It is reasonable to expect to be loved but what form and expression that takes may be unique to a relationship. Your partner can truly and deeply love you but not be great at showing it in exactly the way you most desire. Who you each are has to be considered as you define what's "reasonable" in your relationship.

To offer a somewhat extreme example, consider a couple for which both partners have a deeply held expectation of being able to have biological children together. After one partner has a serious medical problem that results in infertility, however, they are no longer able to have this experience. Their expectation of having biological children is no longer reasonable for their relationship.

Acting on unreasonable expectations is likely to lead to conflict. Brett and Josh are a good example of this problem. Both had high-pressure jobs in accounting, so it was very critical that they learn how to handle conflict well.

In counseling, they made tremendous progress with all the techniques we presented in the first section of this book. They were handling what had been significant conflicts far better than they ever had before. But their progress was held back by Josh's expectation that because they had these techniques under their belts, they wouldn't have any more unpleasant arguments. That's just not reasonable.

Josh's expectation for zero conflict actually generated *a lot more* conflict until he took a hard look at it. To overcome it, he had to become aware of his unrealistic expectation, and challenge it within himself. It wasn't an expectation the couple had to meet; it was one that Josh had to change—and he did.

Be Clear About What You Expect

Even an expectation that is perfectly reasonable can get you into trouble if it's never clearly expressed. We all tend to assume that our model of an ideal marriage is the same as our partner's. *Why should we have to tell them what we expect?* In effect, we assume that our spouse knows what we expect, and failures to meet our expectations can therefore be interpreted as intentional (i.e., bad).

For example, how many people make the assumption that their partner should just know what they find sexually pleasing? As we explained in the last chapter, we see this time and time again. One or both partners are angry that the other is failing to meet a desire or expectation. But more often than not, they've never expressed what they want. In effect they are expecting their partner to be good at mind reading.

Priti and Jay had regular eruptions of conflict whenever they went to his parents' house. Priti had the expectation that he'd stay close by when at his parents. She didn't like being left alone in conversations with his mother, whom she perceived as prying into the secrets of their marriage. By contrast, Jay was thinking that he should give Priti as much opportunity as possible to get to know his parents. He often sensed that Priti was distant after these visits but didn't understand why.

Priti's expectation for Jay to stay nearer when visiting his mother was perfectly reasonable. Yet, until she told him what she wanted, he was left to his own assumptions. He thought Priti would like it when he went off with one parent, leaving her with the other. Once she expressed her real expectation, he could act on it to help her have a better time.

The bottom line is that you can't work from any kind of shared perspective if you don't, well, share your perspective!

Be Motivated to Meet Your Partner's Expectations

As we note in our chapter title, which references a famous Rolling Stones song, you can't always get what you want, but you can do your part to help your partner get what they want (within reason). Why not try to meet your partner's reasonable and doable expectations?

One of the major reasons most relationships go so well early on is that both partners are motivated to please each other. You try to figure out what your partner likes, and you try to give those gifts in inventive ways. These gifts can be small or large; what matters is that they show you are paying attention to each other.

Working to meet each other's expectations, when you can, will increase happiness and joy for both of you. If you have been together for a while, this is an area where you might redouble your efforts. It's too easy to quit paying close attention to what the other likes or expects. You just get too busy with other things, you just don't see it as important any longer, or you make the mistake of taking your partner for granted. You can decide (right now would be a good moment) to focus some of your energy on meeting some of your partner's expectations, just to please them. Try that with something specific today. You can do it.

HEALTHY GRIEVING: THE DEEPEST ACCEPTANCE

One of the most painful experiences in life is coming to the realization that a reasonable expectation you've communicated clearly to your mate is never going to be met. We all have a list of things we would like to have in our relationships. Some items are more important, some less. None of us will get everything we wished for, even in a strong, happy, relationship. In his work on commitment, coauthor Scott argues that loss of some things is a natural outcome of committing to someone or something. That means some feelings of grief are a reasonable expectation in a committed relationship.

As we'll discuss further in Chapter Sixteen, commitment involves making a choice to give up some things for what you have chosen to have. It entails leaving some things behind to have what you decide is most important. That doesn't mean that we don't ever feel the loss of what we left behind or did not get on the path that we chose. Some grief is normal in a healthy relationship. We are not talking about your partner giving you grief. We're talking about healthy, normal grieving over not having, or losing, something you wanted in life.

One of the most powerful types of acceptance two people can experience in is the awareness that each has some expectations that the other does not meet or meet very well, that neither is perfect nor perfect for the other. The couples who have the most deeply satisfying relationships have two partners who love and accept each other and hang onto the joy of life together despite not getting everything they wanted.

The most amazing marriages we've seen are ones in which the partners not only can accept their disappointments but also reach a point where they can do it together. In other words, they are able to join together in acknowledging things over which each feels some grief in a way that is accepting and intimate. For example, one partner might say, "I know this is one of those times when you wish I'd chosen a different career. I know this is not the type of schedule you wanted for us." The other might say, back, "Yeah, it's hard for me, but it does mean a lot to me that you get this. I chose you."

When you see a couple who can say things like this—and feel closer as a result—you are looking at a deep and tested love.

Work together to be clear and realistic about expectations. Work to meet them. Face the disappointments while also looking for the larger meanings in your life together. Expectations can go from being the source of deep frustration to a better understanding of who you each are and what you can build together.

Talking Points

1. Expectations can be filters that affect how you perceive your partner and your marriage.

2. Expectations come from our experiences in our families of origin, our past relationships, and our culture.

3. Disappointment is one of the best clues that you have an expectation that is not being met.

4. Awareness and communication about important expectations can help transform frustration into understanding and acceptance.

Suggested Activity

This activity is one that many people have found to be especially valuable. It takes some time to do it well, so allow yourself an hour or two over a few days to work through this list. Getting the most out of this activity also takes considerable follow-up, but the return on your investment of time and energy can be significant.

Analyze Your Expectations

What follows is a series of prompts about areas of your relationship that can be especially affected by expectations. There may be other areas where you have expectations, and some of the areas listed here may not be especially important to you, but this can be a very illuminating exercise, and many couples have found it extremely beneficial. According to our research, it's consistently rated one of the best exercises we offer.

Write down what you expect, regardless of whether or not you think the expectation is realistic. Be truthful when you put down what you think, not what sounds like the "correct" or least embarrassing answer.

Each of you should think about your own answers before sharing what you come up with. You may feel awkward sharing some of your expectations, or may not feel comfortable sharing them at all at this point in your relationship. Take your time to think clearly about how you will handle this situation.

What do you expect when it comes to . . .

1. *The longevity of this relationship.* Is it "Till death do us part"?

2. *Sexual fidelity.* What does that mean to you? What do you expect? What behavior (of yours or your partner) would violate your expectations?

3. *Monogamy.* What do you expect or desire about monogamy? Most couples in the past could assume they were (likely) on the same page about this. That's not necessarily the case for all couples today.

4. *Love.* What kinds of things tell you most clearly you are loved?

5. *Your sexual relationship.* Frequency? Practices? Taboos?

6. *Romance.* What is romantic for you? What do you expect in your relationship?

7. *Children.* Do you want children? More children?

8. *Children from a previous relationship.* If you have children from a prior relationship, you likely have important expectations as to how things are handled when they are home with you. What role do you expect your new partner to play in their lives?

9. *Work, careers, and provision of income.* Who works outside the home? Both of you? One or the other? If you both have jobs outside the home, is either of your jobs more important? In what ways?

10. *Basic approach to life.* Do you see the two of you as a team or as two independent individuals?

11. *Communication about problems in the relationship.* Do you want to talk these out? Everything or just the most important things? If so, how?

12. *Power and control.* Who do you expect will have more power and in what kinds of decisions? Who disciplines the kids, or does so the most? What happens when you disagree in a key area? Who has the power now? How do you feel about that?

13. *Money management.* Does one of you control the money? Does one partner have more of a say in how money is spent, or is it equal? How does that fit your expectations?

14. *Household tasks.* Who does what? How much household work do you expect each of you to do?

15. *Religious beliefs and observances.* Do either of you have a religious commitment? How, when, and where do you expect to practice your faith? If there are differences in religious beliefs, cultural backgrounds, or family traditions, how would you like them to be resolved? In which tradition—or both—will you raise your children (or are raising them)?

16. *Time together.* How much time do you want to spend together (as opposed to with friends, at work, with family, and so on)?

How acceptable is spending time apart? What type of activities do you prefer to do together, and which do you prefer not to?

17. *Social media and other forms of online sharing.* Do the two of you have similar expectations about what can be shared with others on social media? Do you have concerns about sensitive, personal things being shared in this way with the world?

18. *Sharing feelings.* How much of your feelings do you expect should be shared? How much is okay to be kept private?

19. *Friendship with your partner.* What is a friend? What would it mean to maintain or have a friendship with your partner?

20. *The little things in life.* Where do you squeeze the toothpaste? Should the toilet seat be left up or down? Who sends the holiday cards? Really think about the little things that could irritate you or have irritated you (or have been going really well). What do you want or expect in each area?

21. *Forgiveness.* How important is forgiveness in your relationship? Is there anything you consider to be unforgivable? How should forgiveness be dealt with in your relationship?

22. *Other relationships.* Which ones are OK? Friendships with members of the opposite sex (or same sex, etc., depending on who you each tend to be attracted to)? Relationships with coworkers? When you are not together, how much time spent with friends is OK with you?

Rate Your Expectations

Now go back to each of the areas you looked at in the preceding exercise and rate each expectation on a scale of 1 to 10 according to how reasonable you think it really is. A 10 would be "Completely reasonable" and 1 means "Completely unreasonable."

Decide which of the areas are important to your relationship and find a time to discuss them together.

14

Beliefs, Values, and Life Experiences

Navigating Differences and Cultivating Connection

Thus far in the book we've focused a lot on how to handle conflict. We've looked into ways to enhance your relationship with a focus on friendship, support, fun, and your love life. We have also examined the importance of clarifying basic expectations about your relationship. This chapter shares some overlapping themes with Chapter Thirteen (expectations), but our focus here is more granular: the importance of deeply examining your core beliefs, ideology, values, identity, and life experiences (i.e., the elements that so strongly influence your expectations). Along the way, we will show how you can use what you learn about yourself to deepen your relationship with your partner—or, if needed, resolve differences related to these core aspects of yourself.

Couples who have strong differences in who they are and where they come from will get the most out of this chapter. But even couples who have similar cultural and life experiences or almost identical worldviews will find much to think about and usefully apply to their lives. Which camp do you and your partner fit into?

SHARED WORLDVIEWS

Shared worldviews will typically reflect shared values. They might include and emphasize the importance of core values such as commitment, respect, intimacy, honesty, and forgiveness—values that are clearly associated with good relationships. They might also include sharing a sense of important causes to support, or the importance (or lack of importance) of family. The more similar your core belief systems, the more likely it is that you and your partner will agree on the values that should be incorporated in your marriage and lives.

Perhaps the most important way your worldview can affect your marriage is by shaping your expectations in areas such as parenting and discipline practices, holiday celebrations, decisions on who does what around the house, and marital roles in general. There's that word again—*expectations*. We repeat it again because expectations are that important (and, if not directly addressed, incredibly likely to spark conflicts). The simple fact is that when two people share key relationship expectations, they are going to have an easier time negotiating life together, and vice versa. So, just like Chapter Thirteen(expectations) advises, you and your partner must make your expectations clear, no matter what they are or where they come from.

This discussion is not relevant to just a small group. Since the first edition of this book, the United States has become a much more diverse country, and today residents are more likely than ever to meet and fall in love with someone who does not come from the same place or have the same basic life experiences or worldview. Even as society has become more accepting of many types of personal differences, many couples still need to navigate important differences in their worldviews and values to ensure their relationships can stand the test of time.

Here is just a sampling of the types of differences (or similarities) couples may have to confront, and what we consider in this chapter:

- Race
- Ethnicity
- Cultural background

- Religious beliefs and practices
- Political views
- Beliefs about society
- Economic status of self or family growing up

Don't get us wrong: conflict is certainly not guaranteed! On the contrary, people can have many obvious differences but still discover that they mutually embrace a sense of what is important in life. Important differences can be the basis of division, or they can be a springboard for growth and acceptance, bringing you closer together. Our goal here is to focus on ways partners can handle such differences (or similarities) to make their connection all it can be.

HOW DO THESE DIFFERENCES AFFECT COUPLES?

There are a variety of ways the differences affect couples. They matter because they are often tied to what one believes is the best way to handle this or that, or how to prioritize things in life. When two people are on the same page, life might get difficult but they will have an easier time agreeing on how to view the situation in front of them. When they're not on the same page, there is more potential for distance and disconnection. This often shows up in the form of misaligned expectations (covered in Chapter Thirteen) or potent hidden issues (covered in Chapter Seven).

When two people are on the same page, life might get difficult but they will have an easier time agreeing on how to view the situation in front of them. When they're not on the same page, there is more potential for distance and disconnection.

These differences can also affect the level of acceptance and support the couple receives from family and friends (or doesn't). Regardless of how good things are between the two partners, how friends and family view their relationship can be a source of great strength or vulnerability. Suppose your families are quite different culturally and religiously. Do your families and friends support the two of you being together? Do they accept your partner?

If there is a loss of support, it may be based on racial or religious differences, or any number of other dimensions. Many couples are rejected by their families because of their political viewpoints. For others, rejection is based on their gender or sexual identity. Whether motivated by fear, judgment, or loving concern, however, this type of rejection can divide partners and add additional stress to a relationship that can feel enormous.

As you read though this chapter, consider how the dimensions we focus on (and others) affect your worldviews, your expectations, hidden issues, and the type of support you have from family and friends for your relationship. We hope that will help you in deciding on the best ways to protect and strengthen your relationship.

RACE, ETHNICITY, AND CULTURE

First, an important caveat: race, ethnicity, and culture is a very broad category deserving of a more nuanced discussion. But for our brief purposes here, we can place these items under the broad umbrella of differing cultural identities. Consider as you read ahead just how many ways fundamental differences in identity can affect a life partnership.

Although the research is somewhat narrow, historical data on marriage has shown that interracial couples have been more likely to struggle in marriage. That said, such findings are often based on older studies and simple comparisons like Black-white versus white-white marriages. Not only are there reasons to believe the pattern could have weakened in recent times, but there is also a lot more complexity in modern pairings that large studies do not capture very well. At the same time, the finding does fit a broader literature suggesting that couples may struggle more when there are greater differences between partners on the dimensions we listed previously.

One obvious reason why race or ethnicity differences might lead to unique challenges is that partners may experience more discrimination and stress. Although the legal prohibitions against interracial marriage have been gone from the US since 1967, views against it still exist in some areas and among some groups. Another important explanation for why people in racially mixed marriages are somewhat more likely to struggle is that differences in race and/or ethnicity are associated with differences in worldviews, customs, family support, and other practices that affect couples and families. Those differences can, quite understandably, be hard for couples to navigate.

Even though interracial relationships and marriages are more accepted now than in the past, that does not mean that some such couples don't have to work through their differences. As mentioned, our family and cultural backgrounds have an enormous impact on our values, beliefs, and behaviors—even in ways we don't realize. We not only pick up all sorts of mundane expectations from our families (for example, do we have a holiday meal around a big table or in front of the television watching football?), we also absorb a culture.

Here's a real-life example from a couple we've worked with that illustrates what this tension looks like. Kate and Ahmed (names have been changed) met online and found each other attractive in many ways. But they started out with very different life experiences and backgrounds. Kate comes from a large family who runs a popular restaurant where Kate works and spends most of her time. Her family's background, and the restaurant, is Italian. Ahmed is of African descent and works in a nursing home. He lives in a communal house with his relatives, including his cousins (whom he calls his brothers) and auntie (whom he refers to as mama). Over their first few months of dating they grew closer in many ways, but after things settled down (and the honeymoon period ended) they began to run into major differences stemming from their very distinct backgrounds.

For example, their food preferences and eating habits were completely different and somewhat unappealing to each other. Because eating is such an unavoidable and regular part of life, this became a big issue for them. For that and other reasons, Ahmed didn't feel comfortable going to Kate's family's restaurant, causing Kate's family to wonder if he would ever fit in with them or be able to embrace the family business. As well, their worldviews were formed by vastly different life experiences. Ahmed also admitted some inner doubts that Kate could ever really understand the stress he experienced solely because he is a Black man in the US.

The good news for their relationship was that they loved each other and wanted to work things out. They discovered that, beneath these differences, most of their core values overlapped even though they might express things differently. Both valued family above all else and believed in being kind to those in need. Both valued independence and self-sufficiency and shared a strong work ethic. Both of them respected and didn't judge differences and believed in having open communication with no secrets. Because of these shared values, they've been able to discuss their needs and either compromise or accept their differences when they can't.

In the end, people can't erase the influence their backgrounds have on them. What they can do, however, is develop a shared view of life that embraces and respects these differences.

POLITICS, IDEOLOGY, AND SOCIAL ISSUES

It's not exactly news that American society is hugely polarized about politics. Although this has probably always been the case to some extent, and this phenomenon exists in most societies around the world, the dynamic here in the US has taken on special intensity in recent years. People are deeply divided and even cutting off associations over differences in political viewpoints. There are many possible explanations. Social media is a popular culprit, but there are many other sources of social upheaval in play. What isn't in dispute, though, is that in such a digitally overconnected world, people are significantly less connected to real-world communities and organizations than in the past. This further fuels division.

The result is that some people are less willing to even consider being with someone who votes differently from themselves. Many people now put in their dating profile that they are only interested in partners who are in the same political party as themselves. Not only that, but parents have also become less accepting of their children marrying into the wrong party. In 2017, Voice of America writer Kevin Enochs summarized findings showing that between 1958 and 2016 there was a dramatic increase in parents reporting it would be unacceptable for their child to marry someone from an opposing political party. This may not have happened to you, but surely some people have been rejected or judged by friends and family for partnering with someone across the political divide.

Why does this matter? Well, for some people, politics is a core expression—even *the* core expression—of their views, beliefs, and life expectations. Their political views have taken on importance akin to religion. It is a huge and inseparable part of their identity, as much or more so than their ethnicity or cultural background.

Despite these changes, love works like it ever did. Two people meet, have an attraction, and form an attachment before their political opinions have a chance to be explored. That means a lot of couples will need to have the skills to handle these types of differences well in order to protect their relationship. That is, if they're even willing to be part of a politically mixed relationship!

Some studies suggest political differences can be pretty hard for a couple to manage. Others, including one by our team headed up by Troy Fangmeier, suggest a lot of couples in inter-political relationships are handling things just fine. Our study, however, uses a sample from about 2011—which, given recent political events, can seem like a lifetime ago. No one knows how much more polarized things may become. There is a great need for more research on this subject. The question here is if this matters for you and your partner.

It did matter for Lucy and Collin. They fell in love at a liberal arts college and have been together for twenty-five years. Over the course of their relationship, Lucy became more involved in her counseling career and had a long-standing women issues reading group. Collin became a banker and joined an investment club. Over time their interests and peer group involvements became increasingly polarizing for the two of them, with Lucy becoming more politically liberal and Collin becoming more conservative. Try as they might to respect each other's viewpoints, their emotions would invariably enter the conversation and things would get heated.

Eventually, and in a loving way, Lucy and Collin decided that the best way to handle these differences was to avoid talking politics with each other entirely, turning instead to their respective peer groups for understanding. Note that this is a solid option for couples who find it's a threat to their relationship to allow these differences to push them apart. That's not avoidance or withdrawal as much as an agreed-on decision not to slide into letting these kinds of differences destroy all that's great about their connection.

Closely connected to political views (or even driving them) are peoples' views and beliefs about big-picture topics such as climate change, social policy, or even their philosophy on the "right" types of government or economic systems. As with everything we write about in this chapter, these dimensions can be the source of closeness and identification between partners, or differences that threaten their bonds.

What about you? Do you and your partner vote differently? Do you have heated discussions about candidates or policies? Do you have different views of climate change and what should be done about it? How about energy? Fracking? Social policy regarding families? Family planning, abortion, when life begins? These are just some of the most volatile, polarizing issues of our day and age.

If you have different views, do you avoid such topics or end up in conflict together over them? If you see things similarly, does that form part of your connection? Whatever you come up with thinking about these questions, think about how you could do all you can to make sure it's safe for you both to connect.

RELIGIOUS AND SPIRITUAL BELIEFS AND PRACTICES

Many people express their worldview through their religion, typically the faith of their parents. Others relate more to spiritual beliefs and practices than religion, per se. For some, these two domains are highly overlapping and for others, they are quite separate. For our purposes here, it is easier to discuss religion merely because it is such a clearly defined domain that is responsible for teaching specific moral codes, ethical practices, rituals, and behavioral practices. But being part of a religion, it's important to note, involves much more than just adhering to the doctrines and practices of a particular faith. It is also a major source of someone's culture and identity.

Statistics show that the number of American adults who say religion is important to their lives has been steadily trending downward in recent years. Nevertheless, religion still exerts a profound impact on the lives and belief systems of many people. The effect of religion on marriage has been studied for years. Most of this research has been conducted with those involved in Western religious traditions, especially within the Judeo-Christian spectrum. Despite this, the findings we will discuss here may well apply to most couples, no matter their faith, given that our central focus is how differences in worldviews can lead to differences in expectations and priorities in life.

Many studies show that religious involvement is modestly associated with lower odds of divorce and/or higher relationship happiness. The differences are not large, though. For example, couples who are more religious tend to be a bit more satisfied in their marriages and less likely to divorce, and they have lower levels of conflict and higher levels of commitment.

Annette Mahoney and colleagues have shown that couples who find ways to engage together in religious and spiritual activities together have stronger relationships. Her thesis is that such practices add depth of meaning and connection to how two people view their marriage and how they connect in life. Such practices are clearly not of interest to those who are not religious but can be a strong way to protect one's relationship and family for those where such views and beliefs are shared.

Another protective factor for couples engaging in a practice of faith together is social. Research by sociologist Paul Amato and his colleagues shows that, even as the trend has been for couples to become more isolated from others in how they live (e.g., not joining outside groups or activities), religious couples are more likely to be involved in community activities and efforts (i.e., less likely to become socially isolated) than other couples. That alone may account for most of the edge some religious couples may have over their nonreligious counterparts.

Such deep ties to a religious community may not be for you, but it's very important for all couples to have strong support systems for their relationships. Connections to a community are important for you as a couple—no matter how you obtain them. There are so many options, from bowling leagues, book clubs, softball teams, gourmet cooking groups, and so forth. There are many ways for you to pursue a stronger social support network for your marriage. Some may be easier to develop than others, but the goal is worthy regardless.

What should you take away from all this? If you share a common faith, engaging with it more strongly may protect and strengthen your relationship. If you don't share a common faith, but it's important to one or both of you, that could be a source of disconnection. There may be ways the two of you can work together to manage that better using skills and strategies (or mindsets) covered in this book.

Either way, most couples could stand to put more thought and action into being involved—as a couple—with others in the community.

WHAT TO DO WHEN YOUR VIEWS ARE NOT YOUR PARTNER'S VIEWS

When couples don't share their faiths or worldviews, the impact on the relationship can be demoralizing and distressing. This may not be surprising given how important one's beliefs and values are to one's sense of identity. That makes it doubly important that couples handle such differences with care.

The good news—as you have heard us point out time and time again—is that when it comes to how your relationship will do over time, any of your actual differences in worldview may not be as critical as how you *handle* those differences. As we have stressed, staying friends and showing respect do not depend on your seeing everything the same way.

Here are some challenges and solutions to handling nonshared core beliefs and worldviews. Note that we will refer to couples with important differences in culture, race, religion, or other profound life experience as intermarriages, which could be interfaith, interracial, and so on.

Nonshared but Respected Views

Many couples do not share a number of beliefs, but they handle their differences well, and with respect. In fact, the very differences that divide some couples can be a source of intimacy if two partners are able to enjoy the exchange and delight in who each other is.

For example, Jean and Margaret fell in love in college fifteen years ago. Now they are in their late thirties, with two children and busy lives. Neither was religious. Margaret was raised in a somewhat religious home, but she never really connected with her parents' faith. Jean grew up in a completely nonreligious home and has never become interested. However, Jean and Margaret have walked different paths as they've shared a life and family together.

Over the years, Jean has become something of an environmental activist. She's a passionate defender of nature, an adamant recycler, and a vegetarian. Although Margaret isn't opposed to these passions, she doesn't share any of them. She's willing to put cans and bottles in the recycling bin, but that gives her none of the deep feelings of responsibility that Jean feels. Also, Margaret really loves her burgers and steak.

Margaret has her own interests. She's always been into film, and on the suggestion of a friend she joined a film club a few years ago that meets regularly to discuss the movies they view. In general, she's much more into arts and culture than Jean, who could take it or leave it.

Margaret and Jean don't share all of the same values and passions. As a result, their various activities take some time away from being together. But they have not let their differences cause any rift between the two of them. If either started actively pestering the other to share the same interests or to give up one in favor of the other, their relationship could deteriorate in a hurry. Wisely, they have not gone this route.

For a couple to handle differences in beliefs, values, or passions well, the partners need at least three things: (1) the skills to maintain respect in light of the differences, (2) enough personal security about their own beliefs and values, and (3) a strong and clear commitment to being together and sharing life, even when they don't share all the things that matter in life.

When One Is Religious and the Other Is Not

There are many married couples who share a similar faith but not a similar focus on religious practice. Sometimes differences develop over time, as one person becomes more involved or the other one begins to drop out.

Whatever the reasons, this isn't an easy challenge to resolve. For some couples, this misalignment becomes a source of conflict. The more religious partner pushes and cajoles the nonreligious partner to come along or can't stop from nudging their partner to become more active in the practice of their faith.

Here's the really tricky part. A number of researchers, such as Vaughn Call and Tim Heaton of Brigham Young University, have found that the more the religious partner attends services relative to the less religious partner, the higher the couple's risk for divorce. Such a finding could merely indicate that attendance is a strong marker of how great the difference between the partners really is. But it seems to us that there is something more involved.

If you are the religiously involved one, you need to think about where you want to draw the line. We would not for a minute suggest that you back off from your beliefs. However, you might want to make sure that you don't cross a line where your involvement at religious services and events takes up so much time that it harms your marriage. Odds are, having a healthy, respectful marriage is an important part of your faith.

If you are the one who's not religiously involved, give some serious thought to what you are willing to do that taps into your partner's desire to do things together. For example, although you may not be interested in attending services, perhaps you are willing to join with your partner in a volunteer service activity.

Nonshared Views with Conflict

Many intermarriages start out just fine, with couples thinking they can beat the odds. Love will conquer all, and all that. Although love can conquer a lot—especially if translated into loving and respectful behavior—the more there is to conquer, the greater the risk of failure.

One of the common dilemmas for partners who have commitment to different faiths comes into play with observances and rituals related to family life. In fact, marriage, birth, and death have a habit of bringing us more in touch with our core beliefs. Most religions specify specific rituals about such events, which help families move through the transitions with meaning and support. So, when conflict arises in differences in worldview, couples are often unable to take advantage of the support offered by their religious system of choice, much to their unhappiness.

For example, Ava and Josh married at twenty-seven after meeting at work some years before. He grew up in an observant Jewish home and she in a Catholic home. Both sets of their parents were unhappy about their choice. But they really did love each other and believed that religion didn't really matter that much. What about children? No problem. "We'll let them choose for themselves what to believe." What about their parents? Also no problem. "They'll learn to accept our marriage." Religious practice? Again, no problem. Neither was particularly involved or observant at this point in life, so they figured, "You do your thing, and I'll do mine." Of course, none of these things were so simple as life moved forward.

Despite their threats, both sets of parents showed up for the wedding, which was conducted by a judge in a lodge. Things went along fairly well for Josh and Ava until the fourth year of marriage, when they were expecting their first child. What were once abstract questions about faith and practice suddenly became very real.

For Ava, the idea of having a child was wonderful but at the same time marred by concerns: "What kind of world am I bringing my child into?" These natural anxieties led her to seriously reevaluate her lack of faith. It seemed to her there was no better guide for grappling with such questions than by returning to her religious practices. She decided she wanted their baby to be baptized. For Josh, his vision of himself as a daddy returned him to an interest in *his* faith.

"What if I have a son? I want a mohel to do the circumcision, not a doctor." Suddenly, each had an interest in spiritual things—for their child and themselves—that hadn't seemed important a few years before. Children can do that to you. They decided to seek both rituals but had trouble finding a Mohel who would do the circumcision and a Catholic priest who would do the baptism (without a strong commitment to their respective religions). So, they ended up doing neither.

The couple made compromises that worked for a few years. Both parents read Bible stories to Benjamin, and he certainly enjoyed celebrating both Hanukkah and Christmas. But the balancing act got tougher and tougher. By the time Benjamin was four, negative feelings intensified to the point that conflicts about him were erupting into all sorts of other relationship events. One by one, key areas of intimacy suffered under the weight of these conflicts.

Eventually Ava suggested they get some professional help and Josh agreed. Their counselor helped them work through their differences, using a lot of the strategies in this book. Most important, the counselor guided them to work toward a much more thorough understanding of who each was, where they had each come from, and what they hoped would happen now. Ava and Josh both started to feel some confidence again—and some closeness, because they deepened their understanding of what was important to the other. It wasn't that they saw eye to eye on everything; the difference was they were working the challenges respectfully and as a team, which reinforced all of what they loved about each other in the first place.

Whatever your background, it can be important for you and your partner to understand one another's core belief systems and related differences—whether those are based on spiritual or religious beliefs, cultural differences, or other important differences in where you came from or what you have come to value. If you are intermarried (or thinking about becoming so), you should accept that your challenges in marriage may be somewhat greater than for other folks. Does that mean couples with differences in backgrounds are doomed? Of course not. But for such couples, it's especially important to be able to handle differences and clarify expectations well. If you have very different beliefs and traditions, you reduce the risks these differences can cause by facing them as a team and employing the skills you've learned.

Where differences occur, there are many ways to decide what to do if you remember to respect what's important to your partner and not to jump to decisions prematurely. Only by having safe and open conversations about what you each believe can you build intimacy and trust and create your own unique family traditions.

Conversations about worldviews, basic values, and core beliefs are often the most compelling and stimulating conversations couples can have, because it allows them to celebrate what's meaningful in each other's lives and create their own couple or family culture.

You can do this. We believe in you!

Talking Points

1. Our worldviews go far beyond just a set of beliefs about how we understand the world—they influence our values and expectations.

2. Having a different worldview than our partner can mean an opportunity for growth or conflict, depending on the extent of the difference and each partner's willingness to accept the other. This is possible when two partners can talk about their beliefs and differences skillfully and with emotional safety.

Suggested Activity

The following questions are designed to get you thinking about a broad range of issues related to your core beliefs. We would like you to write down an answer to each question as it applies to you.

That will help you to contemplate how various beliefs and viewpoints affect your relationship. If you and your partner choose to talk more fully about such matters, you will each be better prepared by taking this time to consider your own thoughts.

Questions for Reflection

1. Do you have a core belief system? What types of beliefs make up your worldview? What do you believe in?

2. How did you come to have the worldview you hold?

3. What is the meaning or purpose of life in your core belief system?

4. What were your beliefs growing up? How were these core beliefs practiced in your family of origin? What religious observances did you practice?

5. Do you make a distinction between *spiritual* and *religious*? What is your view on these matters? Which has the greater influence on your relationship?

6. What is the meaning of marriage in your belief system?

7. What vows will you say, or what vows did you say? How do these tie into your belief system?

8. What is your belief about divorce? How does this fit in with your belief system?

9. How do you practice—or expect to practice—your core beliefs in your relationship? (This could mean religious involvement, spiritual practices, cultural traditions, or something else, depending on your belief system.)

10. What do you think the day-to-day impact of your belief system should be on your relationship?

11. Are there specific views on sexuality in your belief system? What are they? How do they affect the two of you?

12. If you have children—or plan to have children—how are they being raised or how will they be raised with respect to your belief system?

13. Do you give, or expect to give, financial support to a religious institution or causes related to your belief system? How much? Do you both agree?

14. Do you see potential areas of conflict regarding your belief systems? What are they?

15. What do you believe about forgiveness in general? How does forgiveness apply in a relationship such as the one with your partner?

16. In your belief system, what is your responsibility to other humans?

17. How do you observe (or expect to observe) religious holidays?

18. In your belief system, what is the basis for respecting others?

19. How do you view final matters of life? The meaning of death? Is there an afterlife? What about organ donation and the use of living wills?

20. Are there any other questions you can think of and answer?

After you and your partner have finished the entire activity, plan time to talk about your answers—and views of the world. You may find that you deepen your connection by learning more about each other.

PART 4

Staying the Course

15

Forgiveness
Restoring Hope

Few things in life hurt as much as feeling let down or betrayed by a friend or coworker. But when this happens at the hands of your life partner, the pain can be exponentially worse.

This gets at a paradox at the heart of marriage: you risk more hurt in this kind of relationship than you do in less intimate ones. You expect more and you are more vulnerable because more is riding on how the relationship works out. In most cases, an acquaintance who treats you poorly can be shrugged off without any lingering effects. But a partner who acts the same way can cause lasting damage and resentment.

Fact is, being in a relationship means you will get hurt from time to time. If you and your partner have known each other for a while, it's all but guaranteed that they've let you down or hurt you—and that you've done the same. It couldn't be otherwise; after all, you're both human. The only way to avoid any kind of hurt is to never get deeply involved with anyone. Most people choose to reject this kind of safety.

Even if unintentionally, so many things we do can cause minor or major hurts: put-downs, avoidance, negative interpretations, abusive comments, forgetting something important, making decisions without regard for the needs of our partner, affairs, addictions, impoliteness, and so on. That's quite a list, with quite a range of possible impacts.

237

The million-dollar question is, why are some couples able to move through *and beyond* these kinds of events while others get bogged down in despair? That's our focus here: how to think about and act on forgiveness when it's needed to restore your relationship.

TWO PERSPECTIVES ON FORGIVENESS

Before we get into the nitty-gritty of defining and dissecting forgiveness and the best ways to encourage it, let's look at two examples of couples who have experienced relationship wounds.

Both stories showcase actions in need of forgiveness. But the infractions are very different: one is minor and one is major. Accordingly, they have very different implications for the future and how forgiveness can proceed.

Oops, I Forgot: The Domicos

Beth and Nicolas Domico met each other in a Parents Without Partners support group and later married. Each had been married once before, and each shared custody of the children from their first marriages. When they met, they discovered they had much in common, including a desire to marry again. And that's just what they did.

There's been nothing remarkable about their marriage and blended family except that they have done a great job of it. They've handled myriad stresses of bringing two sets of kids together, and they've become a family. They have their ups and downs, but they handle the problems that come up with respect and skill.

Nicolas was recently chosen to be honored as employee of the year at the company's annual luncheon. He was happy about the award, and happier still to receive a substantial bonus for his good work. When he asked if Beth would like to attend the event, her response was "Absolutely, I would love to be there." Nicolas told his fellow workers and his boss that Beth would be coming, and a place was kept for her at the front table, right beside Nicolas.

In the week leading up to the event, Beth, found herself dealing with an unexpected crisis at work. On the big day she became completely distracted by her project and forgot all about the luncheon. Nicolas was at the party feeling very embarrassed. He was also a little bit worried, because it was unlike Beth to miss things, much less an important event like this. Here were his peers, honoring him, and without explanation his wife failed to show up. He made the best of the embarrassment, explaining to his coworkers that "she must have had a crisis at the office." And he had that right. Still, it hurt.

As soon as Nicolas walked in the door that evening, Beth remembered what she had forgotten:

BETH: (*distressed*) Oh, no! Nicolas, I just remembered—

NICOLAS: (*interrupting*) Where were you? I've never been so embarrassed. I really wanted you there.

BETH: I know, I know. I'm so sorry. I wanted to be there with you.

NICOLAS: So where were you? I called you ten times.

BETH: I was dealing with a crisis at work and my phone was on Do Not Disturb. I completely spaced out on your lunch . . . I'm so sorry. I feel terrible.

NICOLAS: I didn't know what to tell people, but I guessed it was probably a situation at work.

BETH: You were absolutely right, but that doesn't excuse my missing the ceremony. Please forgive me. I really am sorry.

Should Nicolas forgive Beth?

Of course he should. Beth took complete responsibility for her actions and expressed her deep, unqualified regret. Additionally, although the situation Nicolas found himself in was embarrassing, on the scale of partner transgressions it was relatively minor.

Now consider a very different example, one in which the same question ("Should Person 1 forgive Person 2?") has a much more complicated answer.

Maybe the Grass Is Greener: The Swensons

Chris and Tasha Swenson have been together for eight years. They met in college, where both majored in business. They married shortly after they graduated and then moved to the Midwest. After three years they had their first child, a delightful girl named Chloe. Two years later they had another girl, Maya, who was serious, very bright, and a real handful at times.

Everything was sailing along just fine until this year. Not long after their anniversary, Tasha noticed that Chris was gone more and more. His job demanded a lot, but "Does he really need to be gone that much?" she wondered. She became suspicious. Without much time together or communication between them, it was hard to know what was going on. But what began as a feeling that she didn't really know Chris anymore eventually gave way to something darker: suspicion he was having an affair.

She got sick and tired of wondering. So, one night she told him she was going to see a friend and left. They had arranged for a babysitter to watch the kids so he could go into work, in his words. Borrowing her friend's car, she followed him as he left the neighborhood—and continued on to an apartment complex. She watched as he got out of the car and entered one of the units, noting its number. She sat and sat for three hours. Restless, she got up to look at the name on the mailbox that corresponded with the unit number: Jill something-or-other.

"Not good, this is not good," she said to herself. It felt as though gravity were pulling her stomach down through her intestines. Now what? Tasha wasn't the type of woman who liked to wait to find things out. She decided to knock on the door. After fifteen minutes, Jill came to the door in her bathrobe.

JILL: (*seeming quite tense*) Can I help you?

TASHA: (*calm but falling apart on the inside*) Yes. Please tell Chris I'm out here in the car and that I'd like to talk to him.

JILL: *(gaining composure)* Chris? Who's Chris? I'm alone. You have
the wrong address.

TASHA: *(sarcastic)* Maybe I could take a look inside to be sure.

JILL: I don't think so. Look, you have the wrong address, whatever
your problem is. Good-bye!

TASHA: *(yelling out as Jill closes the door)* Tell Chris I'll be at home—
if he still remembers where that is!

Chris rolled in an hour later. He denied everything for about
three days, but Tasha wasn't about to back down. After yet another
denial she told Chris to get out. "An affair is bad enough, but if you
can't even admit it, there's nothing left for us to talk about."

Chris left and then promptly fell apart. He began drinking and
disappeared from work for days at a time. Tasha felt even more alone
and betrayed. Although she still loved Chris, her rage and resentment only grew in his absence. "I thought I could trust him. I can't
believe he would cheat on me!"

Chris's sense of shame was so great that he was afraid to deal with
Tasha head-on. So, he decided he'd just stay away from home. "She
told me to get out, anyway," he told himself. Still, he was really both-
ered that Tasha was being so tough. He wondered if things were
really, truly over. He liked Jill, but he didn't want to spend his life
with her. When he was able to think clearly, it became increasingly
obvious whom he wanted to be with: Tasha.

In a way, he developed a new respect for Tasha; there was no
begging or pleading, just toughness. Tasha didn't actually feel tough
at all. She was in agony. But she was very sure of what she had seen.
There was no chance she'd go on with Chris unless he dealt with her
honestly. She wasn't sure whether she wanted to stay or leave.

Tasha came home one night to find Chris sitting at the kitchen
table with a terrible look of pain on his face.

CHRIS: *(desperately)* Please forgive me, Tasha. I don't know . . . I'll
get help. I don't know . . . I'm not sure what happened.

TASHA: *(cool outside, rage inside)* I'm not sure what happened either, but I think you know a lot more than I do.

CHRIS: *(looking up from the table)* I guess I do. What do you want to know?

TASHA: *(icily, controlling her rage)* I'd like to know what's been going on, without all the BS.

CHRIS: *(tears welling up)* I've been having an affair. I met Jill at work, we got close, and things sort of spun out of control.

TASHA: I guess they did. How long?

CHRIS: What?

TASHA: *(voice raised, anger coming out)* How long have you been sleeping together?

CHRIS: Five months. Since the Christmas party. I couldn't handle things here at home. There's been so much distance between us . . .

TASHA: *(enraged)* So what! What if I couldn't handle it? I didn't go looking for someone else. I don't want you here right now. . . . Just go. *(turning away, heading into the next room)*

CHRIS: If that's what you want, I'll go.

TASHA: *(as she walks away)* Right now that's what I want. Please leave me alone. Let me know where you'll be so I can tell the kids.

CHRIS: *(despondent)* I'll go to my parents. That's where I've been lately.

TASHA: *(sarcastic)* Oh, thanks for telling me.

CHRIS: I'll leave. Please forgive me, Tasha, please.

TASHA: I don't know if I can. I don't owe you anything. *(She goes upstairs and slams the door, and Chris slips out the back door.)*

At this point, Tasha had some big decisions to make. Should she forgive Chris? *Could* she forgive Chris? She'd already decided that she might never be able to trust him again, not fully. He clearly wanted to come back, but how would she ever know he wouldn't do this again the next time they had trouble together?

What do you think? Should she forgive Chris, and what does it mean to forgive?

WHAT IS FORGIVENESS?

Now that we've reviewed two vivid but very different examples of what partner-caused hurt can look like, it's a good time to explore what forgiveness is and isn't. We define forgiveness as a decision to give up your perceived or actual right to get even with, or hold in debt, someone who has wronged you. Similarly, *Webster's New World Dictionary* defines *forgive* this way: "1. to give up resentment against or the desire to punish; . . . 2. to give up all claim to punish; . . . 3. to cancel or remit (a debt)." The picture of forgiveness is a canceled debt.

Note that *forgive* is a verb. It's active; it's something you must *decide* to do. When one of you refuses or fails to forgive, you can't function as a team because the unforgiven partner is kept "one down" by being indebted to the other. The transgression may be brought up time and time again during moments of conflict, used by the hurt partner to "win" the fight of the moment.

An unwillingness to forgive is the ultimate in scorekeeping, the message being "You are way behind on my scorecard, and I don't know if you can every do enough to catch up." If this situation persists long enough, the partner seeking forgiveness may slide into a spiral of hopelessness. And what do people do in the face of debts they see no hope of ever paying off? They walk away.

Hanging onto resentment and bitterness isn't only bad for your relationship, it's harmful to your health. Some say that forgiveness is a gift to oneself, because of the pain and damage it does by holding onto it. Stewing in anger puts you at risk for all sorts of psychological and physical problems, such as depression, ulcers, high blood pressure, and rage—not to mention divorce.

For forgiveness to work, though, especially when there is a serious incident that damages trust, a number of things need to happen. One helpful place to start is to be aware of what forgiveness is not.

WHAT FORGIVENESS ISN'T

We hear the phrase *forgive and forget* so often that it's assumed to be a package deal, but in fact they have nothing to do with each other. Can you remember a very painful wrong someone has caused in your life, for which you feel you have forgiven that person? We bet you can. Just because you have forgiven—and given up a desire to harm the other in return—doesn't mean you have forgotten the event ever happened. That's not how real life works.

> *We hear the phrase* forgive and forget *so often that it's assumed to be a package deal, but in fact they have nothing to do with each other.*

A related misconception is the belief that if a person still feels pain about something that happened, they have not really forgiven. You can still feel pain about being hurt in some way yet have fully forgiven the one who harmed you. That's grief, not unforgiveness. Sometimes there is an irreplaceable loss of some sort, but this doesn't mean that the wronged person hasn't forgiven or cannot forgive.

Generally speaking, the severity of the damage to a relationship or sense of loss is proportional to the degree in which trust was violated. So although forgetting an appointment may create a small sense of debt, it probably doesn't jeopardize one's trust too much. An affair, however, would cause both an enormous sense of debt and a huge loss of trust.

Another major distinction to make is between forgiveness and restoration of the relationship. Forgiving does not assume reconciliation or restoration with the person who caused harm. For a relationship to be restored when there is serious harm or a loss of trust, the partner who did the damage must (1) take clear responsibility and (2) make a sincere effort to regain the hurt partner's trust. There can be many reasons why someone forgives, but it won't make sense for them to restore their relationship unless major changes are made.

And even when forgiveness is granted, sometimes the damage is too great for the relationship to be restored.

TAKING RESPONSIBILITY

About now, some of you may be raising a very common question about forgiveness: "Does forgiveness mean the person who hurts you isn't responsible for what they did? It sounds like you're suggesting letting them get away with it."

This is one of the biggest misunderstandings about forgiveness. When you forgive, you are not saying a person who did wrong is not responsible. The person who committed the infraction is responsible for their behavior, period. Forgiving someone *does not* absolve that person of responsibility for their actions. However, when one partner takes clear responsibility for hurting the other partner, the other person will have an easier time forgiving and moving forward.

In this light, it's important to distinguish between punishment and consequences. You can be forgiven from the standpoint that your partner is not seeking to hurt or punish you, but you can still accept the consequences of your behavior and make efforts to repair the damage. For example, although it may not be required for forgiveness, a great way to show your desire to take responsibility is to make amends for hurting your mate. Making amends takes humility because, if genuinely done, it shows that you accept responsibility. This gives your partner the greatest reason for hope to move forward.

In some cases, explanations may provide context that makes the hurt sting a bit less (e.g., the infraction was the result of good intentions or unique circumstances, as opposed to malice), but explaining is *not* the same as taking responsibility and asking for forgiveness. Too many people try to justify their actions by claiming, "I did X because they were doing or not doing Y." There is virtually nothing your partner can do that justifies your doing something that was wrong and hurt them.

Let's summarize so far. If you've been wronged by your partner, it's up to you to forgive or not. Your partner cannot do this for you; it's your decision alone to make. If you've wronged your partner in some way, it's your job to take responsibility for your actions. You need to apologize and mean it. And, if needed, you must make a plan to change your behavior and take steps to see that whatever you did doesn't happen again. These steps are perfect examples of both doing your part and deciding, not sliding.

TRUST ISSUES

Because trust is so foundational to relationship success, it's important that we understand the *kinds* of trust that matter so much in a relationship. There are two foundations to trust that seem essential to the themes of this chapter. First, there is the fidelity of the partners to each other based on the nature of their commitments and the boundaries in the relationship. Second, there is each partner's ability to follow through on what they have committed to do. Consistent with all of what we wrote in Chapter Thirteen, these are both areas where expectations—and clarity about them—will matter a great deal.

When trust has been broken, it is essential for partners to identify *how* it was broken. The process of forgiveness with restoration can proceed only if two people have a similar view on what they are working through. In the case of the Swensons, it means Chris must take complete and absolute responsibility for his affair if their marriage is to have any chance of surviving. That would be foundational for rebuilding trust.

With significant violations of trust, it can be beneficial for a couple to seek counseling with a therapist who has experience helping couples move toward healing, such as in working through infidelity. Not all couples therapists have this experience, so it is important to ask. Further, when an individual has been victimized by an affair, this is often a traumatizing event (or series of events).

When a person has been deeply traumatized and is struggling to cope with some loss or damage from events in their life, individual therapy with someone having expertise in trauma-informed care can make a real difference. There are also some therapists who help couples deal with infidelity from a trauma-based perspective about the damage that has occurred. The section at the end of the book entitled "Getting More Help" may be useful to you if you are looking for more help.

Here's what happened next for Chris and Tasha. In the few days after Chris's visit, they had some nasty talks on the phone. With so much tension in the air, it was easy to escalate things. Yet Chris persistently stated his desire to rebuild the marriage. He wanted to come back.

Tasha asked Chris to come to the house one night for a talk. She arranged for the kids to be with her parents for the evening. She met with him and poured out her pain and anger. He listened. She focused on how his behavior had affected her, not on his motives and weaknesses. He took responsibility to the point of a sincere apology. He didn't make excuses or blame her for the affair. She started to think there was a chance they could get through this. Their talk concluded this way:

CHRIS: I've had a lot of time to think. I know I made a very bad choice that hurt you deeply. It was wrong of me to begin that relationship.

TASHA: Thank you for the apology. I needed to hear it. I love you, but I can't pick up where we left off. I need to know that you'll get to the root of this problem.

CHRIS: What do you want me to do?

TASHA: I don't want to say. I don't know. I've got so many questions that I don't know what to think. I just know that I needed to hear you say you'd done something very wrong.

CHRIS: Tasha, I did do something wrong. I know it. It's also very clear to me . . . clearer than it's been in a few years . . . that I want this marriage to work. I want you, not someone else.

TASHA: I'd like to make it work, but I'm not sure I can learn to trust you again.

CHRIS: I know I hurt you very deeply. I wish I could undo it.

TASHA: If I'm going to forgive you, I need some way to believe that it won't happen again.

CHRIS: I promise I will work on that. I'd like to come back home.

TASHA: That's OK with me, but I need to know we'll go and get help to get through this.

CHRIS: Like a therapist.

TASHA: Yes, like a therapist. I'm not sure what to do next, but I think seeing someone would be important. If you'll agree to that, I can handle you coming back home. I think.

CHRIS: That makes sense.

TASHA: Don't expect me to go on like nothing's happened. I'm very, very angry with you right now.

CHRIS: I know. I don't expect you to act like nothing happened.

TASHA: OK.

Tasha opened up and didn't hold much back about being angry, and Chris validated her pain and anger. He didn't get defensive even when emotions ran high. If he had, Tasha was prepared to work on forgiveness to free herself up but end the marriage.

Chris did the best he could under the circumstances. The next day, he began calling around to find the best therapist. He wanted a professional who knew what they needed to do to move forward. This showed Tasha that he was serious about repairing their marriage, thereby offering her some evidence of his dedication. Considering how absent it had been recently, it was something she needed to experience.

Things progressed inch by inch, talk by talk. Two steps forward, one step back. Tasha will always remember what Chris did—how could she ever forget?—but the ache in her heart became weaker over time. Some effects of infidelity will be lasting, even where a couple has found a path to healing. Couples therapy can help couples regain more of their connection.

WHAT ABOUT REGAINING TRUST?

We're often asked how you regain trust when something has so damaged it. The question isn't really relevant when it comes to minor breaches. There is no loss of trust in the Domicos' incident. But for the Swensons, there's a huge loss of trust. How do you rebuild it? It's not easy. But there are three key points we like to make about the process.

1. *Trust builds slowly over time.* Trust builds as you gain confidence in someone being there for you over time. A great way to help your partner trust you more is to do all you can to show your commitment to them. That is something over which you have a lot of personal control.

   Tasha can regain her trust in Chris only slowly. The best thing that can happen is for a considerable amount of time to go by without another breach. And any actions Chris takes should demonstrate—loudly—his intention to make things work. We recommend adopting a policy of full transparency, at least at the beginning: about all activities you take and your whereabouts. This is an important way to help alleviate suspicions and show that nothing is being hidden, especially when emotions are so raw and skepticism is high. If Chris has another affair or lies again about the past one, it will probably be impossible for Tasha to trust him ever again.

2. *Trust has the greatest chance to be rebuilt when each partner takes appropriate responsibility.* The most important thing Chris can do to regain Tasha's trust is to take full responsibility for his

actions. If she sees him doing all he can to bring about serious change without her prodding and demanding, her trust will grow. Tasha can also help build Chris's trust that she doesn't plan to hold the affair over his head forever. If she reminds him about the affair, especially during arguments, he won't be able to trust that she really wants him to draw closer and be her life partner again.

3. *Trust is a choice.* When everything is said and done, each person has to *decide* to trust their partner. It's a leap of faith, but not blind faith. Eyes should be wide open looking for evidence of change. To that end, some couples may choose to have a recommitment or "re-trust" ceremony as a way to mark the new beginning of their relationship.

STEPS TO FORGIVENESS AND RESTORATION

We want to give you some steps that can help guide you or your partner as you (or they) walk the rocky, challenging path to forgiveness. The steps should be thought of as signposts more than a process to be rigid about. Keep in mind that in laying out these steps, we are not implying that the process of forgiveness is simple, easy, or linear. This is simply a starting point, but hopefully a useful one.

First thing's first: our guidelines are founded on the assumption that it makes sense to try to restore your relationship. If it feels unsafe or irreparably broken, forgiveness may be possible, but restoration probably will not.

These steps take time. A thirty-minute talk won't do it. Also realize that you may have to work back through some of the earlier steps as you are working through later ones. Additionally, although these steps are for the two of you to do together, the most important work takes place inside each of you as individuals. This includes trying to imagine what your partner was going through or has been through.

The process may involve talking with friends, a counselor or therapist, or a clergy member or other spiritual adviser. As we pointed out previously, many couples will benefit from seeking outside help for making forgiveness happen. A therapist might help you with these steps or work from another model for structuring healing after a large violation of trust. Regardless of your approach, remember that deep listening and understanding will go a long way.

Step One: Schedule a Couples Meeting

If an issue is important enough to focus on in this way, do it right. Set aside times when you will have no distractions. Prepare yourselves to deal openly, honestly, and respectfully. As we said in the chapter on ground rules, setting aside specific times for dealing with issues makes it more likely that you'll follow through on your actions.

Step Two: Discuss the Specific Violation to Be Forgiven

Identify the problem or harmful event you want to work through. Stay focused and be careful not to wander into unrelated issues. You must both agree that you are ready to discuss it in this format at this time. If not, wait for a better time. And be prepared for the process to stretch over a number of talks.

Step Three: Fully Explore Your Pain and Concerns

The goal in this step is to have an open, validating talk—or talks— about what has happened that harmed one or both of you. This means taking all the time needed for both of you to listen, and really hear, what the other has to say. That might take place in one meeting, or it might be something you do over several times meeting together. And no matter how much time you spend in this stage of working toward forgiving, remember that forgiveness takes time. (See Step Seven.)

Obviously, this process will mean the partner who did harm will fully listen to the one harmed about how they have been affected and what they felt and feel now. Less obviously to many, this will also mean that the one who was most obviously harmed will take time to fully listen to their partner who harmed them about what that partner was going through at the time of the transgression. That's hard but important work.

Why is it important for both partners to listen to each other's experience? Because forgiveness and restoration are most likely to happen when two things are true: both partners want the relationship to continue and each partner is working within themself to build empathy for the experience of the other. In essence, forgiveness and restoration are most likely to happen with both love and understanding.

This step is an obvious place where you should consider using the Speaker Listener Technique. If there's ever a time to have a safe and clear talk, this is it. The foundation for forgiveness is best laid through an understanding based in listening.

Step Four: The Offender Asks for Forgiveness

If you have offended your partner in some way, an outward appeal for forgiveness is not only appropriate but very healing. An apology is a powerful addition to a request for forgiveness. A sincere apology validates your partner's pain and should never be followed by a "but" or a rationalization. To say, "I'm sorry. I was wrong. Please forgive me," is one of the most healing things that one person can do for another if done genuinely.

But what if you don't think you have done anything wrong? You can still ask that your partner forgive you. Remember: forgiveness is a separate issue from *why* the infraction or mistake occurred. So even if you don't agree that you did anything wrong, your partner can choose to forgive. That's harder, but it's doable if the incident at stake wasn't experienced as a major violation of trust.

Step Five: The Offended Agrees to Work Toward Forgiving

Ideally, the one wanting to forgive their partner will need to clearly acknowledge their intent to forgive. That's different from pronouncing that forgiveness has happened and, boom, "We're all good now." A simple "I forgive you" will likely be fine for minor hurts, but for anything of significance, it's important to aim for a statement of intention rather than a declaration that forgiveness has been granted. For example, there is a lot of power in saying, "I'm working toward forgiving you."

Making your intent explicit makes it feel more powerful and increases accountability between the two of you. You are letting your partner know that you will do your part when it comes to working toward letting go and do not intend to keep them in a one-down position of debt. You are also conveying that you do not plan to bring up the betrayal in the middle of future arguments or conflicts.

You should both recognize that this commitment to forgive is just the start of a process. It definitely does *not* mean that the offended partner won't feel pain or any effects from what happened. But you're moving on, together. You're working to restore your relationship and repair the damage that's been done to it.

Step Six: If Applicable, the Offender Commits to Change Recurrent Patterns or Attitudes

This step assumes that what happened was part of a pattern, not just a one-time event. It's important to acknowledge harmful behavioral patterns and that stopping them is going to take work. As discussed in Step Five, neither of you can expect the issue to be settled and forgiveness granted immediately. It's not going to help for the partner who committed harm to say, "I've changed, let's move forward." It is much more meaningful if they say they are working on change and then provide specific steps on how (the more detailed the better). That may include individual therapy or other steps that keep them accountable for making change happen (aka, doing their part).

If you have hurt your partner, it also helps to make amends. When you make amends, you make a peace offering of a sort to demonstrate your desire to get back on track. It's a gesture of goodwill. Some of the most potent acts that help to make amends will be those that are symbolic of how you are trying to heal, so they may be examples of the changes you are working on making in yourself, or simple things like giving of your time and attention or remembering a special day and making something happen. This shows your investment in your relationship and desire to build it back up.

Finally, it never hurts to thank your partner for their good-faith efforts to overcome your current challenges. That goes for both sides.

Step Seven: Expect It to Take Time

Following these steps can help make a difference. They provide you with some structure for how to move forward during an emotionally daunting and messy process. Remember, though, that they initiate a process, not conclude it. You may each be working on your side of the equation for some time to come.

Forgiveness is complicated. It's also challenging and scary. Hopefully, however, we have given you some useful ideas when it comes to the hard but invaluable work of rebuilding trust.

Talking Points

1. Acceptance and a willingness to forgive are crucial elements of a happy marriage.

2. Forgiveness is a choice: you can choose to move forward, release your partner from owing you a debt, and work to restore your relationship.

3. One can forgive another without believing it is wise to restore and continue the relationship. Also, just because someone has

granted forgiveness does not mean they can, or should, forget the hurt they suffered.

4. Taking responsibility for your own negative actions and working to change offensive or destructive patterns are essential if forgiveness is to be given.

Suggested Activity

Here you have a chance to apply some of what you have learned in this chapter about forgiveness to your own life. In contrast to the last part of this chapter where we focus on how to work through a path of forgiveness and restoration as a team, the idea here is for your own reflection—as an individual.

Spend some time reflecting on times you may have hurt your partner. Have you taken responsibility? Did you apologize? Have you taken steps to change any recurrent patterns that give offense? Just as you may be holding on to some grudges, you may be standing in the way of reconciliation on some issues if you've never taken responsibility for your end.

16

Commitment in an Ever-Changing World
Staying on the Wonderful, Winding Path

Congrats if you've made it all the way to this final chapter. It really shows your commitment!

Speaking of which: think back to all the weddings you've attended over the years. Each ceremony was surely special in its own way, filled with inspiring poems, beautiful readings of scripture, tender jokes, or heartfelt declarations of love. For all of the uniqueness of each event, however, the same theme no doubt emerged as each partner declared their vows: commitment. A promise to stay together through good times and bad, and an acknowledgment that taking the shared journey of marriage will require deliberate effort and force of will, possibly—hopefully—for the rest of their lives.

More broadly, most married couples rightfully consider commitment the glue that holds their relationship together, which is why it's emphasized so strongly during wedding ceremonies. Research consistently shows that the kind and depth of a couple's commitment affects not only their chances of staying together but also their chances of being happy over many years.

Commitment, of course, means many things to many people. Over the years, you and (or) your partner may even change how you define and embody it. So it's worth taking a few moments to stop and think about what it means to you right now. Take a piece of paper and jot down the words that come to mind when you think of *commitment*.

It won't take long to do it, and you don't have to share your ideas with anyone else. But think about what you wrote down as you make your way through the chapter. It will be illuminating to compare your notes to the ideas about commitment we discuss in these next pages.

WHAT IS COMMITMENT?

In our years of research and practice, we've found that commitment can be boiled down to two core elements. The first is *dedication*, which is the desire to maintain or improve the quality of one's relationship for the benefit of both partners. Dedication is characterized by a desire (and actions) not only to continue in the relationship but also to improve it, sacrifice for it, and invest in it. People who are dedicated look out for and tend to their partner's well-being, not just their own. They are experts at doing their part.

By contrast, *constraint* refers to forces that motivate people to stay in relationships whether or not they are still dedicated. As we discuss in the box "The Binds That Tie," constraint commitment may arise from either external or internal pressures. Constraints help keep couples together by making ending the relationship more costly—economically, socially, personally, or psychologically. Even if dedication is low, constraints can keep people in relationships they might otherwise want to leave.

The Binds That Tie

What constitutes someone's commitment constraints depends on who they are, what they value, and what their circumstances are. Here's a list of common constraints that lead a person to continue on in a relationship regardless of their dedication to it:

- Social pressure from friends and family
- Financial considerations

- Concerns for children's welfare or fear of losing contact
- The difficulty of the steps it'd take to leave
- Moral factors, such as a belief that divorce is wrong or that a person should always finish what they started
- Poor quality of alternatives

Are constraints a bad thing? Not always. Without constraint commitment, many couples would not make it beyond a year or two because of the normal ups and downs they experience in life satisfaction. We can't prove this, but we believe it's true for most couples. One of the helpful things that constraints can do is put the brakes on destructive behavior when one partner is unhappy or frustrated in their marriage. It's only when a marriage is damaging or destructive that constraints become a problem, because they can prevent a person from seeking help or getting out of a dangerous situation.

Why Does Commitment Develop?

Commitment starts to develop when two people meet, enjoy being together, and start to become attached. That leads to a desire to start making their relationship more secure. In its various forms, commitment marks your mutual desire to be an "us" with a future. Of course, this growing commitment is not always mutual at the start. For some, it never actually becomes mutual—a topic we will discuss in a box later in this chapter.

In its various forms, commitment marks your mutual desire to be an "us" with a future.

Most people experience an awkward period in a growing relationship during which the desire to be together may be strong, but the commitment is unclear. In many relationships, one or both partners may feel anxious about whether or not they'll stay together, until the ambiguity and uncertainty resolves. But as their mutual dedication becomes clearer, it starts to feel safer to invest in the relationship emotionally. They have become committed to each other.

Lisa and Joseph had been dating for a few months. Eventually they reached a point where each was feeling in love but not all that secure about where the relationship was headed. They felt great about each other and were becoming attached, but attachment is not commitment. Little signals started to emerge that were emblematic of their mutual desire to make their connection surer. Lisa began to notice Joseph would refer to *we* or *us* when they talked together or were around others. She would bring up things they could do in the future together, and he'd dive right in on the possibilities. Each could see small ways that the other was starting to make sacrifices for their relationship. They were investing emotionally in it.

That stuff is commitment in action. If it keeps growing, it often ends up in some form of a fully and mutually expressed "I do" and "I will . . . be there for you, sacrifice for you, love you into the future," and so forth. That's where Lisa and Joseph ended up. The growing signals of commitment led to them marrying a few years after they first met.

A clear, strong sense of mutual dedication is important for all couples. It is only with a deep sense of security that two people can fully surrender and experience the wonder, magic, and mystery of a great relationship. They can be vulnerable, make mistakes, and take emotional risks without worrying that their partner could leave if they aren't "perfect." After all, who is?

How Does Commitment Erode?

Most couples have high levels of dedication early on, such as when they get engaged or are in their early years of marriage. What happens that reduces dedication for some couples over time? For one thing, if a couple isn't handling conflict well, Communication Danger Signs will steadily erode their satisfaction with their marriage and take dedication along with it. With dedication in jeopardy, a sense of caring for another erodes further, and satisfaction takes a bigger dive. It's a downward spiral from there. Both partners try less and see their partner trying less, and soon their relationship is dying.

Although constraint commitment can add a stabilizing dimension to a relationship, it can't give you a great relationship. It can, however, help you refrain from doing impulsive, damaging things in the short run during times when you are unhappy. Constraints provide some defense against a marriage ending, but upping your dedication game is going on offense to make a relationship all it can be. Our research shows that dedicated couples report not only more satisfaction with their relationships but also less conflict about the problems they have and greater levels of self-disclosure.

The not-so-secret secret to satisfying commitment is to maintain not just constraint commitment but also a high level of dedication. Let's dig in on that.

STICKING, STUCK, OR STOPPING?

Because you're reading this book, we assume you want to stick together with your current or a future partner, which means that you want to thrive in your journey through life together. We also know that many of you feel something closer to stuck than to sticking. And many of you are in danger of stopping altogether: getting a divorce and moving on.

To give you a more concrete understanding of how commitment works, we'll look at examples of two couples, one stuck, the other sticking. In both marriages there is commitment, but, as you'll see, the types of commitment are very different.

Andy and Tricia: Stuck, Not Sticking

Andy and Tricia married thirteen years ago. They have a four-year-old son and a seven-year-old daughter. Andy manages a large outdoor store, and Tricia is a secretary in a doctor's office. Like most couples, Andy and Tricia started out very much in love but have gone through some tough times. Raising two kids has proven more stressful than either of them expected. Combined with the hassle of major job changes for both, child-rearing has left them feeling tired and distant.

Tricia has considered divorce on more than a few occasions, and increasingly finds herself thinking about leaving Andy. Andy also feels unhappy with the marriage but hasn't considered divorce as much of an option. He also hasn't thought of any ways to improve the marriage. He hopes for more, but hasn't told Tricia this, and thinks trying to get closer just doesn't work. When he does try to do something thoughtful, he feels shut out by Tricia. He worries about her leaving, but he senses that any energy put into the marriage at this point is wasted effort.

"Maybe things will get better when the kids leave home," he thinks. "I've just got to stick with it and hope for the best." We'd call this attitude *being stuck*.

Tricia and Andy work around people they find attractive. Jordan is a single, good-looking man at Tricia's work who has made it clear he's interested in her. She finds herself thinking more and more about him and finding herself in more and more situations where something could happen with him.

Tricia is very aware of changes she's gone through over the years, and increasingly thinks that Andy will never be the kind of partner that she hoped for. Furthermore, she feels she is putting a lot more into the marriage than Andy is, with little in return for her time and effort. She resents that he doesn't seem to appreciate and accept all she's done for him. Like Andy, she is thinking it's just not worth the effort to try harder.

As Tricia thinks about leaving Andy, difficult questions plague her. First, she wonders how the kids would respond to divorce. Would it hurt them? Would Andy want custody? Would it be hard to get a divorce? Would Andy try to stop her? How could they afford lawyers? She wonders how she could support herself on her income alone. Who would get the house? Could either afford to keep the house alone? Would Andy pay child support? If she married again, would another man accept her children?

As Tricia considers these questions, she decides that maybe the costs of getting a divorce are greater than she wants to bear, at least for now. Sure, she's in pain, but she balances this against the pain and stress a divorce could bring. A feeling of despair hangs over her. Feeling trapped, she decides that staying is better than leaving. But, staying stuck isn't a very satisfying outcome.

Heather and Cameron: Sticking, Not Stuck

Heather and Cameron have been married for eight years. They have two children, a seven-year-old boy and an eleven-year-old girl. Although they've had their stressful times, they have few regrets about marrying one another. They met when both were working for a large insurance company.

Their kids present some real challenges. Their son has a serious learning disability and requires attention and support. Their daughter is beginning to show more signs of rebellion than they had ever imagined, and this too causes concern. Despite these challenges, Heather and Cameron usually feel the other's support in facing the tasks of life.

Cameron does occasionally become aware of attraction to others at conferences. However, he does not dwell on "what if" or act in ways that may jeopardize the marriage. They genuinely respect and like each other, do things for each other, and talk fairly openly about what they want out of life and marriage. Importantly, Heather and Cameron have regularly made time for their relationship—to play together, to talk as good friends, and to keep their passion alive. Each is willing to help the other reach important goals in life. They stick together.

As you can see, Andy and Tricia and Heather and Cameron have very different marriages. Andy and Tricia are miserable, and Heather and Cameron are enjoying life. Both marriages are likely to continue for the time being, reflecting some kind of commitment. But Heather and Cameron have a much different, deeper kind of commitment.

"Sounds great," you may be thinking. "But how do I become more like Heather and Cameron and less like Andy and Tricia?" This is the focus of the next section.

THE COMMITMENT PLAYBOOK

One of the most important ideas in this book—from the first chapter through this one—is that people have the power to *decide* or *slide* into how they approach important moments or transitions in their relationships. This holds for big and small decisions alike, such as how the next moment might unfold in an argument. For instance, are we going to slide into escalation or do something different (and better)? Doing something different takes a decision.

Similarly, you can decide to make a deliberate effort to preserve and enrich your marriage or just slide along with minimal effort. There are times when commitment requires a decision to do something, believe something, or to act in deliberate ways that enhance your marriage, as opposed to simply believing that love is enough to weather the challenges life will inevitably throw in your path.

Unfortunately for the sliders, love usually isn't enough (as you well know). Relationships rarely go the distance by accident. Find an older couple who seems to be effortlessly in love, and we'll show you two partners who have actively worked to stay in love—and remain committed to each other. This is true even if they aren't fully conscious of their relationship-preserving behavior. Unintentionally or not, they've *decided* to work for their marriage.

When it comes to commitment, we have found that there are four key areas of deciding:

- Choices
- Couple identity

- Sacrifice
- The long-term view

The good news is these are all areas couples have control over, individually and collectively. Let's go over them.

Making (Good) Choices

Commitment involves making a choice to give up other choices. This is true for large and small decisions in life. Even what you had for lunch today was a type of commitment, because you had to choose among alternatives.

Commitment involves making a choice to give up other choices.

When it comes to commitment, we have found that the kinds of decisions partners will have to make often fall under one of two groupings: choices related to prioritizing their relationship and choices related to imagining what life could potentially be like with other partners.

Setting Priorities

We all either make decisions involving competing time and resources or let things slide in ways that may not protect our most important commitments. Those who are more dedicated to their partners are more likely to routinely make decisions that protect their relationships. Most everyone does this early on, in the phases of dating and getting to know one another, during which each partner will often move mountains to spend time with each other. But as the cares and hassles of life take over, too many of us allow our relationship to take a backseat. A great relationship is a front-seat deal (unless you are in the backseat together, but that's closer to the topic of Chapter Twelve).

Problems with priorities can reflect a problem with overinvolvement elsewhere as much as it does a lack of dedication at home. It's easy to slide into prioritizing outside obligations over your relationship and take your partner for granted. Unfortunately, as people get busier and busier, too many end up no-ing each other out of routine or exhaustion: "No, I don't have time to talk tonight"; "No, I'm too tired to even think about having sex tonight"; "No, I promised Aaron I'd come over Saturday and help him put up that new fence."

Scott's son Luke expressed the essence of protecting priorities at age six, when Scott asked him why he said no so often when asked to do this or that. Luke answered, "Because yes takes too much time." He understood that protecting his priorities had a lot to do with saying no to competing activities. That's a lesson many of us are still working to understand long into adulthood. To protect your relationship, you've got to be good at saying no to things that might seem important at the time and saying yes to your partner in ways that matter to them.

Lopsided Love

In 1921, Edward A. Ross defined the law of personal exploitation: "in any sentimental relation, the one who cares less can exploit the one who cares more." In 1938, Willard Waller described this in terms of the "principle of least interest." He argued that in any relationship, deal, or negotiation, the one with the least interest has the most power. This fits in with commitment theory. The one who is least committed in a romantic relationship often has more power.

We have published many studies on what we call *asymmetrical commitment*, which is a fancy way of saying the love and commitment in a relationship is lopsided. Relationships where one partner is much less committed than the other are difficult. There often is less connection and shared priority and a lot of frustration. Some relationships were asymmetrical

in commitment from the get-go, and some people are fortunate enough to have figured this out and moved on before
going further. Other couples start out with similar dedication,
but it wanes for one.

It is difficult to get or keep a relationship on track if both
are not committed to doing what it takes. It's not unusual for
partners to vary over time, with one or the other being
stronger in pushing to make it work for a while. But when
one is consistently less willing to do their part, power balances will inevitably occur that will destabilize, if not erode
your relationship. That is why it's so important to commitment to nurturing your relationship, in big and small ways
alike. Dedicate yourselves to being emotionally generous: it
can be contagious and sustaining, and it can help realign an
imbalance.

Alternative Monitoring: Forsaking All Others?

Just because two people make a choice to give up other romantic
choices, it does not mean that the other options disappear from
the planet. In our research we talk about *alternative monitoring*, or
how much you keep an eye out for other partners in life. The more
you are attracted to or attuned to other potential partners, the
more you erode your dedication to your partner. In a publication
headed up by our colleague Lane Ritchie, we showed that alternative monitoring was greater among those who eventually broke up
with their partners or who had an affair compared to those reporting less alternative monitoring. Probably just as you'd expect.

Do you find yourself frequently or seriously thinking about being
with people other than your spouse? Our research shows that this
aspect of dedication is the most sensitive to your current level of happiness. In other words, when unhappy with their partners, many
people are prone to start thinking about the what-ifs. What if I had

chosen her instead? What would it be like to be with him instead of my partner?" You can what-if yourself to a place of despair and resentment if you choose to do so. Or you can make a conscious choice not to.

Research by Dennis Johnson and Caryl Rusbult suggests that highly dedicated people mentally devalue attractive potential partners. When tempted, do you dwell on the grass that seems greener, or do you figure that every lawn has problems and focus on taking better care of your own? You can choose to attack such thoughts about others rather than allow them a comfortable home in your mind.

Couple Identity: The Story of Us

In some couples, each partner views the relationship as a team. Others, however, believe relationships are made up of two separate individuals who mostly focus on themselves.

As you might suspect, in the happiest and strongest marriages *we* transcends *me* in how partners think and negotiate conflict. If a couple doesn't have this sense of being a team, conflict is more likely, because the spouses see problems as "me against you" instead of "us against the problem." Our research clearly shows that couples who are thriving in their marriages have a strong sense of *us*.

We aren't suggesting that you should merge your identities. Far from it. Rather, we're suggesting that most couples do best when they frame their relationship as two individuals coming together to form a team. What a difference this can make in how you view life together!

Many couples have nurtured and protected their couple identity from the start. If you have it, work at keeping it up. But if you haven't, take this opportunity to openly discuss and plan for how you want to express your we in the years ahead. If you've lost that couple feeling, work at getting it back. You can do it if you want.

Sacrifice

Selfishness may sell in our culture, but it doesn't buy lifelong happy marriages. It seriously undercuts couple identity and elevates the wrong priorities. However, positive attitudes about sacrifice—and sacrificial behavior—gird up a strong relationship over time. In fact, our research has shown that people who are happiest in marriage gain satisfaction from doing things that are largely or solely for their partner's benefit.

Selfishness may sell in our culture, but it doesn't buy lifelong happy marriages.

By this we aren't recommending your being a martyr, but that you try to find the joy that comes from giving to your partner. In the way the term is commonly used, a martyr does things for another not out of concern for what is best for that person but because the martyr wants to put the other in debt or feel righteous. This is not dedication.

Andy and Tricia (the stuck couple from our example) have stopped giving to each other. Andy doesn't think he'll get anything back if he gives more, and Tricia already feels that she's given more than her share for a lifetime. Neither feels like sacrificing anything at this point. They've lost the sense of *us* that promotes giving to one another without resentment. So neither is going to give much at this point, at least not until they think the other person does. That could be a very long wait.

Relationships are stronger when both partners are willing to make sacrifices. In the absence of this willingness to sacrifice, what do you have? A relationship in which at least one of you is in it mostly for what you can get, with little focus on what you can give. That's not a recipe for happiness or growth. People who practice emotional generosity for its own sake generally feel happier than those who keep track of who gives more. Giving can also become contagious, if for no other reason than that no one enjoys feeling in another person's debt. It's also a great way to shift the energy in a faltering relationship.

Do you often feel that your partner owes you? There's nothing wrong with doing positive things and wanting to be appreciated. There *is* something wrong with believing you are owed. In couples who are doing wonderfully well, you'll find two partners who give freely to one another and appreciate what the other gives. It's a beautiful form of teamwork.

The Surprising Research on Living Together Before Marriage

It is commonly believed that living together before marriage improves the odds of success in marriage. This is actually not the case. Scores of studies (including many leading studies by coauthors Galena, Scott, and Howard) show that this conventional wisdom is wrong. In fact, there is no evidence that couples who live together before marriage tend to have better marriages.

How did this misperception become so widespread? If so many people believe that living together before marriage will improve their odds, and if so many couples end up getting married after living together, how can it be that studies do not support this benefit? In our view, many people overlook a very important detail. Living together makes it harder to break up—compared to dating, that is. It can increase the constraints to remain together long before two people have matured in their dedication to having a future together. To break up after moving in together, someone has to move out, possessions may need to be divided up, financial entanglements have to be broken, and so on. That's a form of inertia. Some couples get trapped by it in a relationship they might have otherwise left.

This risk isn't present for everyone who lives together before marriage. Couples who only started living together *after* being engaged to marry show no additional risk. Why? We believe those who are engaged or already married have sealed the deal on their commitment to the future before taking a step that makes it harder to break up.

Further, studies by other scholars (such as Wendy Manning, Pamela Smock, and Jo Lindsay) have shown that couples typically move in together without any clear discussion or decision about why they are doing it and what it means. As Manning and Smock note, they slid into it. That fact—along with our long-time focus on decisions as part of the nature of commitment—was foundational in us coming to emphasize "sliding versus deciding."

Sliding isn't part of the formation of a strong commitment because commitment involves making a clear choice among options. Commitments are decisions but sliding just sort of happens. Decisions at important moments provide an anchor for following through. Many types of ceremonies—especially wedding ceremonies—are built to provide that anchor, publicly. Contrast this with how often couples slide through potentially important transitions as their relationship develops. That's not always harmful, but sometimes, by sliding, people are giving up options before they have made a choice.

As you read this, some of you may be thinking, "That's us. We slid into everything, including living together before being engaged." We want to assure you that this in no way means you are doomed. You might have no added risk or you might; we don't know. What we do know is that you picked up this book and are reading it, a sign of commitment. We also know that the strategies described in this book have been shown to eliminate the kinds of risks couples who have lived together before engagement may experience.

Our advice is pretty simple: even if you slid all the way to this point in your lives together, it's not too late to start making decisions. It's not too late to decide to make your marriage all it can be.

The Long-Term View

When people are more dedicated to their partners, they want and expect the relationship to last. They want to grow old together. This expectation that the relationship will continue over the long term is a core part of dedication and plays a critical role in the day-to-day quality of marriage. It's crucial for one simple reason: no relationship is consistently satisfying. None.

What gets couples through tougher times is the long-term view that commitment brings. How? When you actively decide you are in it and will keep trying, you can more safely deal with the curve balls life throws at you. The long-term view stretches out the time perspective for you, making it easier not to overreact to the small, annoying events in life.

The long-term view stretches out the time perspective for you, making it easier not to overreact to the small annoying events in life.

There's a deep sense of security that comes from knowing you and your partner are in it for the long haul, and that promotes lasting happiness. When you feel secure, you are more likely to interpret a conflict that comes up as exactly what it is: a temporary issue to be resolved and moved on from, not an epic battle that will affect the fate of your relationship. Commitment—dedication in action—nurtures all the best things in a relationship.

In the absence of a long-term view, people tend to focus on immediate payoffs. This is only natural. If the long term is uncertain, we concentrate on what we're getting in the present. The message is, "You'd better produce, or I'll look for someone who can." Most of us resent feeling like we could be abandoned by someone from whom we expected to find security and acceptance. People generally do not invest in a relationship with an uncertain future and reward.

This is why it is also so important to never dangle the threat of divorce or breaking up when things escalate and angry words get spoken. Doing this undermines the whole premise that there is a future to invest in together. Commitment might not mean "never having to say you're sorry" (you do!), but it should mean not living in fear that one bad fight can lead to it all coming apart.

The importance of having a long-term perspective was captured well by M. Scott Peck in *The Road Less Traveled*: "Couples cannot resolve in any healthy way the universal issues of marriage: dependency and independence, dominance and submission, freedom and fidelity, for example, without the security of knowing that the act of struggling over these issues will not destroy the relationship."

We're not saying people should make a Herculean effort to save a marriage, particularly if it is abusive or destructive. However, for the great number of couples who genuinely love each other and want to make their marriages work, a long-term perspective is essential for encouraging each partner to take risks, be vulnerable, and trust that the other will be there when it really counts.

Family communication expert Fran Dickson has studied lifelong married couples. She found that the happier couples reported having talked regularly about their future over their years together. What these couples described is a great way to nurture a vision for a future together. Such talking does not mean locking in all the details, but rather dreaming and reminding one another that the relationship has a future as well as a history. This is one of the powerful things we recommend the two of you try to do together.

Archimedes said that he could move the world with a place to stand and a long enough lever. His point was really about physics and mechanical leverage, but his lesson remains true: making a difference in your relationship is going to involve figuring out where you stand and what levers you are willing to pull to do your part. Harnessing the leverage of commitment will help you take hold of your relationship future. Practice expressing your commitment daily and reap the lifetime rewards.

Talking Points

1. Commitment is a complex concept, involving both external constraints that hold relationships together, and dedication, which helps keep alive the desire to stay in a relationship.

2. Choices about how you think about your partner, how you behave together, and how high a priority you give the relationship determine your level of commitment.

3. You need to believe in the future of your relationship in order to keep it growing and strong.

Suggested Activity

This is an activity you can do on your own, any time you like. It describes small ways you can act in ways that show your commitment.

Make a list of things you can do that fit all three of these characteristics:

1. Small behaviors that you know your partner appreciates

2. Things you could do on just about any given day

3. Things you are unlikely to do all that often

That list will be things that you know make a difference for your partner that you can do but are not likely to do—but you could, and you know it. Why do we emphasize small things? Because they can happen any day. Most days do not provide an opportunity to perform some life-altering act of sacrifice for your partner. But the small stuff? Yeah, you can make those things happen. Your partner won't always notice but they will notice enough, and it will make a difference.

Small beats big. Get going.

17

Moving Forward

A longtime collaborator of ours, Bill Coffin, likes to suggest that couples think about relationship fitness as they might think about physical fitness. Just as you should work out three or four times a week for twenty to thirty minutes, you and your partner should devote at least that much time to working on your relationship.

By *work* we don't just mean having dedicated weekly meetings. It also includes planning fun times together, having friendship talks, being supportive, having sex, hanging out together reading a book or watching TV in the same room, listening to music, or simply being together in some other way. Make the time for your relationship to be regularly renewed in these ways.

One of the annoying facts of life is that as a marriage goes on, the positive aspects of it inevitably diminish, either because they slip away or are killed off by conflict. When this happens, it can seem very hard, if not impossible, to restart the engine. One major purpose of this book is to show you that recapturing what's been lost is far from impossible—and not even as hard as it may seem—if you consciously *decide* to work toward change. To push yourself even if things are uncomfortable at first, as they inevitably will be. To stick to the empirically proven plans laid out in the previous pages. *To fight for your marriage.*

When something that used to happen naturally early on in your marriage (kissing, holding hands, saying "I love you," having sex) stops happening, what do you do? If you're like most couples, probably nothing. So why not try to . . . well, do something? *Decide* to kiss your partner when you leave for work; decide to hold hands while you're on a walk; decide to say "I love you" face-to-face and in texts, e-mails, and phone calls; decide to initiate sensual touching. (As Howard likes to ask couples at his retreats: "Is it illegal where you live to hold hands?") So much of relationship fitness simply involves repeating and reinforcing positive habits, no matter how small, and reducing negative ones.

UNLOCKING THE MARRIAGE YOU WANT

At the beginning of our book we talked about the three keys to a great relationship:

1. Make it safe to connect.
2. Decide, don't slide.
3. Do your part.

They are reinforced throughout the book repeatedly because of how important they are. In light of this, take a look at your relationship right now and ask yourself: Are you making it safe to connect so that you can be supportive in ways that are meaningful to your partner? Are you deciding to act in ways that benefit your relationship and making an effort to control conflict and talk without fighting? Are you doing your part to make sure that fun, friendship, and sexuality are alive and well in your relationship? In brief, are you deliberately focusing on the areas of your relationship that need attention? If you're serious about incorporating these keys into your life, here are some important things to keep in mind.

Review

To get the most out of what we've presented in this book, be sure to review the material whenever you find yourself having an issue in your relationship and unsure how to best proceed. We all learn better when we go over key concepts again and again. For example, it would be a great time to go back to Chapter Nine and review the ground rules. Are you using them? Have you kept at it?

It would be especially valuable to review the rules for the Speaker Listener Technique, the six types of support, how to make positive connections a priority, and the principles of forgiveness. None of these rules or ideas are all that complicated, but you have to master them to really reap their benefits. Better yet, after some time has passed, read through the whole book again.

Keep in mind as you review this book that you can only do *your* part. Also, no one we have worked with over the years has followed every rule and principle—nor would we expect them to. Keep what has worked for you and your partner and ditch what hasn't. Also think about what ideas you'd like to test out more as you continue in your journey.

As you review this book, remember that you can only do your *part.*

Practice

In our humble opinion, the biggest thing that separates this book from so many other marriage books (and there are many out there) is that it details very specific actions you can take. It helps readers develop real skills, not philosophical frameworks or other well-meaning but ultimately abstract solutions. Building a stronger marriage isn't all that different from learning a new language or instrument (though probably a lot simpler!). Anyone can be taught to do it.

The key to such an approach is to practice the skills and ways of thinking we've recommended. It's not enough just to review the ideas, though. You need to practice the techniques and strategies to make them a part of your life. Commit to employing them in your everyday interactions, even when—especially when—it feels hard. Do this enough and they'll become automatic.

A friend and colleague of ours, Bob Weiss, notes the difference between being under *rule control* rather than *stimulus control*. To be under stimulus control means you're constantly *reacting* to the things happening around you, the stimuli of your life. If you don't want to be controlled by outside events but would rather make your own loving and conscious choices (rules) that guide your behavior, you need to practice the strategies that give you more control over how you approach things. No idea we present can help you unless you're ready to put it into action.

Engage Your Skills

As you strengthen your skills through practice and the development of positive rituals, the most important goal is for you to be able to call on your skills when you need them. Knowing how to use the Speaker Listener Technique or the problem-solving model is great, but the real benefit comes from applying these tools when you need them most.

Unfortunately, the times you're most likely to need a skill are often the times it's hardest to use them, so being able to deploy them automatically is critical. That's why we've offered suggested activities throughout the book. That's where practice and good habits really pay off. For example, as you work on the Time Out ground rule, it'll be harder at the start than after using it a few times. Time Outs can seem like a type of avoidance when you start using them, but eventually you will see how powerful it is to hit Pause temporarily when a conflict threatens to spiral out of control. Your relationship will benefit significantly when you and your partner take control over how and when you'll deal with difficult issues.

Reinforce, Reinforce, Reinforce

When we train other professionals and paraprofessionals to work with couples, we emphasize over and over the need to provide positive reinforcement (e.g., praise and appreciation) as couples learn the skills we teach. As important as it is to teach new skills, it's no less critical to reinforce any positive changes that are already happening.

We offer the same suggestion to you. As you work on learning new patterns and ways of thinking, offer positive reinforcement to yourself and your partner. Praise them for listening well, for working with you to handle an issue more productively, for being committed, and so forth. Don't take each other for granted. Show your appreciation for a positive effort. And don't dwell on the past. In other words, don't say, "Why couldn't you have done this seven years ago?" Instead, focus on reinforcing the important changes that are occurring *now*.

When was the last time you said, "I love how you do that" or "I really appreciated it that you dropped what you were doing the other night to listen to me talk about my issues at work"? It's not hard to say "Thanks" or "Great job!" or "I really appreciated that." Best of all, the effects of these small gestures on your relationship can be dramatic.

In life and in marriage, it's way too easy to focus on the negative. Instead, decide to push yourself to reward positive changes and to truly appreciate all the great things about your partner and your relationship. Love with abandon and generosity, and then behold the power of love.

*Love with abandon and generosity, and then behold the
power of love.*

GO CONFIDENTLY INTO YOUR SHARED FUTURE

One result of following the advice in this book is that it will foster confidence in you and your partner. By *confidence* we mean a feeling deep down that you can work through almost any disagreement or disappointment. When you are confident, you boldly move into the future together as a team, secure in the knowledge that things will turn out OK. (And, as you very well know by now, the importance of safety and security in a relationship can't be overstated.)

Now that you've read the book, you know what to do. But will you do it? Your challenge is to put what we have talked about in our book into action in your life.

We are relationship optimists. We believe that it's (almost) never too late to reboot a relationship that's on the ropes, or to take a relationship from "going fine" to "going amazing." We also firmly believe that the principles explored in this edition of *Fighting for Your Marriage* will help you not only in your marriage but also in other key areas of your life, including parenting and work.

Although we have tried to make this book fun and easy to read, relationships are not all fun. They take work. But we hope that with dedication, making the right decisions at critical times, and a strong sense of commitment, you will have every chance to fulfill the dream that most people in the world cherish: to have a healthy, happy relationship that stands the test of time.

As our journey together comes to a close and yours moves forward, keep in mind our keys to a great relationship one last time: make it safe to connect, decide don't slide, and do your part. Focus on being a team and protecting and enhancing the positives: fun, support, and friendship. Remember to keep investing *no matter what*. And if you do decide to fight, fight *for* your marriage and win!

Getting More Help

This book describes strategies and skills that are taught in workshops based on the PREP Approach. There are many situations in which people need a lot more help than can be provided in a book or a workshop. People experiencing serious relationship and individual problems may benefit greatly from seeking more help.

Because you are taking this time to think more about your life and relationships, it may also be a good time to think about other services that you or others you care about may need. Even if your main goal right now is to improve your relationship, difficulties in other areas can make it harder to make your relationship work. Likewise, if you are having really severe problems in your relationship, they can make dealing with any of these other problems that much harder.

Here are some areas where additional help could be important for you and your family. After describing some of the areas where more help can be especially important, we will mention some ways to find some of these types of help.

Financial Problems

- Serious money problems make everything else harder.
- Job loss and unemployment can be key sources of conflict and stress for couples.

- Although this book can help you as a couple work more as a team, you may need more help to learn to manage your finances or find a job.

Serious Relationship or Other Family Problems and Stresses

- If you have ongoing serious relationship or marital problems where more help is needed, you should consider seeking counseling from someone who specializes in helping couples.

- Coping with a serious, life-threatening, or chronic illness or disability in a child or adult can place a lot of stress on caregivers and their family relationships. Community resources often exist to help families with these kinds of issues.

Substance Abuse, Addictions, and Other Compulsive Behaviors

- No matter what else you have to deal with in life, you will find it harder if you or your partner, or another close family member, has a substance abuse problem.

- Drug or alcohol abuse and addiction rob a person of the ability to handle life well, have close relationships, and be a good parent.

- Drug or alcohol abuse can also make it harder to control anger and violence.

- Other problems couples and families sometimes face include eating disorders, sexual addictions, and gambling.

You need to decide to get help with these problems to improve your life and the lives of those you love.

Mental Health Problems

- Mental health problems come in many forms, from anxiety to depression to schizophrenia, and place a great deal of stress on couple and family relationships.

- Depression is particularly common when there are serious relationship problems. And, even when not a result of relationship problems, depression can cause difficulties in a relationship. Couple therapy can be quite helpful when one or both partners is struggling with depression or anxiety.

- Attention deficit disorder affects adults, not just children, and it can lead to more difficulties in a relationship.

- Having thoughts of suicide is often a sign of depression. Seek help if you struggle with such thoughts.

- A history of trauma(s) (such as from abuse, neglect, discrimination, and violence) can lead to symptoms of post-traumatic stress disorder (PTSD) and other chronic impairments in one's ability to feel safe, calm, and focused.

The good news is that there are now many effective treatments for mental health problems, with services available in all counties in the US, including options for those with limited means of paying. There have been advances in the treatment of PTSD and other effects of trauma, with an increasing number of therapists and others in communities being able to provide trauma-informed care.

Domestic Aggression and Violence

- Although domestic aggression and violence of any sort is wrong and dangerous, experts recognize different types and/or differing levels of severity. For example:

  - Some couples have arguments that get out of control, with frustration spilling over into pushing, shoving, or slapping. This can be dangerous, especially if you don't take strong measures to stop the patterns from continuing.

  - The type of domestic violence that gets the most attention in the media is when one partner uses aggression or coercion to control their partner. Fear of one's partner is a hallmark symptom for these abusive relationships. Verbal abuse, threats of harm, and forced sexual activity can be part of this pattern.

- This book is not a treatment program for physical aggression or domestic violence. If you are dealing with aggression and violence in your relationship, you need more help than this book can provide. That might mean seeking marital or relationship counseling or seeking the advice of domestic violence experts.

- If you have any questions about the safety of your relationship, you should contact a domestic violence program or hotline, especially if you feel that you are in danger of being harmed.

You must do what you need to do to ensure that you and your children are safe. If you ever feel that you are in immediate danger from your partner or others, call 911 for help or contact your local domestic violence hotline.

Where to Get More Help

If you, your partner, or your relationship experiences any of these or other difficulties, we strongly recommend that you get more help.

There are many ways to find out about resources in your community. You can ask a trusted physician, caregiver, or wise friend for help in finding resources. For example, your doctor or other caregiver may know of local therapists or counseling centers that they trust. When possible, seek out therapists who have worked with the types of difficulties for which you are seeking help. There are also community mental health centers in cities and counties across the US. Some communities also have programs that help people in managing money or seeking employment. Such help might be provided by the extension department of a local university. Searching the web for local resources in your community might lead you to some of the best resources for your needs.

The following are some of the national hotline numbers or websites that can help when you or someone you love is in crisis.

If you are outside the US, you can search for similar types of resources in your country.

National Resources

National Domestic Violence Hotline: SAFELINE, text START to 88788 or call 1-800-799-SAFE (7233)

SAMHSA: for getting help with mental health and substance abuse/use disorders: https://findtreatment.gov/ or call 1-800-662-HELP (4357)

Suicide & Crisis Lifeline: Text 988 or call 1-800-273-TALK (8255)

Resources Regarding PREP

This book is based on decades of research and development on the Prevention and Relationship Education Program (PREP). There is a business that disseminates materials and resources based on the PREP Approach to relationship education.

You can learn more about these resources at https://prepinc.com/.

PREPinc.com is focused on resources that are widely used by community leaders and agencies to teach workshops for those they serve covering the principles, skills, and strategies of PREP. At that website, you will find the following:

- Descriptions of various curricula for different audiences

- Descriptions of how one can become trained to facilitate and deliver any of the various curricula to their audience

- Background information and history on PREP and the research on which it is based

Couples who are interested in an online course in PREP, called *ePREP*, can access it at the website LoveTakesLearning.com. This online version of PREP is available only in English, and it is not available in most countries outside the US due to the complexities of taxes on digital products.

Books

In addition to the book you are holding, there are many other titles from the PREP team.

12 Hours to a Great Marriage: A Step-by-Step Guide for Making Love Last by Howard J. Markman, Scott M. Stanley, Susan L. Blumberg, Natalie H. Jenkins, and Carol Whiteley

This clear self-guided book provides busy couples with practical steps on how to make their love last.

The Power of Commitment: A Guide to Active Lifelong Love by Scott M. Stanley

Best-selling marriage expert Dr. Scott Stanley shows couples the way to active, lasting love through an understanding of what commitment can do for a relationship.

Why Do Fools Fall in Love? Experiencing the Magic, Mystery, and Meaning of Successful Relationships by Janice R. Levine, Howard J. Markman

This book is a collection of creative essays that is a remarkable mix of science, psychology, personal insight, and passionate stories focused on the chemistry of lasting love.

A Lasting Promise: A Christian Guide to Fighting for Your Marriage by Scott M. Stanley, Daniel Trathen, Savanna McCain, and Milt Bryan

This book was written for those seeking a faith-based, Christian viewpoint on the skills and strategies of PREP.

References by Chapter or Theme

Throughout this book, we sometimes mention specific studies or general summaries of findings from studies related to the topic at hand. We do not use footnotes, but we do put citations we have used or are thinking about, or specifically have referred to, in this section, which we organize by chapter or theme. Some chapters are so distinct that we list them separately. Some are related to broad themes (e.g., communication, conflict management) so we collapse all citations for that topic in one section.

GENERAL CITATIONS OR BACKGROUND RESOURCES

These are just a few of the important citations or resources directly related to the research on PREP (the Prevention and Relationship Education Program), the field of preventive relationship education, or ideas in this book.

For a list of citations of studies on variations of PREP, you can access a document at https://app.box.com/s/eerhvl6vh4cstn59bdt2.

The website for PREP has a number of sections describing its history and content relevant to PREP and this book. There are also descriptions of adaptations of PREP, training opportunities, and curricula that are available for use in relationship education: https://prepinc.com/.

Cowan, P. A., & Cowan, C. P. (2014). Controversies in Couple Relationship Education (CRE): Overlooked evidence and implications for research and policy. *Psychology, Public Policy, and Law, 20*(4), 362–383.

Gurman, A. S., Lebow, J. L., & Snyder, D. K. (2023). *Clinical handbook of couple therapy* (6th ed.). Guilford Press.

Hahlweg, K., Markman, H. J., Thurmaier, F., Engl, J., & Eckert, V. (1998). Prevention of marital distress: Results of a German prospective longitudinal study. *Journal of Family Psychology, 12*(4), 543–556.

Halford, W. K., Markman, H. J., & Stanley, S. M. (2008). Strengthening couple relationships with education: Social policy and public health perspectives. *Journal of Family Psychology, 22*, 497–505.

Hawkins, A. J., Blanchard, V. L., Baldwin, S. A., & Fawcett, E. B. (2008). Does marriage and relationship education work? A meta-analytic study. *Journal of Consulting and Clinical Psychology, 76*(5), 723–734.

Hawkins, A. J., Hokanson, S., Loveridge, E., Milius, E., Duncan, M., Booth, M., & Pollard, B. (2022). How effective are ACF-funded couple relationship education programs? A meta-analytic study. *Family Process, 61*(3), 970–985.

Levine, J. (1998). The Couples Health Program: Overview. Retrieved from http://www.janicelevine.com/CouplesHealth Program.html

Mace, D., & Mace, V. (1980). Enriching marriages: The foundation stone of family strength. In N. Stinnett, B. Chesser, J. DeFrain, & P. Knaub (Eds.), *Family strengths: Positive models for family life* (pp. 89–110). University of Nebraska Press.

Markman, H. J., & Floyd, F. (1980). Possibilities for the prevention of marital discord: A behavioral perspective. *American Journal of Family Therapy, 8*(2), 29–48.

Markman, H., Floyd, F., Stanley, S. & Lewis, H. (1986). Prevention. In N. Jacobson & A. Gurman (Eds.), *Clinical handbook of marital therapy* (pp. 172–195). Guilford Press.

Markman, H. J., Hawkins, A. J., Stanley, S. M., Halford, W. K., & Rhoades, G. (2022). Helping couples achieve relationship success: A decade of progress in couple relationship education research and practice, 2010–2019. *Journal of Marital and Family Therapy, 48*(1), 251–282.

Markman, H. J., & Rhoades, G. K. (2012). Relationship education research: Current status and future directions. *Journal of Marital and Family Therapy, 38,* 169–200.

Markman, H. J., Rhoades, G. K., Stanley, S. M., Ragan, E., & Whitton, S. (2010). The premarital communication roots of marital distress: The first five years of marriage. *Journal of Family Psychology, 24,* 289–298.

Stanley, S. M., Carlson, R. G., Rhoades, G. K., Markman, H. J., Ritchie, L. L., & Hawkins, A. J. (2020). Best practices in relationship education focused on intimate relationships. *Family Relations, 69,* 497–519.

INTRODUCTION

Brown, S. L., & Lin, I. (2022). The graying of divorce: A half century of change. *Psychological Sciences and Social Sciences, 77,* 1710–1720.

Burgess, E. W., & Locke, H. J. (1945). *The family: From institution to companionship.* American Book Co.

Cherlin, A. J. (2014). *Labor's love lost: The rise and fall of the working-class family in America.* Russell Sage Foundation.

Cohen, P. N. (2019). The coming divorce decline. *Socius,* p. 5.

Coontz, S. (2006). *Marriage, a history: How love conquered marriage.* Viking.

Dixon, S. J. (2019). Online dating site or app experiences of users in the United States as of October 2019. Retrieved from https://www.statista.com/statistics/309384/us-online-dating-site-or-app-experiences/

Finkel, E. J. (2017). *The all-or-nothing marriage: How the best marriages work*. Dutton.

Fry, R. (2023). A record-high share of 40-year-olds in the U.S. have never been married. Pew Research Center. Retrieved from https://www.pewresearch.org/short-reads/2023/06/28/a-record-high-share-of-40-year-olds-in-the-us-have-never-been-married/

Guzzo, K. B. (2014). Trends in cohabitation outcomes: Compositional changes and engagement among never-married young adults. *Journal of Marriage and Family, 76*, 826–842.

Kearney, M. S. (2023). *The two-parent privilege: How Americans stopped getting married and started falling behind*. University of Chicago Press.

Kennedy, S., & Ruggles, S. (2014). Breaking up is hard to count: The rise of divorce in the United States, 1980–2010. *Demography, 51*(2), 587–598.

Korhonen, V. (2023). Estimated median age of Americans at their first wedding in the United States from 1998 to 2022, by sex. Retrieved from https://www.statista.com/statistics/371933/median-age-of-us-americans-at-their-first-wedding/

Manning, W. D. (2015). Cohabitation and child wellbeing. *The Future of Children, 25*(2), 51–66.

Nock, S. L. (2009). The growing importance of marriage in America. In H. E. Peters & C. M. Kamp Dush (Eds.), *Marriage and family: Perspectives and complexities* (pp. 302–324). Columbia University Press.

Payne, K. K., (2012). Median age at first marriage, 2010 (FP-12-07). National Center for Family & Marriage Research.

Retrieved from https://scholarworks.bgsu.edu/ncfmr_family_profiles/26/

Rackin, H. M., & Gibson-Davis, C. M. (2018). Social class divergence in family transitions: The importance of cohabitation. *Journal of Marriage and Family*, 80, 1271–1286.

Richards, L., Franks, M., & Shrout, R. (2023, January 13th). Marriage provides health benefits—and here's why. *The Conversation*. Retrieved from https://theconversation.com/marriage-provides-health-benefits-and-heres-why-190731

Rosenfeld, M. J., Thomas, R. J., & Hausen, S. (2019). Disintermediating your friends: How online dating in the United States displaces other ways of meeting. *PNAS*, 116(36), 17753–17758.

Smock, P. J., & Schwartz, C. R. (2020). The demography of families: A review of patterns and change. *Journal of Marriage and Family*, 82(1), 9–34.

Twenge, J. M. (2017). *iGen: The 10 trends shaping today's young people—and the nation*. Atria Books.

US Census Bureau. Median age at first marriage: 1890 to present. Retrieved from https://www.census.gov/content/dam/Census/library/visualizations/time-series/demo/families-and-households/ms-2.pdf

US Census Bureau. National marriage and divorce rates declined from 2011 to 2021. Retrieved from https://www.census.gov/library/stories/2023/07/marriage-divorce-rates.html

US Census Bureau. Provisional number of marriages and marriage rate, divorces annulments and rate 2000–2020. Retrieved from https://www.cdc.gov/nchs/data/dvs/national-marriage-divorce-rates-00–20.pdf

Wilcox, B. (2024). *Get married: Why Americans must defy the elites, forge strong families, and save civilization*. Broadside Books.

Wolfinger, N. H. (2023). Family change in the context of social changes in the U.S. In M. Daly, N. Gilbert, B. Pfau-Effinge, & D. Besharov (Eds.), *The Oxford handbook of family policy: A life-course perspective*. Oxford University Press.

THREE KEYS

Cordova, J. V., Gee, C. G., & Warren, L. Z. (2005). Emotional skillfulness in marriage: Intimacy as a mediator of the relationship between emotional skillfulness and marital satisfaction. *Journal of Social and Clinical Psychology, 24*, 218–235.

Doss, B. D., Thum, Y., Sevier, M., Atkins, D. C., & Christensen, A. (2005). Improving relationships: Mechanisms of change in couple therapy. *Journal of Consulting and Clinical Psychology, 73*(4), 624–633.

Sibley, D. S., Kimmes, J. G., & Schmidt, A. E. (2015). Generating new stories of commitment in couple relationships by utilizing the sliding versus deciding framework. *Journal of Family Psychotherapy, 26*, 68–73.

Stanley, S. M., & Markman, H. J. (2020). Helping couples in the shadow of COVID-19. *Family Process, 59*, 937–955.

Stanley, S. M., Markman, H. J., Jenkins, N. H., Rhoades, G. K., Noll, L., & Ramos, L. D. (2006). *Within our reach leader manual*. PREP Educational Products, Inc.

Stanley, S. M., Rhoades, G. K., & Markman, H. J. (2006). Sliding versus deciding: Inertia and the premarital cohabitation effect. *Family Relations, 55*(4), 499–509.

LOVE

Buscaglia, L. F. (1982). *Love*. SLACK, Inc.

Levine, J. R. (2001). Behold: The power of love. In J. R. Levine & H. J. Markman (Eds.), *Why do fools fall in love?* (pp. 3–7). Jossey-Bass.

Levine, J. L., & Markman, H. J. (2001). *Why do fools fall in love: Experiencing the magic, mystery, and meaning of successful relationships.* Jossey-Bass.

Markman, H. J. (2001). Unraveling the mysteries of love. In J. R. Levine and H. J. Markman (Eds.), *Why do fools fall in love?* (pp. 199–206). Jossey-Bass.

Noller, P. (1996). What is this thing called love? Defining the love that supports marriage and family. *Personal Relationships, 3,* 97–115.

Sternberg, R. J. (1986). The triangular theory of love. *Psychological Review, 93*(2), 119–135.

Sternberg, R. (2000). *Cupid's arrow: The course of love through time.* Cambridge University Press.

COMMUNICATION AND CONFLICT

This section includes references related to the content of the chapters on Communication Danger Signs, communication techniques, the issues and events model, problem-solving, and ground rules.

Amato, P. R., & Previti, D. (2003). People's reasons for divorcing. *Journal of Family Issues, 24,* 602–626.

Baumeister, R. F., Bratslavsky, E., Finkenauer, C., & Vohs, K. D. (2001). Bad is stronger than good. *Review of General Psychology, 5,* 323–370.

Birchler, G., Weiss, R., & Vincent, J. (1975). Multimethod analysis of social reinforcement exchange between maritally distressed and nondistressed spouse and stranger dyads. *Journal of Personality and Social Psychology, 31,* 349–360.

Bradbury, T. N., Beach, S.R.H., Fincham, F. D., & Nelson, G. M. (1996). Attributions and behavior in functional and dysfunctional marriages. *Journal of Consulting and Clinical Psychology, 64,* 569–576.

Bradbury, T. N., & Fincham, F. D. (1992). Attributions and behavior in marital interaction. *Journal of Personality and Social Psychology, 63*(4), 613–628.

Carrere, S., & Gottman, J.M. (1999). Predicting divorce among newlyweds from the first three minutes of a marital conflict discussion. *Family Process, 38*(3), 293–301.

Christensen, A., & Heavey, C. L. (1990). Gender and social structure in the demand/withdraw pattern of marital conflict. *Journal of Personality and Social Psychology, 59*, 73–82.

Clements, M. L., Stanley, S. M., & Markman, H. J. (2004). Before they said "I do": Discriminating among marital outcomes over 13 years based on premarital data. *Journal of Marriage and Family, 66*, 613–626.

Cummings, E. M., & Davies, P. (1994). *Children and marital conflict.* Guilford Press.

Emery, R. (1982). Interparental conflict and the children of discord and divorce. *Psychological Bulletin, 92*, 310–330.

Fincham, F. D., & Beach, S. R. (1999). Marital conflict: Implications for working with couples. *Annual Review of Psychology, 50*, 47–77.

Fisher, R., Ury, W. L., & Patton, B. (2011). *Getting to yes: Negotiating agreement without giving in.* Penguin Books.

Gottman, J. M. (1993). The roles of conflict engagement, escalation or avoidance in marital interaction: A longitudinal view of five types of couples. *Journal of Consulting and Clinical Psychology, 61*, 6B15.

Gottman, J. (1994). *What predicts divorce? The relationship between marital process and marital outcomes.* Lawrence Erlbaum.

Gottman, J. M., Coan, J., Carrere, S., & Swanson, C. (1998). Predicting marital happiness and stability from newlywed interactions. *Journal of Marriage and the Family, 60*(1), 5–22.

Gottman, J., & Levenson, R.W., (2002). A two-factor model for predicting when a couple will divorce—Exploratory analyses using 14-year longitudinal data. *Family Process, 41*(1), 83–96.

Gottman, J., Levenson, R., & Woodin, E., (2001). Facial expressions during marital conflict. *Journal of Family Communication, 1*(1), 37–57.

Gottman, J., Notarius, C., Gonso, J., & Markman, H. (1976). *A couple's guide to communication.* Research Press.

Grych, J., & Fincham, F. (1990). Marital conflict and children's adjustment. *Psychological Bulletin, 108,* 267–290.

Heavey, C. L., Christensen, A., & Malamuth, N. M. (1995). The longitudinal impact of demand and withdrawal during marital conflict. *Journal of Consulting and Clinical Psychology, 63,* 797–801.

Heyman, R. E., & Smith Slep, A. M. (2001). The hazards of predicting divorce without crossvalidation. *Journal of Marriage and Family, 63,* 473–479.

Johnson, M., Lavner, J., Mund, M., Zemp, M., Stanley, S. M., Neyer, F. J., Impett, E., Rhoades, G. K., Bodenmann, G., Weidmann, R., Bühler, J., Burriss, R., Wünsche, J., & Grob, A. (2022). Within-couple associations between communication and relationship satisfaction over time. *Personality and Social Psychology Bulletin, 48*(4), 534–549.

Karney, B. R., & Bradbury, T. N. (1995). The longitudinal course of marital quality and stability: A review of theory, method, and research. *Psychological Bulletin, 118,* 3–34.

Kiecolt-Glaser, J. K., Malarkey, W. B., Chee, M., Newton, T., Cacioppo, J. T., Mao, H. Y., & Glaser, R. (1993). Negative behavior during marital conflict is associated with immunological down-regulation. *Psychosomatic Medicine, 55,* 395–409.

Kiecolt-Glaser J. K., & Wilson, S. J. (2017). Lovesick: Couples' relationships and health. *Annual Review of Clinical Psychology, 13,* 421–443.

Kline, G. H., Wood, L. F., & Moore, S. (2003). Validation of revised measures of family and interparental conflict for use with young adults. *Journal of Divorce & Remarriage, 39* (3–4), 125–142.

Lawrence, E., Orengo-Aguayo, R. E., Langer, A., & Brock, R. L. (2012). The impact and consequences of partner abuse on partners. *Partner Abuse, 3,* 406–428.

Markman, H. J. (1981). The prediction of marital distress: A five year follow-up. *Journal of Consulting and Clinical Psychology, 49,* 760–762.

Markman, H. J., & Hahlweg, K. (1993). The prediction and prevention of marital distress: An international perspective. *Clinical Psychology Review, 13,* 29–43.

Markman, H. J., & Kraft, S. A. (1989). Men and women in marriage: Dealing with gender differences in marital therapy. *Behavior Therapist, 12,* 51–56.

Markman, H. J., Rhoades, G. K., Stanley, S. M., Ragan, E., & Whitton, S. (2010). The premarital communication roots of marital distress: The first five years of marriage. *Journal of Family Psychology, 24,* 289–298.

Matthews, L. S., Wickrama, K.A.S., & Conger, R. D. (1996). Predicting marital instability from spouse and observer reports of marital interaction. *Journal of Marriage and the Family, 58,* 641–655.

McNulty, J. K., & Karney, B. R. (2002). Expectancy confirmation in appraisals of marital interactions. *Personality and Social Psychology Bulletin, 28,* 764–775.

Notarius, C., & Markman, H. J. (1993). *We can work it out: Making sense of marital conflict.* Putnam.

Owen, J., Manthos, M., & Quirk, K. (2013). Dismantling study of Prevention and Relationship Education Program:

The effects of a structured communication intervention. *Journal of Family Psychology, 27*(2), 336–341.

Scott, S. B., Rhoades, G. K., Stanley, S. M., Allen, E. S., & Markman, H. J. (2013). Reasons for divorce and recollections of premarital intervention: Implications for improving relationship education. *Couple and Family Psychology: Research and Practice, 2*(2),131–145.

Snyder, M., & Swann, W.B. (1978) Behavioral confirmation in social interaction: From social perception to social reality. *Journal of Experimental Social Psychology, 14*, 148–162.

Stanley, S. M., Markman, H. J., & Whitton, S. (2002). Communication, conflict, and commitment: Insights on the foundations of relationship success from a national survey. *Family Process, 41*, 659–675.

Storaasli, R. D., & Markman, H. J. (1990). Relationship problems in the early stages of marriage: A longitudinal investigation. *Journal of Family Psychology, 4*, 80–98.

van Eldik, W. M., de Haan, A. D., Parry, L. Q., Davies, P. T., Luijk, M.P.C.M., Arends, L. R., & Prinzie, P. (2020). The interparental relationship: Meta-analytic associations with children's maladjustment and responses to interparental conflict. *Psychological Bulletin, 146*(7), 553–594.

Weiss, R. L. (1980). Strategic behavioral marital therapy: Toward a model for assessment and intervention. *Advances in Family Intervention, Assessment and Theory, 1*, 229–271.

FILTERS

Bradbury, T. N., Beach, S.R.H., Fincham, F. D., & Nelson, G. M. (1996). Attributions and behavior in functional and dysfunctional marriages. *Journal of Consulting and Clinical Psychology, 64*, 569–576.

Bradbury, T. N., & Fincham, F. D. (1990). Attributions in marriage: Review and critique. *Psychological Bulletin, 107,* 3–33.

Bradbury, T. N., & Fincham, F. D. (1992). Attributions and behavior in marital interaction. *Journal of Personality and Social Psychology, 63*(4), 613–628.

Fincham, F. D. (2001). Attributions and close relationships: From Balkanization to integration. In G. J. Fletcher & M. Clark (Eds.), *Blackwell handbook of social psychology* (pp. 3–31). Blackwell.

Kahneman, D., & Tversky, A. (1990). Prospect theory: An analysis of decision under risk. In P. K. Moser (Ed.), *Rationality in action: Contemporary approaches* (pp. 140–170). Cambridge University Press.

Loftus, E. F. (2017). Eavesdropping on memory. *Annual Review of Psychology, 68,* 1–18.

McNulty, J. K., & Karney, B. R. (2002). Expectancy confirmation in appraisals of marital interactions. *Personality and Social Psychology Bulletin, 28,* 764–775.

Mynatt, C. R., Doherty, M. E., & Tweney, R. D. (1977). Confirmation bias in a simulated research environment: An experimental study of scientific inference. *Quarterly Journal of Experimental Psychology, 29,* 85–95.

Snyder, M., & Swann, W. B. (1978). Behavioral confirmation in social interaction: From social perception to social reality. *Journal of Experimental Social Psychology, 14,* 148–162.

Tversky, A., & Kahneman, D. (1974). Judgment under uncertainty: Heuristics and biases. *Science, 185*(4157), 1124–1131.

Weiss, R. L. (1980). Strategic behavioral marital therapy: Toward a model for assessment and intervention. *Advances in Family Intervention, Assessment and Theory, 1,* 229–271.

Zadra, J. R., & Clore, G. L. (2011). Emotion and perception: The role of affective information. *Wiley Interdisciplinary Reviews–Cognitive Science, 2*(6), 676–685.

FUN AND FRIENDSHIP, SUPPORT, AND SENSUALITY

Amato, P. R., Booth, A., Johnson, D. R., & Rogers, S. J. (2007). *Alone together*. Harvard University Press.

Beach, S.R.H., Fincham, F. D., Hurt, T. R., McNair, L. M., & Stanley, S. M. (2008). Prayer and marital intervention: A conceptual framework. *Journal of Social and Clinical Psychology, 27*, 641–669.

Burgess, E. W., & Locke, H. J. (1945). *The family: From institution to companionship*. American Book Co.

Centers for Disease Control and Prevention (CDC). (2023). Health risks of social isolation and loneliness. Retrieved from https://www.cdc.gov/emotional-wellbeing/social-connectedness/loneliness.htm

Cordova, J. V., Gee, C. G., & Warren, L. Z. (2005). Emotional skillfulness in marriage: Intimacy as a mediator of the relationship between emotional skillfulness and marital satisfaction. *Journal of Social and Clinical Psychology, 24*, 218–235.

Cordova, J. V., & Scott, R. (2001). Intimacy: A behavioral interpretation. *The Behavior Analyst, 24*, 76–86.

Cox, D. A. (2021). The state of American friendship: Change, challenges, and loss. Findings from the May 2021 American Perspectives Survey. The American Enterprise Institute. Retrieved from https://www.americansurveycenter.org/research/the-state-of-american-friendship-change-challenges-and-loss/

Crawford, D. W., Houts, R. M., Huston, T. L., & George, L. J. (2002). Compatibility, leisure, and satisfaction in marital relationships. *Journal of Marriage and Family, 64*, 433–449.

Cutrona, C. (1996). *Social support in couples: Marriage as a resource in times of stress.* Sage.

Dehle, C., Larsen, D., & Landers, J. E. (2001). Social support in marriage. *American Journal of Family Therapy, 29*, 307–324.

Denby, D. (2018). Portrait of an artist as an old man: Mel Brooks in his 90s. The Atlantic. Retrieved from https://www.theatlantic.com/entertainment/archive/2018/07/portrait-of-an-artist-as-an-old-man-mel-brooks-in-his-90s/564683/?curator=MediaREDEF

Diener, E., Tamir, M., & Scollon, C. N. (2006). Happiness, life satisfaction, and fulfillment: The social psychology of subjective well-being. In P.A.M. Van Lange (Ed.), *Bridging social psychology: Benefits of social psychology.* Psychology Press.

Dutton, D. G., & Aron, A. P. (1974). Some evidence for heightened sexual attraction under conditions of high anxiety. *Journal of Personality and Social Psychology, 30*, 510–517.

Finkel, E. J. (2017). *The all-or-nothing marriage: How the best marriages work.* Dutton.

Gable, S. L., & Reis, H. T. (2010). Good news! Capitalizing on positive events in an interpersonal context. *Advances in Experimental Social Psychology, 42*, 195–257.

Grewen, K., Girdler, S., Amico, J., & Light, K. (2005). Effects of partner support on resting oxytocin, cortisol, norepinephrine, and blood pressure before and after warm partner contact. *Psychosomatic Medicine, 67*, 531–538.

Hahn, C. M., & Campbell, L. J. (2016). Birds of a feather laugh together: An investigation of humour style similarity in married couples. *European Journal of Psychology, 12*(3), 406–419.

Hall, J. A. (2017). Humor in romantic relationships: A meta-analysis. *Personal Relationships, 24*(2), 306–322.

Halpern-Meekin, S. (2019). *Social poverty*. NYU Press.

Harlow, H. F. (1958). The nature of love. *American Psychologist, 13*(12), 673–685.

Mahoney, A., Pargament, K. I., Jewell, T., Swank, A. B., Scott, E., Emery, E., & Rye, M. (1999). Marriage and the spiritual realm: The role of proximal and distal religious constructs in marital functioning. *Journal of Family Psychology, 13*, 321–338.

Pasch, L. A., & Bradbury, T. N. (1998). Social support, conflict, and the development of marital dysfunction. *Journal of Consulting and Clinical Psychology, 66*, 219–230.

Relationship success tied not to joking but shared sense of humor, researcher says. (2017). *University of Kansas News*. Retrieved from https://news.ku.edu/news/article/2017/02/08/ relationship-success-tied-not-joking-shared-sense-humor

Sullivan, K., & Davila, J. (Eds.). (2010). *Support processes in intimate relationships*. Oxford University Press.

EXPECTATIONS

Baucom, D. H., & Epstein, N. (1990). *Cognitive behavioral marital therapy*. Brunner/Mazel.

Burgess, E. W., & Locke, H. J. (1945). *The family: From institution to companionship*. American Book Co.

Sager, C. J. (1976). *Marriage contracts and couple therapy*. Brunner-Routledge.

Wilcox, W. B., & Dew, J. (2010). Is love a flimsy foundation? Soulmate versus institutional models of marriage. *Social Science Research, 39*, 687–699.

FORGIVENESS

Allen, E. S., Atkins, D., Baucom, D. H., Snyder, D., Gordon, K. C., & Glass, S. P. (2005). Intrapersonal, interpersonal, and contextual factors in engaging in and responding to extramarital involvement. *Clinical Psychology: Science and Practice, 12,* 101–130.

Donovan, L.A.N., & Priester, J. R. (2017). Exploring the psychological processes that underlie interpersonal forgiveness: Replication and extension of the model of motivated interpersonal forgiveness. *Frontiers in Psychology, 11,* 10–13.

Fincham, F. D. (2019). Forgiveness in couple and family therapy. In J. Lebow, A. Chambers, & D. C. Breunlin (Eds.), *Encyclopedia of couple and family therapy.* Springer.

Fincham, F. D. (2022). Towards a psychology of divine forgiveness. *Psychology of Religion and Spirituality, 14*(4), 451–461.

Fincham, F. D., Hall, J. H., & Beach, S.R.H. (2005). 'Til lack of forgiveness doth us part: Forgiveness in marriage. In E. L. Worthington (Ed.), *Handbook of forgiveness* (pp. 207–225). Wiley.

Fincham, F. D., Stanley, S. M., & Beach, S.R.H. (2007). Transformative processes in marriage: An analysis of emerging trends. *Journal of Marriage and Family, 69,* 275–292.

Gámiz, M., Fernández-Capo, M., Buechner, V. L., Marlos, C., & Worthington, E. L. (2022). The role of making a decision to forgive in the process of forgiveness: A longitudinal study. *Current Psychology, 41,* 3363–3373.

Gordon, K. C., Baucom, D. H., & Snyder, D. K. (2004). An integrative intervention for promoting recovery from extramarital affairs. *Journal of Marital & Family Therapy, 30,* 213–231.

McCollough, M. E., Worthington Jr., E. L., & Rachal, K. C. (1997). Interpersonal forgiving in close relationships. *Journal of Personality and Social Psychology, 73,* 321–336.

Snyder, D. K., Gordon, K. C., & Baucom, D. H. (2023). *Getting past the affair: A program to help you cope, heal, and move on—together or apart.* Guilford Press.

Worthington, E. L. (2013). *Forgiveness and reconciliation: Theory and application.* Routledge.

Worthington, E. L. (2021). Forgiveness considered as virtue. In J. R. Peteet (Ed.), *The virtues of psychiatric practice.* Oxford University Press.

Worthington, E. L. (n.d.). The REACH forgiveness workbook. Retrieved from https://www.discoverforgiveness.org/tools/the-reach-forgiveness-workbook#downloads

Worthington Jr., E. L., & Sandage, S. J. (2016). *Forgiveness and spirituality in psychotherapy: A relational approach* (pp. 21–36). American Psychological Association.

BELIEFS, VALUES, AND LIFE EXPERIENCE

Afifi, T. D., Zamanzadeh, N., Harrison, K., & Torrez, D. P. (2020). Explaining the impact of differences in voting patterns on resilience and relational load in romantic relationships during the transition to the Trump presidency. *Journal of Social and Personal Relationships, 37*(1), 3–26.

Amato, P. R., Booth, A., Johnson, D. R., & Rogers, S. J. (2007). *Alone together.* Harvard University Press.

Call, V. R., & Heaton, T. B. (1997). Religious influence on marital stability. *Journal for the Scientific Study of Religion, 36,* 382–392.

Crohn, J. (1995). *Mixed matches: How to create successful interracial, interethnic, and interfaith relationships.* Ballantine Books.

Enochs, K. (2017). In US, 'Interpolitical' marriage increasingly frowned upon. Retrieved from https://www.voanews.com/usa/us-interpolitical-marriage-increasingly-frowned-upon

Fangmeier, T. L., Stanley, S. M., Knopp, K., & Rhoades, G. K. (2020). Political party identification and romantic relationship quality. *Couple and Family Psychology: Research and Practice, 9*(3), 167–180.

Haidt, J. (2012). *The righteous mind: Why good people are divided by politics and religion.* Pantheon/Random House.

Heaton, T. B. (1984). Religious homogamy and marital satisfaction reconsidered. *Journal of Marriage and the Family, 46,* 729–733.

Heaton, T. B. (2002). Factors contributing to increasing marital stability in the United States. *Journal of Family Issues, 23,* 392–409.

Hetherington, M., & Weiler, J. (2018). *Prius or pickup: How the answers to four simple questions explain American's great divide.* Houghton Mifflin Harcourt.

Hohmann-Marriott, B. E., & Amato, P. (2008). Relationship quality in interethnic marriages and cohabitations. *Social Forces, 87*(2), 825–855.

Iyengar, S., & Westwood, S. J. (2015). Fear and loathing across party lines: New evidence on group polarization. *American Journal of Political Science, 59*(3), 690–707.

Kalmijn, M., de Graaf, P., & Janssen, J. (2005). Intermarriage and the risk of divorce in the Netherlands: The effects of differences in religion and in nationality, 1974–94. *Population Studies, 59,* 71–85.

Klofstad, C. A., McDermott, R., & Hatemi, P. K. (2013). The dating preferences of liberals and conservatives. *Political Behavior, 35*(3), 519–538.

Mahoney, A. (2010). Religion in families, 1999–2009: A relational spirituality framework. *Journal of Marriage and Family, 72,* 805–827.

Mahoney, A., Pargament, K. I., Jewell, T., Swank, A. B., Scott, E., Emery, E., & Rye, M. (1999). Marriage and the spiritual realm: The role of proximal and distal religious constructs in marital functioning. *Journal of Family Psychology, 13*(3), 321–338.

Mallinas, S., Crawford, J., & Cole, S. (2018). Political opposites do not attract: The effects of ideological dissimilarity on impression formation. *Journal of Social and Political Psychology*, 6, 49–75.

PRRI Staff. (2023). Religion and congregations in a time of social and political upheaval. Retrieved from https://www .prri.org/research/religion-and-congregations-in-a-time-of-social-and-political-upheaval/

Smith, G. (2021). About three-in-ten U.S. adults are now religiously unaffiliated. Pew Research Center. Retrieved from https://www.pewresearch.org/religion/2021/12/14/about-three-in-ten-u-s-adults-are-now-religiously-unaffiliated/

Stanley, S. M., & Markman, H. J. (1992). Assessing commitment in personal relationships. *Journal of Marriage and the Family*, 54(3), 595–608.

Zhang, Y., & Van Hook, J. (2009). Marital dissolution among interracial couples. *Journal of Marriage and the Family*, 71(1), 95–107.

COMMITMENT

Dickson, F. C. (1995). The best is yet to be: Research on long-lasting relationships. In J. Wood & S. Duck (Eds.), *Understanding relationship processes: Off the beaten track* (pp. 22–50). Sage.

Fincham, F. D., Stanley, S. M., & Beach, S.R.H. (2007). Transformative processes in marriage: An analysis of emerging trends. *Journal of Marriage and Family*, 69, 275–292.

Impett, E. A., Beals, K. P., & Peplau, L. A. (2001). Testing the investment model of relationship commitment and stability in a longitudinal study of married couples. *Current Psychology*, 20(4), 312–326.

Joel, S., et al. (2020). Machine learning uncovers the most robust self-report predictors of relationship quality across 43 longitudinal couples studies. *Proceedings of the National Academy of Sciences, 117*(32), 19061–19071.

Johnson, M. P., Caughlin, J. P., & Huston, T. L. (1999). The tripartite nature of marital commitment: Personal, moral, and structural reasons to stay married. *Journal of Marriage and the Family, 61*, 160–177.

Johnson, D. J., & Rusbult, C. E. (1989). Resisting temptation: Devaluation of alternative partners as a means of maintaining commitment in close relationships. *Journal of Personality and Social Psychology, 57*, 967–980.

Jones, W., & Adams, J. (1999). *Handbook of interpersonal commitment and relationship stability*. Plenum.

Kline, G. H., Stanley, S. M., Markman, H. J., Olmos-Gallo, P. A., St. Peters, M., Whitton, S. W., & Prado, L. (2004). Timing is everything: Pre-engagement cohabitation and increased risk for poor marital outcomes. *Journal of Family Psychology, 18*, 311–318.

Knopp, K. C., Rhoades, G. K., Stanley, S. M., & Markman, H. J. (2015). Stuck on you: How dedication moderates the way constraints feel. *Journal of Social & Personal Relationships, 32*(1), 119–137.

Levinger, G. (1999). Duty toward whom? Reconsidering attractions and barriers as determinants of commitment in a relationship. In W. Jones & J. Adams (Eds.), *Handbook of interpersonal commitment and relationship stability* (pp. 37–52). Plenum.

Lindsay, J. M. (2000). An ambiguous commitment: Moving into a cohabiting relationship. *Journal of Family Studies, 6*(1), 120–134.

Manning, W. D., & Smock, P. J. (2005). Measuring and modeling cohabitation: New perspectives from qualitative data. *Journal of Marriage and Family, 67*, 989–1002.

Peck, M. S. (1978). *The Road Less Traveled: A New Psychology of Love,* Traditional Values and Spiritual Growth. Simon & Schuster.

Pew Research Center. (2010). The decline of marriage and rise of new families. Retrieved from https://www.pewresearch.org/social-trends/2010/11/18/the-decline-of-marriage-and-rise-of-new-families/

Rhoades, G. K., Stanley, S. M., & Markman, H. J. (2009a). Couples' reasons for cohabitation: Associations with individual well-being and relationship quality. *Journal of Family Issues, 30*, 233–258.

Rhoades, G. K., Stanley, S. M., & Markman, H. J. (2009b). The pre-engagement cohabitation effect: A replication and extension of previous findings. *Journal of Family Psychology, 23*, 107–111.

Rhoades, G. K., Stanley, S. M., & Markman, H. J. (2009c). Working with cohabitation in relationship education and therapy. *Journal of Couple and Relationship Therapy, 8*, 95–112.

Rhoades, G. K., Stanley, S. M., & Markman, H. J. (2012). The impact of the transition to cohabitation on relationship functioning: Cross-sectional and longitudinal findings. *Journal of Family Psychology, 26*(3), 348–358.

Rhoades, G. K., Stanley, S. M., Markman, H. J., & Allen, E. S. (2015). Can marriage education mitigate the risks associated with premarital cohabitation? *Journal of Family Psychology, 29*(3), 500–506.

Ritchie, L. L., Stanley, S. M., Rhoades, G. K., & Markman, H. J. (2021). Romantic alternative monitoring increases ahead of infidelity and break-up. *Journal of Social and Personal Relationships*, 38(2), 711–724.

Ross, E. A. 1921. *Principles of sociology*. Century.

Rusbult, C. E. (1983). A longitudinal test of the investment model: The development (and deterioration) of satisfaction and commitment in heterosexual involvements. *Journal of Personality and Social Psychology*, 45, 101–117.

Rusbult, C. E., Zembrodt, I. M., & Gunn, L. K. (1982). Exit, voice, loyalty, and neglect: Responses to dissatisfaction in romantic involvement. *Journal of Personality and Social Psychology*, 43, 1230–1242.

Sprecher, S., Schmeeckle, M., & Felmlee, D. (2006). The principle of least interest: Inequality in emotional involvement in romantic relationships. *Journal of Family Issues*, 27(9), 1255–1280.

Stanley, S. M. (2005). *The power of commitment*. Jossey-Bass.

Stanley, S. M., Lobitz, W. C., & Dickson, F. (1999). Using what we know: Commitment and cognitions in marital therapy. In W. Jones & J. Adams (Eds.), *Handbook of interpersonal commitment and relationship stability* (pp. 411–424). Plenum.

Stanley, S. M., & Markman, H. J. (1992). Assessing commitment in personal relationships. *Journal of Marriage and the Family*, 54, 595–608.

Stanley, S. M., & Rhoades, G. K. (2023). Maybe I do. *Retrieved from* https://ifstudies.org/blog/maybe-i-do

Stanley, S. M., Rhoades, G. K., Kelmer, G., Scott, S. B., Markman, H. J., & Fincham, F. D. (2019). Unequally into "us": Characteristics of individuals in asymmetrically committed relationships. *Family Process*, 58, 214–231.

Stanley, S. M., Rhoades, G. K., & Markman, H. J. (2006). Sliding vs. deciding: Inertia and the premarital cohabitation effect. *Family Relations*, 55, 499–509.

Stanley, S. M., Rhoades, G. K., Scott, S. B., Kelmer, G., Markman, H. J., & Fincham, F. D. (2017). Asymmetrically committed relationships. *Journal of Social and Personal Relationships, 34*, 1241–1259.

Stanley, S. M., Rhoades, G. K., & Whitton, S. W. (2010). Commitment: Functions, formation, and the securing of romantic attachment. *Journal of Family Theory and Review, 2*, 243–257.

Stanley, S. M., Whitton, S. W., Low, S. M., Clements, M. L., & Markman, H. J. (2006). Sacrifice as a predictor of marital outcomes. *Family Process, 45*, 289–303.

Stanley, S. M., Whitton, S. W., & Markman, H. J. (2004). Maybe I do: Interpersonal commitment and premarital or nonmarital cohabitation. *Journal of Family Issues, 25*, 496–519.

Surra, C. A., & Hughes, D. K. (1997). Commitment processes in accounts of the development of premarital relationships. *Journal of Marriage & the Family, 59*(1), 5–21.

van Lange, P.A.M., Rusbult, C. E., Drigotas, S. M., Arriaga, X. B., Witcher, B. S., & Cox, C. L. (1997). Willingness to sacrifice in close relationships. *Journal of Personality and Social Psychology, 72*, 1373–1395.

Waller, W. (1938). *The family: A dynamic interpretation.* Gordon.

Whitton, S. W., Stanley, S. M., & Markman, H. J. (2007). If I help my partner, will it hurt me? Perceptions of sacrifice in romantic relationships. *Journal of Social and Clinical Psychology, 26*, 64–92.

Wieselquist, J., Rusbult, C. E., Foster, C. A., & Agnew, C. R. (1999). Commitment, pro-relationship behavior, and trust in close relationships. *Journal of Personality and Social Psychology, 77*, 942–966.

About the Authors

*H*oward J. Markman, PhD, is a distinguished professor of psychology at the University of Denver. He is a Fellow of the American Psychological Association Division of Family Psychology and the Association for Behavioral and Cognitive Therapies. His awards include the Distinguished Contributions to Family Therapy Research Award from American Association for Marriage and Family Therapy.

Dr. Markman is the founder of the internationally known evidence-based couples relationship education program, PREP (Prevention and Relationship Education Program). The PREP program is widely used in the US military and in more than fifteen countries around the world. PREP has been cited by the CDC as a research-based program that can prevent or ameliorate inter-partner violence.

Dr. Markman is one of the leading researchers in the areas of couples, marriage, divorce prevention, and couples relationship education and therapy in the world. He has written more than one hundred books and scientific articles in the couples and family field including earlier editions of the bestselling couples relationship education book, *Fighting for Your Marriage*. He has numerous grants with the University of Denver and has a practice in couples relationship education and couples therapy

Dr. Markman has appeared in national media, including *The Oprah Winfrey Show*, *The Today Show*, *20/20*, the *New York Times*,

CNN, the *Wall Street Journal*, the *Washington Post*, and NPR, and is available to give talks and workshops.

Scott M. Stanley, PhD, is a research professor at the University of Denver. He has published extensively on subjects including commitment, cohabitation, relationship development, and the prevention of relationship distress.

Along with colleagues Dr. Howard Markman, Dr. Galena Rhoades, and Dr. Elizabeth Allen, Dr. Stanley has conducted research on relationship education since the early 1980s, mostly funded by grants (to one or more of these scholars) from the National Institutes of Health and the Administration for Children and Families. Dr. Stanley and Dr. Rhoades have conducted research focused on relationship development, cohabitation, and commitment, also funded by the National Institutes of Health. This line of research has influenced efforts to help individuals improve their relationship decision-making.

Dr. Stanley has regularly contributed to stories in major media outlets as an expert on relationships. Dr. Markman and Dr. Stanley co-own the PREP Companies, an enterprise founded with the goal of disseminating research-informed and evidence-based relationship education materials. Dr. Stanley publishes blog articles in a number of outlets including at slidingvsdeciding.com.

Galena K. Rhoades, PhD, is a research professor and the director of the Institute for Relationship Science in the Department of Psychology at the University of Denver. Her research focuses on romantic relationship formation processes, such as dating and living together, and predictors of relationship success. She also conducts studies on the effectiveness of relationship interventions offered by community organizations across the United States. She has more than 140 publications in these areas.

Dr. Rhoades founded a nonprofit in Denver called Thriving Families. This organization offers MotherWise, a relationship education program for women during pregnancy and postpartum, as well as mental health services for families.

Dr. Rhoades is also a practicing clinical psychologist. In her private practice, she primarily sees couples and families.

Janice R. Levine, PhD, is a clinical psychologist who specializes in couples relationships and family development. She received her undergraduate degree from Yale University and her graduate degrees from Harvard University, where she later joined the faculty in Psychology and was Instructor in Psychiatry at Harvard Medical School. Dr. Levine is coauthor of the books *Why Do Fools Fall in Love?* and *Beyond the Chuppah: A Jewish Guide to Happy Marriages*, and is founder of The Couples Health Program, a nationally recognized curriculum that teaches couples how to achieve greater intimacy through communication and conflict-resolution skills. She is featured in the "Best in Massachusetts" magazine as a Top Doc.

Dr. Levine lectures nationally on all aspects of couples and family development, has hosted a Parent Education TV and Lecture Series, and has been a frequent contributor to major broadcast and print media. She is the founder of Partners for ACCESS, a nonprofit organization dedicated to growing a sustainable medical center in rural Uganda. A former concert violinist, Dr. Levine has two adult children with her husband of forty years, and currently lives in southern Maine.

Index